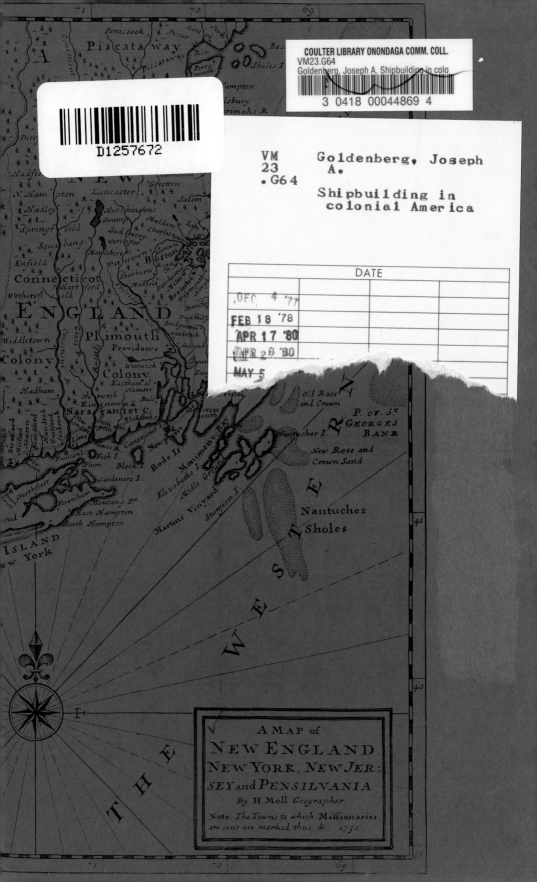

A MAP of
NEW ENGLAND,
NEW YORK, NEW JER-
SEY and PENSILVANIA
By H. Moll Geographer.
Note. The Towns to which Missionaries
are sent are marked thus ⌖ 1730

*Shipbuilding*
*in*
*Colonial America*

# Shipbuilding
# in Colonial America

*Joseph A. Goldenberg*

Published for The Mariners Museum
Newport News, Virginia
by the University Press of Virginia
Charlottesville

THE UNIVERSITY PRESS OF VIRGINIA
Copyright © 1976 by The Mariners Museum

First published 1976

Museum Publication Number 33

Library of Congress Cataloging in Publication Data

Goldenberg, Joseph A.
  Shipbuilding in colonial America.

  (Museum publication no. 33)
  Bibliography: p. 287
  1.  Ship-building—United States—History.
  2.  United States—History—Colonial period.
I.  Title.  II.  Series: Mariners Museum, Newport News, Va.
Museum  publication  33.   VM23.G64   623.82'03   74–32136
ISBN  0–8139–0588–5

Printed in the United States of America

*Endpapers:* Maps by H. Moll,
1730. (Library of Congress)

*To*
*Miss Cerinda W. Evans*
*who,*
*as Librarian of*
*The Mariners Museum*
*from 1935 to 1946,*
*organized the library's*
*remarkable resources*
*of ships and the sea*

# Contents

Illustrations

# Preface

S AILING vessels have been the subject of much nostalgic literature. Writers yearn for the "wooden ships and iron men" of bygone days, and artists show the old sailing ship being towed at sunset to the breaker's yard by an iron steam tug. The people closest to the wooden sailing ships of the colonial era, however, found it difficult to be romantic about their means of livelihood. West Indian sailors referred to island trading schooners as "holes in the water," while to the settlers of this country, ships were of interest only for the goods they could transport. William Bradford and John Winthrop, for example, recorded the arrival of ships from England and the activities of colonial-built boats, but they seldom mentioned a vessel's appearance.

Of course, their attitudes are understandable. One might as reasonably expect a diarist of today to enthusiastically describe the manufacture of trucks and freight trains. But the practical outlook of the colonists makes it difficult to gather much evidence about the form and construction of colonial-built vessels. The noted naval architect and maritime historian Howard I. Chapelle has found and analyzed a dozen or so plans of colonial vessels, but even this small sample is confined to the years after 1730 because no earlier plans have been uncovered. Another naval architect, William Baker, who specializes in seventeenth-century ships, is compelled to work from scattered references in printed colonial records and a few contemporary paintings because of the lack of ship plans. The papers of less than a dozen colonial shipbuilders have been preserved, and most of these are only brief account books.

There are a number of fine general volumes about ships and their construction, but the few detailed studies of shipbuilding during the colonial years are essentially local histories, written after much research, by descendants of shipbuilders.[1] Several regional histories provide information on shipbuilding activity along the Chesapeake Bay and the Piscataqua River,[2] and John G. B. Hutchins includes a brief but excellent summary of colonial shipbuilding in his standard work, *The American Maritime Industries and Public Policy*. Although it appeared after this book was written, and therefore is not referred to in the text, William Baker's *A Maritime History of Bath, Maine, and the Kennebec River Region* must be included in any survey of the literature of colonial shipbuilding as it is already the model for all regional histories to follow.

The absence to date of a general study of the growth of the shipbuilding industry in colonial America may be attributed to the sketchy records now available. In order to offer a useful study of colonial shipbuilding, several untapped sources had to be referred to and a wide range of information coordinated to form a coherent general picture. Merchants' papers provide information about contracts, costs, the relationship between shipbuilder and merchant, and the markets for colonial vessels. From legal papers, such as wills and inventories, one may determine the property of shipbuilders and gather details about their tools, slaves, building yards, and financial positions. Lawsuits offer useful information about contracts, construction practices, payments, and labor problems. Colonial tax records usually lack sufficient detail to be valuable in the study of any particular occupation. Philadelphia, however, is a fortunate exception, and the detailed tax assessments available for the years 1773–75 allow interesting comparisons between the wealth of Philadelphia shipbuilders and that of colonists in other professions. Information from newspapers includes accounts of accidents and other shipyard activities seldom mentioned in other sources. Finally, the type, size, and building site for thousands of colonial vessels can be found in various shipping lists, such as port records, shipping registers, and the Lloyd's of London insurance register. Although these records are incomplete, they enable the historian to study the shipbuilding industry from a statistical point of view and to compile tables revealing definite shipbuilding patterns.

At first glance, the variety of sources seems impressive, but there are serious limitations. The great bulk of material is limited to the eighteenth century, and usually to the years after 1720. Most of this material deals with ocean-going vessels built in documented shipyards. A study of the wide variety of small craft, from Indian dug-outs to river craft and fishing boats, and even some larger vessels built outside the shipbuilding centers, awaits the uncovering of new information. Furthermore, the geographic distribution of material is admittedly unbalanced. Although Chesapeake Bay was the scene of much mercantile activity throughout the colonial period, merchants' papers for that region are relatively rare. Similarly, there are few merchants' papers for the Carolinas and Georgia. South Carolina has only one set of merchants' papers useful to the historian of shipbuilding; however, the existence of good legal documents, ship registers, and a newspaper permits the study of shipbuilding in that colony. The South is well represented by legal documents, newspapers, and port records, but the result is still far from satisfactory. A similar situation exists in New York. Compared with the postrevolutionary period, there are few colonial merchants' papers, and those New York merchants whose papers have been preserved were not connected with shipbuilding. Abundant and balanced material may be found in Massachusetts; and Pennsylvania, or more particularly Philadelphia, has a variety of excellent sources. In Rhode Island there are several extensive collections of merchants' papers for the eighteenth century, but, as in New Hampshire, other sources are scanty. Colonies are represented in this study to the extent that available materials allow.

To fill in gaps in the resources, several tempting courses present themselves to the maritime historian. Why not presume, for example, that well-documented nineteenth-century practices were also common in the seventeenth and eighteenth centuries? Some methods may well have been popular in the earlier period, but the frequent technological developments which characterize the nineteenth century make this a hazardous assumption. Why not rely, then, on British and European sources? To some extent I have done so, for the American colonies did, to a certain degree, follow the economic as well as the cultural styles of the mother county. But continental leadership, at least for shipbuilding, cannot be assumed without qualification; differences in resources and needs, for example, must be taken into account. Just the fact that American shipping became more popular in time shows that Americans gradually learned to adapt and then distinguish themselves in this field.

Finally, why not apply to the shipbuilder and his craft contemporary theories on profitability, growth, and social or economic organization? The fact is that shipbuilding in this early period has often been theorized about, especially in general works, but infrequently examined within the restrictions of what can actually be documented. The purpose of this study is to provide a detailed evaluation of shipbuilding within the limits of available material.

This study originated as a dissertation under the direction of Prof. E. P. Douglass at the University of North Carolina. The staffs of many historical societies and other depositories were very helpful in locating appropriate material. The individuals I would like most to credit for the time and knowledge they so freely shared are: Mrs. Eleanor Bishop and Mr. Robert Lovett of the Manuscript Room in Baker Library, Harvard School of Business; Mr. and Mrs. Leo Flaherty of the Massachusetts Archives; Mrs. Norbet Lacy of the New Hampshire Historical Society; Dr. Charles Lee of the South Carolina Archives; Miss Mary Quinn of the Rhode Island Archives; and Mr. Murphy Smith of the American Philosophical Society, who introduced me to another graduate student working on the same subject. To my parents there is a special debt for the moral, not to mention financial, support which they gave with characteristic generosity and enthusiasm.

Mr. Howard I. Chapelle not only allowed me to use many of his notes but also gave valuable advice on revising the work of a nervous graduate student into a book. Likewise, Prof. John Mc-Cusker of the University of Maryland and Dr. Norman Fiering of the Institute of Early American History and Culture at Williamsburg read the manuscript in one of its early stages and provided both intelligent and practical guidance. I am also happy to mention: Mr. Walter Cheatham, a former student at Virginia State College, who redrew the plan of the ship *Lord Camden*; and the editors of *The American Neptune* for permission to incorporate portions of two of my articles, "Names and Numbers: Statistical Notes on Some Port Records of Colonial North Carolina" and "A Forgotten Dry Dock in Colonial Charlestown," into this work.

The largest acknowledgment is to Judi, my wife and editor in residence. Her tasks of reworking the manuscript and retyping it several times paled before her partially successful efforts to drag conclusions from a reticent mate.

For their decision to publish this work, begun some nine years ago, and patience in carrying the project forward, I am most grateful to the staff of The Mariners Museum.

*Shipbuilding*
*in*
*Colonial America*

# CHAPTER I

# Ships and Shipbuilding
# in the First Colonial Settlements

THERE had been paved roads since the Roman Empire, but seventeenth-century Americans were compelled to use cleared paths which were alternately dusty or muddy according to the season. Such roads were adequate for a farmer's cart going to a local market or for a touring carriage, provided the passengers were hardy. Otherwise both people and goods traveled by water; it was cheaper and usually faster than to go by land. North-south trade in the colonies, for example, was carried in coastal vessels wherever possible, for merchants found it far less expensive to hire a small, twenty-ton vessel with a crew of four than to pay for ten or more large wagons, each drawn by four or six horses and led by a driver, which would carry the same load at a slower rate.

Seventeenth-century craft were relatively small in size. The *Sparrow Hawk*, which was wrecked on Cape Cod in 1626 and whose remains were discovered in 1863, was a vessel of about 40 feet overall length that was used to transport twenty-five people across the Atlantic. Evidence indicates that the size of the *Sparrow Hawk* was not unusual for its time.[1] The *Mayflower*, reconstructed in 1956, on the other hand, is small by modern standards (about the size of a New York City harbor tug), yet early seventeenth-century sailors would have considered it a large ship.

Exact dimensions for seventeenth-century ships are rarely found. The number of tuns of wine a vessel could carry was called her tonnage. For two centuries tonnage was ascertained by actually filling a vessel with wine tuns. This inconvenient method was replaced by a formula based upon the vessel's dimensions. According to the English tonnage rule of 1582, devised by Matthew Baker, the length of the keel was multiplied by the beam and, in turn, this product was multiplied by the depth of the hold. The final product was divided by 100, and the result accepted as the vessel's measured tonnage, or tons burden. This tonnage formula was commonly used by shipwrights such as Baker to determine the size of a proposed vessel and to give the merchant a cost estimate based on an agreed price per ton. Results, however, could vary several tons or even more on the same ship. To complicate matters, measured tonnage, or tons burden, did not equal a vessel's actual cargo capacity. Matthew Baker's formula provided that the measured tonnage be increased by one-third to determine the capacity figure.[2]

Baker's rule may have been convenient, but its accuracy is questionable. The formula assumed that all hulls, regardless of size, had the same general form and proportions—but that obviously was not the case. Some ships were built on a "sharp" model for fast sailing and consequently had less cargo capacity than a "full-built" vessel of the same dimensions. Even among Baker's contemporaries, there was disagreement about the relationship of measurements to capacity, and throughout the colonial period variations of Baker's tonnage rule were proposed.[3]

In recent years maritime historians have made a determined effort to eliminate some of the confusion concerning tonnage, but they still disagree about the correlation between measured tonnage and actual capacity. Many ships were designed during the eighteenth and nineteenth centuries as "rule-cheaters," and they frequently had a cargo capacity one-third greater than their measured tonnage. Some writers assume that the same was true in previous centuries; this assumption is backed by Baker's formula. However, Ralph Davis, who has done extensive research in English shipping, maintains that in the seventeenth century the ratio was reversed, and that measured tonnage was often one-third greater than capacity.[4] His reason is that English merchant vessels of that century were still built in the warship tradition. Whereas the Dutch constructed the economical flyboat of large volume and small spread of sail, English shipwrights produced an all-purpose vessel which sacrificed hull capacity for speed and armament. Not until toward the end of the century did the English begin to follow the Dutch pattern of designing merchant vessels with greater cargo capacity.

Out of this confusion of tons and tonnage, several considerations must be emphasized. Builders and merchants contracting for vessels used measured tons to determine hull size and price. But once they owned or hired a vessel, merchants thought of it in terms of cargo capacity. Thus most correspondence between merchants refers to the capacity instead of the measured tonnage of a vessel. The shipping tables in the Appendix list measured tonnage, not cargo capacity, because the former is the measurement used by builders and recorded by port collectors. In this book, when a vessel is described as a 60-ton ship, the figure refers to her size and not her cargo capacity.

By the mid-eighteenth century, sailing vessels were categorized according to their rigs, but few such definite divisions existed for early seventeenth-century craft. The best-defined and most common vessel for ocean voyages was the *ship*, which was identified by square sails on the fore- and mainmasts and a lateen-rigged mizzen mast. A ship's tonnage might be as little as 40 or greater than 400.

Next in size to ships were vessels intended for coastal service but capable of ocean passages. The *pinnace* was a lightly constructed vessel designed to move easily under sails or sweeps (long oars). Light draft and good maneuverability made pinnaces especially useful for trading and exploration ventures. Pinnace rigs varied in size from a single mast with main- and staysails for a smaller model to a full ship rig for a 50-tonner. In contrast to the pinnace, both the *bark* and the *ketch* were heavily constructed vessels designed primarily as sailing craft. Both were single-decked and were employed for fishing or coastal trading. While both had two masts, the bark was square-rigged and the ketch fore-and-aft-. The *shallop*, heavily constructed and undecked, was the smallest colonial-built craft capable of coastal navigation. Usually a single-masted vessel carrying main- and staysails, its small size (about 30 feet or less in length) enabled it to be carried aboard ships in sections and reassembled when needed. The *Mayflower*'s shallop was utilized in this manner.[5] The pinnace, bark, ketch, and shallop remained in use throughout most of the seventeenth century.

The early seventeenth century was a period of steady expansion for English shipbuilding. All sea routes were increasingly traveled, and new ships were required for Mediterranean, East Indian, and American trade, and for the English coal trade. The first vessels Europeans built in America, however, were not designed to profit from expanding trade, but merely to replace wrecked ships and to aid in coastal exploration. In 1526 a Spanish expedition tried to establish a colony along the Cape Fear River in North Carolina.

When one of the ships was wrecked, the colonists built a replacement, and later they launched a second vessel.[6] The two vessels were probably small simple craft that disappeared from view when the settlement was abandoned.

The first English vessel was also built in a temporary colony. In 1607 "a pretty pynnace of about some thirty tonne, which they called Virginia," was constructed by the Popham colonists at the mouth of the Kennebec River, in Maine. A London shipwright named Digby directed the work. A map of the colony depicts a small single-masted vessel, which historians believe to be the pinnace *Virginia*. The vessel in the picture has a simple fore-and-aft rig consisting of a mainsail and a staysail. Such a sail arrangement makes a vessel more maneuverable than a square-sail rig and thus better suited for explorations along the irregular coast. Naval architect William Baker estimates that the *Virginia* was about 50 feet in length. The pinnace made several coastal voyages before the colony was abandoned, in 1608, and for the next twenty years she sailed regularly between Virginia and London. Finally, the *Virginia* was wrecked along the Irish coast.[7]

There are other examples of simple craft built by early settlers. When colonists bound for Virginia were shipwrecked off Bermuda in 1609, they built two small vessels in order to complete the voyage to Jamestown. A Dutch expedition to New Netherland lost one of its ships by fire in 1614, and, to replace it, a small "yacht" was built at Manhattan. The yacht was about 16 tons and had a simple fore-and-aft rig similar to that of the pinnace *Virginia*. She was named *Onrust* (*Restless*) and, like the *Virginia*, was used in coastal explorations. Later the *Onrust* sailed to Holland with a cargo of furs.[8]

Little is known about the first vessels built in Virginia. A couple of small coastal craft were constructed before 1614, but four years later the colony seems to have been almost without any boats. Vessels were needed, but settlers faced with the more immediate problem of survival did not attempt to build their own ships. The London Company provided little leadership and less aid. Finally, in 1622, the company sent Capt. Thomas Barwick and twenty-five ship carpenters to Virginia to construct small vessels for local use. Besides answering the general need for communication, such craft could carry tobacco from the various plantations to Jamestown. The ship carpenters are known to have built at least one shallop, but the artisans eventually succumbed to the diseases that plagued the colony. Captain Barwick died soon after his arrival in Virginia "and the plan, like so many other apparently good ones devised by the Company, came to naught."[9]

A similar but less ambitious plan was also tried in Plymouth Colony. The London investors who were financing the plantation expected profits from fishing and coastal trade. Seeking an appropriate vessel, the Pilgrims purchased the 60-ton pinnace *Speedwell*, but she leaked badly and was unable to accompany the *Mayflower*. In 1623, the London investors sent over the pinnace *Little James*, "a fine, new vessel of about 44 tun, which the Company had built to stay in the country." The pinnace suffered a series of mishaps and was sent back to England. The company then decided it was cheaper to send a shipwright than another pinnace, and in 1624, William Bradford records, the London investors sent "an honest and very industrious" ship carpenter to the colony.[10] Aided by several sawyers (also sent by the company), a local house carpenter, and the unskilled but willing colonists, the shipbuilder soon produced two shallops for fishing and a cargo lighter for transporting goods between ship and shore. Soon after the completion of the vessels, the shipwright began preparing the timbers for two ketches, but he caught a summer fever and died.

The shallops were perhaps 30 feet long and quite suitable for local fishing; but since they were open boats, any cargo aboard could easily be ruined by the sea. In 1625 the colonists wished to send a cargo of corn to a settlement at the Kennebec River and, for this purpose, laid a deck over the midships of one shallop. The voyage was a success; in exchange for the dry corn the colonists received 700 pounds of beaver fur.[11]

Due to the success of the Kennebec voyage, the limited capacity and seaworthiness of a partially decked shallop, and the high prices demanded by Indians for furs, the Plymouth colonists decided to get a larger decked vessel. But the London stockholders were unwilling to risk another pinnace, and there were no vessels for sale in New England. The plantation was without a shipbuilder, so the house carpenter who had worked on the construction of the shallops was requested by the colony "to make a trial . . . of his skill." His solution was simple and effective: he sawed the larger shallop in half amidships and "lengthened her some five or six foot, and strengthened her with timbers, and so built her up and laid a deck on her."[12] The rebuilding was successful, and the vessel served the colony for seven years.

Following the example of Virginia and Plymouth, the New England Company sent six shipwrights to John Endecott's colony at Salem in 1629 to build three shallops which the colony would then use for fishing. Such an assignment could not have taken long, especially since Endecott was ordered to assist the builders by assigning to them any men he could spare. It is unknown whether the shallops were completed, but later in the year another builder and more tools were sent to Salem.[13] Correspondence indicates that the company intended to construct larger vessels, probably for coastal trading. There is no further material about the seven shipwrights, yet doubtless they were on hand when the Winthrop fleet arrived in 1630.

The most notable of the earliest colonial-built vessels was John Winthrop's *Blessing of the Bay*. The governor had this 30-ton bark built to serve the colony's need for communication with other plantations and to gather caches of fish and furs. She was launched into the Mystic River at Medford on July 4, 1631, to be used as a coastal trader, but she does not seem to have been long in service.[14] The bark was typical of the first efforts of colonial builders in that she was a relatively small and simple craft capable of coastal voyages.

Records of shipbuilding in the Massachusetts Bay Colony during the 1630s are sparse. Shipbuilders settled in various towns and were presumably producing boats for local use as well as some small coasting vessels, but larger vessels are known to have been built. John Winthrop records in his *History* that in November 1633 "a small ship of about 60 tons was built at Medford and called the *Rebecca*." Three years later the 120-ton ship *Desire* was built at Marblehead.[15] Unlike previous colonial vessels, these two ships were built for trans-Atlantic voyages, as the industrious colonists were now ready to extend themselves beyond the fishing and coastal trades.

Although the contribution of Indian craft and vessels built by unskilled colonists must be acknowledged, several colonial leaders sought out shipwrights wherever possible. This demand for skilled workmen at the very beginning of colonization implies that shipbuilding, or at least competent repair work, was deemed essential to the survival and prosperity of a settlement, or in some cases to provide escape for colonists when their settlement failed. Any sustained building effort required training, experience, and the luck to survive on the part of the shipwright.

It is possible to follow the travels of one shipbuilder during that period. William Stevens, a skillful and successful shipwright in London, had built many large vessels and was considered to be one of the three or four leading builders in England. However, he worried more about his ships than his wages and soon found himself in debt. Seeking employment abroad, Stevens was preparing to leave for Spain when the Massachusetts Bay Company recruited him. He arrived in Boston, moved to Salem, and in 1637 the town of Salem granted him land "for the building of Shipps, provided that it shall be imployed for that ende." Such grants of free land to shipbuilders were common. As a matter of fact, next to Stevens was another shipwright, Richard Hollingsworth, who also had received land from the town. After a year in Salem, Stevens moved three miles away to the village of Marblehead, where he remained several years. In 1638, he repaired a bark owned by Winthrop and was promised to be paid for the job when the vessel was sold. In the following year he was involved in a dispute concerning an apprentice. In 1642 Stevens made one last move, this time to Gloucester. The town granted him the unusually large sum of 500 acres, and he became active in local politics.[16] He is the only shipbuilder for whom reasons for emigration can be found. His high reputation, debts, and readiness to embark for Spain no doubt played a part in his decision, but his own restlessness, suggested by his moving about during the first ten years in Massachusetts, also must have influenced him.

That Stevens found work plentiful wherever he chose to settle may be an estimation of his personal skills. But it also reflects the colonists' high regard for skilled craftsmen in general and in particular for the shipwright who could adapt his training to building ventures in the new American environment.

# CHAPTER II

# Shipbuilding Patterns in Seventeenth-Century America

## Massachusetts

MASSACHUSETTS was flooded with newcomers during the 1630s. In 1639, when the Great Migration began to abate, the colony's economy suddenly fell into turmoil. Early immigrants had avoided high freight costs by converting their possessions into cash while still in England and then purchasing new farming tools and other necessities on arrival in Massachusetts. Gradually, local merchants grew dependent upon the immigrants' money to pay for shiploads of English manufactured goods. When political and religious changes in England made it possible for many would-be colonists to remain at home, Massachusetts merchants were left without a source of specie.[1]

In 1640 English ships arrived in Boston, as usual, with expectations of good markets and hard cash for their cargoes. But the shippers found little specie. Reluctant to accept promises or agricultural produce, English merchants warned the colonists that their credit was near exhaustion. Massachusetts merchants, unable to receive credit from their English correspondents, were in turn unwilling to accept anything but specie from fellow colonists. Prices for farm produce fell; land prices dropped 80 percent.[2] Depression threatened to turn Massachusetts into an economic backwater ignored by English merchants and their ships.

To meet the emergency, the Massachusetts government passed laws aiding debtors and requiring the acceptance of commodities when cash was unavailable. Efforts were directed to expand the fur trade, and legislation promoting the iron and cloth industries was passed. As a fundamental part of their economic program, Gov. John Winthrop and the General Court advocated the creation of a Massachusetts-built and -owned merchant fleet.[3] By providing their own vessels, Massachusetts merchants would not have to depend on

English shipping; they might even try to open their own ocean trades.

The first response to the plea for local shipbuilding came from Salem, where the Reverend Hugh Peters persuaded some individuals to cooperate in the construction of a vessel under the builder Richard Hollingsworth. Suitable ship timber in the area was being used mostly for barrel staves and clapboards; in October 1640, the Salem town meeting ordered that such timber be reserved for the use of shipbuilders. Several months later, the Reverend Mr. Peters wrote to Governor Winthrop that the town still had difficulty protecting timber for the two or three ships then being built. Aside from timber problems, Hollingsworth became involved in several lawsuits originating in shipyard disputes with other carpenters. The most serious incident was the death of a man in the shipyard: a worker was helping to raise a timber when the tackle broke and he was crushed. Hollingsworth was fined £10, to be paid to the deceased's wife and children. Despite difficulties, the 300-ton vessel, named the *Mary Ann*, was launched in June 1641.[4]

Inhabitants of the Boston Bay area soon surpassed Salem's accomplishment. There was little money in the colony, but shipwrights went ahead with their work, willing to accept whatever form of payment people could make. In 1641 one Boston shipwright, Nehemiah Bourne, was granted an area adjoining his home for a shipyard. At the same time, the £3 10s. paid by a certain Mr. Wright of Braintree for a 60-acre plot was used to help finance the construction of Bourne's ship. As the first vessel of its type built in Boston and a symbol of the colony's new economy, she was appropriately named the *Trial*. Her tonnage was about 160. The launching, early in 1642, was a great occasion. In August, when the *Trial* was ready to sail, John Cotton was asked "to preach aboard her, but upon consideration that the audience would be too great for the ship, the sermon was held at the meeting house."[5]

Boston was well on its way to becoming an active shipbuilding center. Within four years at least six more large ships were constructed in the Boston area, and by the end of 1643 two ships of 300 tons each were launched. In the following year a 250-ton ship was built in Cambridge and one of 200 tons in Boston. Both vessels

were laded with barrel staves and fish and were sent to the Canary
Islands. In 1645 Boston citizens witnessed the launching of one
of the largest colonial ships of the seventeenth century—the 400-ton
*Seafort*. Though paint and ornamental carvings were too expensive
for most early colonial vessels, the *Seafort* had both, plus a heavy
armament. She was built by a former London shipwright, Capt.
Thomas Hawkins. On October 17, 1646, another 300-ton ship was
launched. Meanwhile, Nehemiah Bourne, now a major in the militia, was preparing to build a twenty-gun ship of 250 tons—perhaps
for privateering.[6]

As far as ladings were concerned, timber was a popular export; in
1643, for the first time, eleven New England vessels set sail for the
West Indies, all carrying lumber. Agricultural products also constituted an important cargo; the sale of local produce abroad enabled farmers to get credit from town merchants, who in turn
could then reestablish credit with English exporters.[7] Fish, in the
long run, became the most important cargo, because it encouraged
the growth of shipbuilding. Local fishermen used small open boats,
such as shallops; those who fished offshore grounds required larger
vessels—ketches and barks. Ships carried the salted fish to European
and West Indian markets, while more and more vessels of various
types had to be built for the expanding maritime trades.

Free land offered shipbuilders an opportunity unavailable in
England. Farmers avoided low land next to a river and coves that
were likely to be flooded, just the type of land suitable for shipbuilding. Nor did builders seek valuable land near the center of
town, though occasionally they did receive such grants. Usually,
yards were located away from the central cluster of houses and
nearer the stands of timber. Two Salem shipbuilders, Richard
Hollingsworth and William Stephens, received land about one
mile from Salem Village.[8] William Stevens was satisfied that his
one and a third acres would be sufficient for shipbuilding, for a shipyard did not require a vast area. Thus the needs of a shipbuilder and
the composition of the small agricultural communities of Massachusetts complemented each other.

The government of Massachusetts had recognized the value of
shipbuilding even before its 1641 program. In 1639, for example,
the General Court had exempted all ship carpenters from militia

training, though they were to provide themselves with the usual weapons. Others in this privileged category were fishermen and millers, the tradesmen considered most important to the economy and the least replaceable.[9] On the other hand, the skills of the shipwright did not exempt him from service when the colony needed vessels. There is at least one known instance during the eighteenth century when the Massachusetts government drafted ship carpenters and ordered them to work on a warship for the defense of the colony.

With the beginning of the shipbuilding program of 1641, individual towns became more active than the colonial government in encouraging trade. Salem had difficulty enforcing its law to restrict the cutting of trees suitable for ship timber, and in 1641 both John Endecott and the Reverend Hugh Peters appealed to Gov. John Winthrop in the hope that the General Court would pass an act for the protection of ship timber. When the governor failed to take action, the Salem town meeting passed a new ordinance providing a heavy, 20-shilling fine for each tree cut contrary to the law.[10]

The General Court did pass some legislation to ensure the quality of vessels. The preamble to an act of 1641 states that "the country is nowe in hand with the building of ships, which is a business of great importance for the common good, and therefore suitable care is to be taken that it bee well performed." The act provided that when a vessel was under construction, the owners could appoint a man to survey the work in order to see that the ship was well built and that it conformed to the wishes of the owners. If he found anything amiss, the surveyor would report to the governor, deputy governor, or any two magistrates, who were authorized to appoint two of the leading shipwrights in the colony as viewers to inspect the construction in dispute. If the viewers found bad timbers or poor workmanship, the persons responsible would bear the cost of replacement. Records indicate that the act was enforced in the 1660s and 1670s. The last known instance occurred in 1695, when the lieutenant governor ordered two Boston shipwrights to Newbury to inspect a vessel.[11] They found the hull unfit for sea.

An interesting extension of the inspection act of 1641 is found in a law passed by the General Court in 1698. Instead of leaving inspection to the initiative of the owners, the 1698 act required shipbuilders to have their work viewed by inspectors at specific stages of construction. If the builder neglected to have his work inspected or to replace defective material and workmanship, he was subject to heavy fines. This act is not mentioned in other sources, and so there is no indication as to its reception or observance by shipbuilders. Acting on the Lords Commissioners for Trade and Plantations, the King in Council repealed this inspection act in 1700.[12]

There were other difficulties in establishing standards for the new industry. Several years after the passage of the inspection act of 1641, the Commissioners for the United Colonies of New England reported that builders and owners had frequent disagreements with each other, as well as some problems in common. Meeting at Boston in 1644, the Commissioners authorized the organization of a shipwright's company "with powers to regulate the building of ships, & to make such orders & laws amongst themselves as may conduce to the public good." Presumably, the company would enforce standard shipbuilding practices among its members, assuring Massachusetts of well-built shipping and freeing merchants from numerous court actions at the same time. Guilds of this type had long been common in London and other shipbuilding centers of England. In 1612 James I had chartered a company that was to include all English and Welsh shipwrights. Whether Massachusetts shipwrights actually organized their own company is unknown. There were probably some loose associations among shipbuilders of the larger towns, but there are no records of any formal activity or regulation. Although the commissioners invited builders to present laws for the company, apparently the shipwrights neither appeared nor formulated any regulations.[13] The dispersal of population in colonial Massachusetts must have been a severe handicap to the formation of guilds.

In 1667, the General Court reported that "divers unskilled persons, pretending to be shipwrights, doe build shipps & other vessels . . . which are very defective."[14] Aside from the immediate danger that the vessels might sink, such craft could give all Massachusetts shipping a bad reputation. The General Court appointed a committee to consider the problem and to prepare legislation for the next session, but no report was made.

During the 1667 session, the General Court also considered an act to encourage the construction of a dry dock in Boston or Charlestown. Any person who built a dry dock able to hold a 300-ton ship was promised a fifteen-year monopoly. The reason for this privilege, as stated by the members of the General Court, was that several ships had been lost and others damaged because of the lack of any facilities for extensive examination and repair. Although the act was passed, there is some question as to whether a dry dock was necessary. The nine-foot tide at Boston allowed the small merchant ships of the day to be examined and repaired "on the ebb." For major work, a vessel could be hauled onto the ways of a shipyard. It is doubtful that a shipowner would ignore these customary and relatively cheap methods and pay any charge for dry-docking. Perhaps the dry dock was to be a symbol of an expanding merchant fleet, proof that Massachusetts had port facilities comparable to those of England, or perhaps the dry dock might attract more shipping to Boston. In any event, it was built in 1678 by a group of Charlestown residents, and their company was granted a thirty-year monopoly by the General Court.[15] Little is known about the dry dock, as it did not survive and no other was built. It was probably a financial failure.

While the Massachusetts government recognized the value of a colonial-built merchant fleet, and towns and individuals tried to encourage its construction, shipwrights still faced several problems. Early explorers to the New World had noted the immense forests and their value to shipbuilding. The tall white pines of northern New England were especially impressive, and such trees furnished masts for the largest English warships. But much American timber was unfamiliar to shipwrights. Whereas in England they knew which oak tree to cut and which to avoid, in America they encountered unknown species of oak. In New England and the Middle Atlantic regions, both red and white oak trees abound. The heartwood of white oak is resistant to decay and water, while that of red oak is not.[16] Obviously, white oak should be the preferred timber for shipbuilding. Throughout much of the seventeenth century, however, some colonial builders used red oak, giving all American oak a bad reputation. Shipwrights could learn to judge the qualities of American woods only by experience, and that took time.

The difficult task of hewing trees into timbers for a ship's frame was accomplished with broadax and adz. Even more hard labor was required to saw the planks that covered the frame. Sawmills did not become common in England until the end of the eighteenth century, although they were in use in Europe by the seventeenth. A sawmill was built in northern Massachusetts, however, as early as 1623, perhaps because the high price and scarcity of labor made hand sawing uneconomical. Other mills were built on waterpower sites, sometimes far from the major settlements.[17]

Most of the timbers and planks in a ship were fastened together with wooden dowels called treenails, pronounced "trunnels." In England, treenails were fashioned out of carefully seasoned oak. The colonists found a substitute in locust wood, which has unusual strength, resistance to decay, and low shrinkage. In fact, locust treenails were probably superior to oak ones, and most colonial shipbuilders were using them by the 1630s. Iron bolts were used to hold the keel to the rest of the ship's frame. In the *Sparrow Hawk*, only six or seven bolts were needed for the entire frame. Even when iron became cheaper and more common in the eighteenth century, treenails were still used to attach planking to a ship's frame, because iron nails could rust and rot the surrounding wood.[18]

Iron was used in the superstructure of a vessel when planking was less than $1\frac{1}{2}$ inches thick. Iron braces held the rudder to the ship, and rigging was attached to the hull with iron bolts. A 100-ton vessel would use about 1 ton of iron.[19] This meant that a vessel such as the 300-ton ship *Mary Ann*, built at Salem in 1641, would require 3 tons of ironwork. Iron fittings became more numerous during the eighteenth century. To complicate matters, most ironwork had to be fashioned and fitted for each particular ship and therefore could not be made in England to standard sizes and then sent to the colonies. Before sailing, a vessel also had to be equipped with several anchors.

Governor Winthrop and the General Court advocated the establishment of a Massachusetts iron industry as part of the economic program of 1641. Fortunately, there were plenty of deposits of bog

iron along the Massachusetts coast. John Winthrop, Jr., went to England in 1641 and formed a company to finance ironworks in Massachusetts. The first opened at Braintree in 1645, and a second was completed two years later at Lynn, on the Saugus River. The works produced excellent ironware in a limited quantity; but suffering from mismanagement and competition from imported English bar iron, they earned little profit and caused much litigation among the owners. Before the Saugus and Braintree works closed in the 1660s, others went into operation in Taunton, Providence, and New Haven. In general, though, the attempt to establish a New England iron industry was unsuccessful in the seventeenth century. Doubtless some colonial-built vessels were furnished with iron from the Saugus works. Yet judging from the limited and intermittent production of Saugus and other works, it is safe to say that most iron for early colonial vessels was imported from England. English iron bars were, according to one historian, cheaper than those produced in Saugus and Braintree.[20] Dependence upon English iron was largely eliminated during the eighteenth century.

The last problem Massachusetts shipbuilders had to consider was obtaining cordage and sailcloth. Projects to produce both were included in the economic program of 1641 but never came to fruition. There was no choice but to import the two items. Completion of a vessel frequently was delayed pending the arrival of cordage or sailcloth, and disagreements often arose over the cost, quality, or quantity of the materials. Nevertheless, colonial merchants continued to import them until the Revolution. Paint was less of a concern to shipbuilders, for during most of the seventeenth century it was considered an unnecessary expense; a vessel could be protected by a coat of pine oil, to which time and dirt eventually gave a dark brown appearance.[21] The little paint that was used for decorative purposes usually came from England, though some was made in the colonies.

Since hulls could be constructed of native materials, and with the labor of only about half a dozen men, shipwrights had the resources to complete this part of the building on their own. For outfitting, which required expensive, imported materials, they had to secure financial aid from merchants. And upon these merchants rested the ultimate success of the shipbuilding program of 1641.

Little is known about the details of financing the shipbuilding program, but Governor Winthrop commented that "the work was hard to accomplish."[22] Merchants were asked to fund large ocean-going ships rather than small simple coastal craft. To minimize risk, investors divided the cost of a vessel into shares—quarters, eighths, and sixteenths. However, unlike the case in England, where ownership of trade goods and that of vessels were not always in the same hands, colonial merchants were compelled to ship cargoes in their own vessels. Luckily, the early ventures in timber and farm produce to the West Indies were successful enough to encourage more voyages.

The outbreak of civil war in England disrupted old trade patterns, especially between the Newfoundland fisheries and the West Country. London merchants wanted to take advantage of the situation and seize control of the fisheries from the West Country; but London shipping was already engaged in other trades and London merchants lacked the necessary experience. They found a solution by financing a New England–based fishing industry. Backed by English capital, colonial merchants were now able to enter a profitable and expanding trade. They sent fish to Spain, the Canary Islands, and the West Indies in exchange for specie and bills of credit, with which they could pay for English imports.[23]

The establishment and success of these early trades spurred colonial merchants to greater activity. Now that they had firm credit with English correspondents, they could invest in more shipping to further increase trade. In 1646 two London merchants ordered a ship captain to New England "to buy or build a Ketch of 40 or 50 tons."[24] The captain was to follow the advice of a Boston merchant as to cargo and destination of the vessel. Sending a captain to supervise the construction of a vessel for English merchants became quite common in the eighteenth century. As early as 1651, however, English merchants were purchasing shares in Massachusetts vessels, and ten years later William Stevens built a 150-ton ship for three British merchants on the island of Jersey.[25] Between meeting the needs of an active colonial merchant community engaged in various foreign trades and constructing or repairing vessels for British merchants, Massachusetts shipwrights had more than enough work.

Massachusetts had developed a lively shipbuilding industry by the 1670s. Edward Randolph wrote in 1676 that the Massachusetts colonists

build yearly several ships of good burthen besides ketches and barques, and for these seven last years . . . they have launched 20 ships (annually), some of 100 tons, and this year 30 were ordered to be set on the stocks by the merchants in England, who make their returns from hence in new shipping, but the wars have prevented that number: yet there are at Boston, Charlestown, and other places, above 12 building, some he is informed, upwards of 160 tons.[26]

Another report in 1676 stated that several vessels were annually sent to England and other countries and sold as "merchandise, which they build very cheap." The report listed Massachusetts-built and -owned tonnage as:

    30 vessels between 100 and 250 tons
    200 vessels between 50 and 100 tons
    200 vessels between 30 and 50 tons
    300 vessels between 6 and 30 tons

The main building centers, the report concluded, were Boston, Charlestown, Salem, Ipswich, Salisbury, and Portsmouth, which constructed good ships for £4 per ton.[27]

The above list shows that most Massachusetts vessels were less than 50 tons each. Among these small coastal craft, the ketch seems to have been the most common. In the printed court records of Essex County, for example, one finds the ketch mentioned much more frequently than any other vessel. Besides making coastal and fishing voyages, ketches were also used in the West Indian trade: after the 30-ton ketch *Dove* was launched at Ipswich in the fall of 1673, the owners sent her to Barbados. These small vessels were particularly suited to a merchant community of limited means. A merchant could own several ketches and have shares in others; and so the loss of any one vessel could not ruin him. Such was the practice of Jonathan Curwen, a Salem merchant whose ketches were engaged in the fisheries and West Indian trade. One Boston merchant of 1670 owned one ketch and three shallops, while holding shares in another seven ketches and two ships.[28]

Both reports of 1676 emphasize the practice of building ships for sale in England. Such vessels could be ordered directly by a British merchant, or the colonial merchant might finance them himself and then try to sell them in England or elsewhere. After 1670 the construction of ships for sale expanded and attacted more attention from British merchants. Several circumstances encouraged them to look to the colonies for new shipping. First, British shipwrights failed to supply merchants with an economical cargo carrier. The English custom of building merchant vessels on a warship pattern forced British merchants to try to make extensive use of the many flyboats captured in the Dutch wars of the third quarter of the seventeenth century. But the refusal of British builders to copy the practical Dutch vessel and the restrictions of the Navigation Act of 1662 on foreign-built shipping left English merchants without a source of flyboats. Not until the 1680s did shipwrights on the northeast coast of England begin to build vessels in the flyboat form. Second, a shortage of ship timber became a problem for English merchants after the fire of 1666 because of the huge amount of wood required to rebuild London. The timber reserves were further reduced by an extensive, shortsighted government program begun in 1677 for the construction of warships. A shortage of oak timber meant higher building costs. The prices for shipbuilding in England during this period are unknown, but they were certainly higher than in New England.[29]

The second report of 1676 lists the cost per ton of Massachusetts vessels as £4. In 1676, a Charlestown, Massachusetts, builder charged £3 18s. per ton to construct a 182-ton ship. After adding the cost of masts and other fittings, the price came to a fraction over £4 per ton. Three years later the same shipwright charged a basic price of £3 14s. per ton for a 102-ton ship. The difference was probably due to the larger timber requirements of the first ship. During the same decade, Massachusetts shipwrights were building smaller vessels, such as ketches, for as little as £3 5s. per ton.[30] Prices obviously varied with the size and quality of the vessel, yet samples indicate that the price cited in the second report of 1676 was accurate, at least for larger ships—the type most likely to be purchased by a British merchant.

A final portion of the two reports considers geographic distribution. The heaviest concentration of shipwrights was in Boston and Charlestown. Timber prices were probably higher in the Boston area than in towns to the north, but that would have been balanced by the availability of capital from an active merchant community. Following Boston and Charlestown was Salem, a small town with a group of merchants able to support the building of coastal craft. In 1672, a British merchant who had settled in Salem financed the construction of a 140-ton ship for his six partners—all London merchants. The reports also list Salisbury and Ipswich as shipbuilding centers. Even allowing for local pride, town historians seem to substantiate the shipbuilding activity in Salisbury. But with the exception of a small yard in 1673, there seems to have been little if any shipbuilding in Ipswich during the seventeenth century. In fact, when an Ipswich merchant needed a small ketch in 1677, he contracted with a shipwright in Salisbury. The last town listed is Portsmouth, until 1680 best known for sending "ten mast cargoes a year to England." Records are scarce, but there does seem to have been some shipbuilding. In 1649 a 100-ton ship was under construction. And one active shipwright, John Jackson, settled in Portsmouth in 1645. His son Richard was also a shipwright, and the house he built in 1664 still stands, overlooking the cove into which he launched vessels.[31]

Whereas little information is available about general trends in Massachusetts shipbuilding during this period, the careers of several shipwrights are recorded. William Stevens participated in Gloucester's local government and was elected to the General Court in 1665. A bitter opponent of the Restoration government in England, he became deranged in his last years and lost much of his property. One of his sons, James, was a shipbuilder and, like his father, became active in local politics. James ably served in the General Court for ten years.[32]

By the 1670s Salem had at least a dozen shipbuilders. Two brothers, John and Jonathan Pickering, built vessels at South River on land granted for that purpose by the town. In 1664 the town granted land downstream for the construction of a dam and mill. The proposed dam would cause all shipyards above it to close, since vessels would no longer be able to reach the harbor. The Pickering brothers wrecked some preliminary work on the dam. When construction continued despite their efforts, they went to court, charging the proprietors of the dam with blocking a waterway, The brothers lots their case; when the mill was built, they moved their yard downstream, below the dam, to an area called Ruck's Village.[33]

Ruck's Village, a community of shipwrights, was located on a cove in the South River less than 300 yards from the center of Salem. Despite its nearness to town, the land seems to have been uninhabited until one shipbuilder, Daniel Bacon, established a yard there in 1664. Bacon, who had probably learned the shipwright's trade on the Isle of Jersey, came to Salem at the age of twenty-three. His three sons became shipwrights, and, in turn, two of their sons followed the same trade. By the 1670s there were at least six builders launching vessels into the cove. Related tradesmen also lived in Ruck's Village. Capt. Nicholas Manning and two other anchorsmiths were working there, and Samuel King, a blockmaker, was another village resident.[34] With the skills of such men available, Salem shipwrights were less dependent on British fittings than colonists of the previous generation had been.

Bartholomew Gedney, born in Salem about 1640, was the best-known shipwright at Ruck's Village. A colonel in the militia, Gedney served as a judge and later as a member of the provincial Court of Assistants. Recently, his house has been identified as one standing on a rise overlooking the site of his shipyard. Near the house stood the home of Eleazer Gedney, a shipwright and brother of Bartholomew.[35] Little is known about Eleazer. Following his death, in 1683, his eldest son continued the family shipbuilding tradition.

Although most Salem shipwrights lived in Ruck's Village, others settled along the harbor's edge. Of unknown background, John Becket had settled in Salem by the early 1660s. He and Bartholomew Gedney were appointed by the court to survey a poorly constructed vessel in Gloucester. Becket built his own house on the harbor's edge about half a mile from the center of town on a small site sufficient for a shipyard. Although a leading shipwright, Becket's inventory shows only a modest estate, totaling £358. His house and land account for more than two-thirds of the estate; and after clothing and household furnishings, there remains about £20 worth of shipbuilder's tools, a large number of tools as compared with those listed in later eighteenth-century inventories. The house and yard were used by four generations of Beckets. In 1800 the most famous of all Salem shipwrights, Retire Becket, moved his yard to a nearby location, and Beckets continued to practice shipbuilding in Salem until the late 1880s.[36]

The success of colonial-built shipping in England and America was of great economic importance to New England merchants. At last Massachusetts colonists had a commodity that British merchants would accept in payment for exports to America. True, colonial shipbuilding was in competition with British shipbuilders and therefore dependent upon market conditions in England; but it still must have provided a welcome change for New England merchants, whose sources of specie had previously been limited to the sale of fish and provisions chiefly in the West Indies. The growth of Massachusetts shipbuilding, however, was not welcomed by all observers. In his book on mercantilism published in 1669, Sir Josiah Child warned:

Of all the American Plantations, his Majesty has none so apt for the building of Shipping as New-England, nor none more comparably so qualified for the breeding of Seamen, not only by reason of the natural industry of that people but principally by reason of their Cod and Mackeral Fisheries: and in my poor opinion, there is nothing more prejudicial, and in prospect more dangerous to any Mother-Kingdom, than the increase of Shipping in her Colonies, Plantations, or Provinces.[37]

## Virginia

Virginia had good timber and iron ore. But in 1649 there were still no sawmills in the colony; and after the destruction of the Falling Creek ironworks in the Indian massacre of 1622, no iron was produced locally until the eighteenth century. Virginia long remained dependent on British-built vessels and visiting shipwrights. A Captain Yong, for example, arrived in Virginia on July 3, 1634, and immediately began the construction of two shallops. Thirteen days later he completed his task and left the colony. When a leaking Dutch ship arrived at Jamestown in 1635, there were no shipbuilders to repair her and the vessel had to go on to New Amsterdam. Of course, during the 1630s and 1640s some half dozen ship carpenters were building small boats on the Eastern Shore of Virginia. Two of these men, William Stevens and William Berry, repaired and built a few shallops during the period when Massachusetts builders were launching 300-ton ships. By the middle of the seventeenth century more boats and some coasting craft were built—but no ships.[38]

Seeking a diversified economy for Virginia, Gov. William Berkeley visited England in 1663 to obtain government aid for the cultivation of commodities other than tobacco. He urged that ships built in Virginia be allowed to trade anywhere, doubtless hoping to follow New England's example and have Virginia build ships to carry tobacco and other products to West Indian and European ports. With the same natural resources for shipbuilding as New England, plus the advantages of a valuable staple, Virginia seemed in a good position to construct and own its own shipping. It was probably due to Governor Berkeley's efforts, in fact, that the Virginia House of Burgesses passed an act in March 1662 for the "encouragement of building vessels in this country and the promoting of trade." The law provided that any person who constructed a decked vessel would receive 50 pounds of tobacco for each ton of her burden. At the December meeting of the same year, the encouragement act was expanded and more precisely defined. The builder of a decked vessel greater than 20 but less than 50 tons would receive 50 pounds of tobacco per ton, as in the earlier act. But if the vessel was greater than 50 but less than 100 tons, the bounty would be 100 pounds of tobacco per ton. And for any greater than 100 tons, the builder would be entitled to 200 pounds of tobacco per ton. The act tried to ensure that the shipping would be Virginia-owned by making anyone selling a vessel to a person living outside the colony forfeit the bounty.[39]

There is record of only one person ever receiving the bounty. In 1663 Governor Berkeley awarded Peter Peterson 1,300 pounds of tobacco for building a 26-ton vessel. In general, these acts not only failed to inaugurate a boom in shipbuilding but probably failed as well to affect Virginia's economy at all. At least one large ship was built in Virginia during this period, and perhaps it is more than a coincidence that the bounty act was repealed shortly before the vessel was launched. The ship went to England and was described in a London news letter of 1667: "A frigate of between thirty and forty guns, built in Virginia, looks so fair that it is believed that in a short time they will get the art of building as good frigates there as in England."[40] Probably the frigate was built as a privateer, rather than a regular warship, for service in the second Anglo-Dutch war. A frigate of that armament would measure at least 600 tons and therefore might have earned its builder a 60-ton tobacco bounty—if the act had not been repealed.

Writing to the Commissioners of Foreign Plantations in 1670, Governor Berkeley reported that nearly eighty English tobacco ships arrived annually in Virginia, plus a few New England ketches; "but of our own, we never yet had more than two at one time, and those were not more than twenty tons burden." Explaining "why no small or great vessels are built here," Berkeley commented that "we are most obedient to all laws, whilst the New England men break through, and trade to any place that their interest lead them." The lack of activity in shipbuilding in seventeenth-century Virginia was not, as Berkeley argued in 1670, a result of Virginians' respect for the Navigation Acts. The governor gave better reasons in his essay of 1663, where he suggested that disinterest in shipbuilding and other potential industries was due to "the vicious ruinous plant of Tobacco," for which "Planters neglect all other accessions to wealth." Massachusetts colonists had to turn to shipbuilding—they had no alternatives. But Virginians did not worry about being cut off from England because of a lack of credit; they had no need to build their own shipping or to seek out new trade routes. Tobacco was highly profitable and desired by English merchants; and Dutch merchant ships also sought out the tobacco plantations along the Chesapeake until they were prohibited from doing so by the Navigation Acts of 1660 and 1663.[41] Virginia had a profitable export commodity, and transportation was provided by English merchants; there was little need or incentive for domestic shipbuilding.

### Other Southern Colonies

By 1680 colonists were settled in the Carolinas, but there is no record of any shipbuilding there. Like colonists in other settlements, they probably constructed small craft for communication along the bays and rivers of the coastal regions. Such craft may have been simply large canoes dug out of pine logs. Copied from local Indian craft, dugouts were easily built and used in all the colonies.[42]

Gov. Charles Calvert likewise wrote in 1678 that no ships were being built in Maryland. He tried to encourage the inhabitants to construct small craft for collecting tobacco from plantations and delivering it to the large British merchant ships. But the governor's efforts were unsuccessful, and the colony remained dependent on British-built ships and smaller vessels as well.[43]

### New York

Shipbuilding in early New Amsterdam resembled that in Virginia. The Dutch colonists found good timber but no sawyers, let alone a sawmill; there were iron and wood for charcoal, but only a few smiths and no ironworks. Occasionally some ship carpenters visited the colony, but apparently they never settled permanently. During the early 1630s several shipwrights launched half a dozen "yachts" —small decked vessels capable of coastal navigation—and builders constructed small boats and repaired several larger vessels; but no one built oceangoing ships. In 1652, when the Dutch settlement on the island of Aruba, near the northern coast of South America, lost its only trading vessels, the directors of the company in Amsterdam wrote to Gov. Peter Stuyvesant advising him that it would be cheaper to build a small sloop in his colony and send it to Aruba than to sail the vessel directly from Holland. Apparently shipbuilders were available and the sloop could have been built. But five years later, in 1657, when Governor Stuyvesant asked the directors to send ship carpenters to the colony, he was informed that it was expensive and unnecessary since there was only a small amount of shipping at New Amsterdam. When the Dutch colony on the Delaware River needed a small sloop, there was no one in New Amsterdam to build it.[44]

Under English rule, shipbuilding activity increased. In 1669 Gov. Richard Nicolls and several partners financed the construction of a 120-ton ship, the *Good Fame*, "a very stronge and handsome vessell but costly." The same year, a 60- or 70-ton ship was also launched in New York. But while shipbuilding continued to grow, construction remained limited mostly to small vessels. In 1678 Gov. Sir Edmond Andros wrote that of the ten to fifteen ships of about 100 tons each trading with New York, four of the smaller ones had been built in the colony.[45] New York shipping was not to expand until the eighteenth century.

### Connecticut

Timber was available in Connecticut, and more could be secured by floating wood down the Connecticut River. As his father had done in Massachusetts, Gov. John Winthrop, Jr., promoted the iron industry in Connecticut by constructing a successful ironworks—in his case, at New Haven in 1657.[46] But like other economic efforts in seventeenth-century Connecticut, shipbuilding activity was merely an unsuccessful attempt to emulate Massachusetts.

Connecticut had a small number of shipbuilders; there were half a dozen ship carpenters in New Haven alone by the early 1640s. Like other Connecticut settlers, these shipbuilders came from Massachusetts—some having lived there several years and others just having arrived from England. The wanderings of one early shipbuilder were rather extensive. Thomas Tracy settled in Watertown, Massachusetts, after arriving from England. In 1636 he moved to Salem, where he received five acres of land, presumably for a shipyard. But two years later Tracy was in Saybrook, at the mouth of the Connecticut River, and, after a couple of years there, he moved upriver to the Hartford area. Finally, he settled permanently in Norwich, on the Thames River about fifteen miles above New London.[47]

Of the several settlements in Connecticut, New Haven appeared the most promising. The leaders from urban backgrounds intended to make the town a commercial center as well as a holy experiment, and the site was chosen for its fine harbor and central location between other Connecticut settlements and New Amsterdam. Yet expectations for commercial profit were never realized. The supply of fur, the first export, decreased rapidly, and merchants had to seek a new source. In 1641 they tried to establish a trading post along the Delaware River, "but the settlement was broken up by the Swedes and Dutch, and a pestilence."[48] Their own funds fast disappearing, New Haven merchants had yet to find an export capable of attracting English shipping. Stimulated to undertake shipbuilding by the threat of isolation if they did not, Connecticut merchants probably were heartened by the success of the Massachusetts shipbuilding program.

New Haven already had a small group of shipwrights, and merchants financed the construction of a 100-ton ship. Contemporaries charged that the ship was poorly designed and ill laden, with the light cargo at the bottom of the hull and the heavier part above. The top-heavy vessel left New Haven for England in January 1646 and was never seen again except as an apparition appearing to anxious townspeople. Undaunted by the severe loss, merchants built another ship, which was launched in October 1647. Named the *Fellowship*, the vessel was still active in 1652, but nothing about her voyages was recorded. The history of a smaller ship built at New Haven in 1648 also remains unrecorded. Despite the Connecticut merchants' high hopes for a commercial career, their inability to establish direct trade with England doomed them to remain an agricultural community.[49]

Other Connecticut towns continued to build small coasting vessels; since trade was mainly with Boston, there was no need for large ships. New London became the center of activity in the second half of the seventeenth century, as John Coit with his two sons and a son-in-law built pinnaces and shallops for the coasting trade during the 1660s. When New London merchants began a small but active provisions trade with the West Indian islands, Coit and his partners built three barks ranging in size from 12 to 20 tons. At the same time, merchants started a provisions trade with Newfoundland; this was carried on in small vessels usually owned by one or two men. Such coastal vessels were better investment risks than the cumbersome ships of New Haven. Besides Coit and his relatives, there were several other shipbuilders in the New London area.[50]

Although small vessels were usually sufficient for the provisions tradings of Connecticut, shipwrights occasionally built larger craft.

In 1666 Coit and his partners launched a 70-ton ship, the *New London*, the largest vessel built in New London up to that time, to be used for voyages to Europe. In 1678 the same builders launched a 90-ton ship. This shipbuilding activity obviously does not compare with that of Massachusetts, but Connecticut did build enough for its own needs. Writing to the Lords of Trade in 1680, Gov. William Leete explained that except for some direct export to the West Indies and an occasional ship to Madeira or Fayal, there was little commerce: altogether, Connecticut owned only twenty-seven vessels. The governor concluded that lack of capital and the high cost of labor in the colony were the main obstacles to advancement.[51]

## Rhode Island

In view of the colony's widespread maritime activity in the eighteenth century, it is surprising that few vessels were owned or even built in Rhode Island before 1690. Gov. Peleg Stanford reported in 1680, "We have no shipping belonging to the colony, but only a few sloops." It has been argued that the governor was attempting to disguise an extensive coastal and West Indian trade. That suspicion, however, is not supported by the records. The first known shipwright did not settle in Rhode Island until 1680. Similarly, shipbuilding contracts and bills of sale do not appear in Rhode Island until after 1690.[52] One must conclude that there was little shipbuilding in seventeenth-century Rhode Island.

Due to its unusual geographic position and prevailing winds, sailing ships could enter Newport harbor for shelter when storms closed most other ports. But one finds very few instances of vessels seeking shelter in Newport harbor and little evidence of vessels regularly trading at Newport. Newport at this time was neither the active shipping town nor even the useful haven for emergencies it was to become in its later history. Rhode Island did have a limited coasting and West Indian trade, and therefore some small vessels were probably built in the colony. Yet, overall, the economy of seventeenth-century Rhode Island was agricultural.

## Summary

In the seventeenth century, wood was abundant and iron available in most of the colonies, while many items such as cordage, sailcloth, and other fittings had to be imported from England. But to initiate colonial shipbuilding, men had to be willing to invest their limited resources. In the tobacco-centered economies of Virginia and Maryland, the potential success of seeking new trade was ignored as long as English shipping was readily available. In New England, merchants had little choice but to undertake shipbuilding; for if they wished to secure specie or credit with which to purchase English imports, the merchants had to establish their own trade routes and provide their own carriage. Yet the failure of the New Haven shipbuilding program is evidence that economic need did not guarantee success. The unique combination in Massachusetts was need plus a merchant community with the resources to back a sustained effort.

Shipbuilders were established in various towns from Boston to the north, though the main centers were Boston, Charlestown, and Salem. The craftsmen and their yards were well suited for life in the coastal New England towns, where they provided the fundamental industry for a growing maritime economy in return for a small amount of land and support from the merchant community. The career of at least one shipwright indicates a restlessness common to that age, but employment was at hand wherever he chose to settle. Like other colonists, shipwrights were increasingly native-born, and, in the case of Salem, families often maintained a shipbuilding tradition.

Massachusetts launched at least ten large ships in the 1640s and sent other vessels to the West Indies and the Canary Islands. But, in general, colonial vessels were small craft designed for the coastal and West Indian trades. Ketches less than 50 tons seem to have been the most popular of all. Among the limited number of ships launched, some were built for British merchants as a form of remittance for goods sent to Massachusetts. This practice was still limited in the sevententh century and seemed a convenient source of mutual benefit to most observers. Only Sir Josiah Child sounded the warnings of future economic rivalry between Britain and New England.

# The Early Eighteenth-Century Expansion of Colonial Shipbuilding

## Massachusetts

THE rapid expansion which characterized Massachusetts shipbuilding during the first three decades of the eighteenth century is well documented in the Massachusetts shipping register, 1697–1714.[1] With the exception of fishing vessels and small coasters trading within the colony, the register includes all Massachusetts-built shipping. Table 1, covering the years 1674–96, does not include vessels built and sold outside the colony or lost before registration began, in 1697, but nevertheless may be considered representative, as it does record all shipping based in Massachusetts at that date. Tables 2–4 reflect the remainder of the register, divided into three six-year periods based upon a vessel's construction date.

According to the tables, Massachusetts-built shipping grew from 18,329 tons for the years 1697–1702 to 24,294 for 1703–8, an increase of 32.5 percent. Massachusetts shipwrights launched 27,690 tons during the third six-year period, 1709–14, a gain of about 14 percent. Although the tonnages recorded before 1697 represent only a portion of an unknown total, certain general trends are undeniable. From 6,708 tons, recorded for the years 1674–96, the tonnage increase to 1697–1702 represents a jump of 173.2 percent.[2]

What caused this sudden growth in Massachusetts shipping? During the three brief Dutch wars of the third quarter of the seventeenth century, England had captured between 2,000 and 3,000 prizes and had lost less than 500 of its own merchant ships, but this convenient method of securing tonnage was reversed in the War of the League of Augsburg. Perhaps as many as 4,000 English vessels were captured; and all but 500 were taken in the last years of the struggle, 1694–97. These concentrated losses resulted from the French policy of avoiding naval battles in order to pursue merchant ships. The destruction of British commerce was further hastened by

Atlantic coast shipbuilding centers

increasing numbers of French privateers. English convoys tried vainly to give merchant ships better protection in the War of the Spanish Succession, as the French proceeded to capture at least 2,000 vessels. In comparison, France lost about 1,300 of its own ships. British merchants wanted to replace their many lost vessels, but shipbuilding costs rose sharply in England during the wars. Known for its cheap building rates since the mid-seventeenth century, New England could provide the necessary tonnage at less cost than English shipyards. Bostonians, the governor of New York reported in 1700, claimed they could build merchant vessels for 40 percent less than they could be built in England. When the extensive purchase of colonial-built vessels by English merchants fell off with the coming of peace in 1713, inexpensive New England ships continued to find a market in Britain.[3]

Boston, Charlestown, Scituate, and Salem were the main shipbuilding centers of Massachusetts in 1700.[4] The tables emphasize Boston's domination of building activity in the colony. From 1674 to 1696, Boston produced 25.6 percent of all the Massachusetts tonnage. That figure increased to 31.8 for the years 1697–1702, and then to 34.0 percent for the years 1703–8. Between 1709 and 1714, Boston shipwrights launched 48.8 percent of all Massachusetts-built tonnage. The major portion of Boston's increase was in ships: their number jumped from thirty-four between 1697 and 1702 to fifty between 1703 and 1708 and then to ninety during the next six years. While the number of ships increased, tonnage average declined slightly. Boston not only produced more ships than any other Massachusetts town; it usually launched more of the other types of vessels as well.

In terms of natural resources, Boston was poorly situated for shipbuilding, since timber and iron had to be transported from the surrounding countryside. But as the economic center of New England, Boston offered an amount of capital ready for investment that more than outweighed its lack of timber. Merchants able to finance construction, builders in town waiting for contracts, and numerous workmen also on hand all made Boston the most likely shipbuilding site. Furthermore, cordage and other fittings which had to be imported from England were more readily available at Boston than at other ports. A 1722 map of Boston shows fifteen shipyards, all but two of which are crowded along the town's north-east shoreline. In fact, lack of space caused several builders during the 1720s to lay out their yards at the ends of streets. Sometimes the selectmen allowed the builder to remain, but more often they ordered him to clear the roadway as soon as his ship had been launched. A 1722 engraving of Boston harbor by William Burgis depicts more than seventy sailing vessels in detail and thirteen busy shipyards. Three of the yards have two vessels each on the stocks, while eight yards are building one vessel each. In two other yards, repair work is under way.[5]

Because Charlestown is directly across the Charles River from Boston, one would expect similar shipbuilding patterns for both towns. Records indicate, however, that after the rapid expansion of activity in the two settlements during the late 1690s, Charlestown building leveled off while Boston continued to increase its lead. Charlestown was second to Boston in the construction of ships but, unlike Boston, launched few other types of vessels. In each of the three six-year periods, the smaller town built nineteen or twenty ships averaging 15 to 30 tons larger than those of Boston. Charlestown had a small group of merchants, such as John Phillips and James Russell, who occasionally invested in ship construction, but Boston merchants usually provided the capital for Charlestown shipbuilding. A merchant might have the vessel built for his own use, as did Capt. Elisha Bennett in the early 1690s, or, probably more common, the Bostonian might act as agent for a British merchant. For example, in 1700 two Boston merchants, Thomas Cooper and John Barnaby, contracted with a Charlestown builder for a large ship on the account of a London merchant, Jeremiah Johnson.[6]

Charlestown building prices seem to have been lower than those of Boston. After failing to secure a suitable builder in Boston, Thomas Moffat found a Charlestown shipwright who agreed to charge 2 shillings less per ton than the Boston rate. Later in the same year, 1715, Moffat had another ship built in Charlestown for a Bristol correspondent. This second vessel was smaller than the first, and consequently the building price was even less. "This," Moffat wrote, "is much cheaper than I could get it done in Town [Boston]."[7] The cost difference was probably responsible for larger ships' being constructed in Charlestown, since, for the price of a

Boston-built vessel, a merchant could go across the river and get extra tonnage.

About 16 miles from Plymouth, Scituate was one of half a dozen small towns scattered along the coast south of Boston. Small coasting vessels, mostly for fishing, were built in all the towns. Yet thirty of the thirty-four ships and fifty of the fifty-seven brigantines listed in the register for this area were launched in Scituate; the town built nearly all the oceangoing vessels of its region. Boston merchants provided the capital for the Scituate vessels; but Scituate ships were consistently smaller than those of Boston, while other types of Scituate vessels equaled those from any other Massachusetts town. Perhaps the ships were financed by the less wealthy Boston merchants.[8] Certainly, the town's untapped timber and iron resources offered a cheap alternative to Boston merchants seeking to avoid the city's high building costs. Scituate built 18.6 percent of all Massachusetts tonnage recorded between 1674 and 1696. During the next six years, the town's shipwrights launched 16.6 percent of the Massachusetts total, just a fraction less than Salem, which was second to Boston at that time. Afterward, building in Scituate quickly diminished. In the period ending 1708, Scituate was down to 8.0 percent of the Massachusetts total, and six years later the percentage was 2.6. Why Scituate declined as a shipbuilding center is unknown, but, most likely, builders simply moved to other towns after they had exhausted the area's supply of usable timber and bog iron.

Salem, the fourth Massachusetts shipbuilding center at this time, experienced a rise in construction through the years 1703–8 and then a sharp decline.[9] Like Boston, Salem produced all types of vessels. At first the Salem merchant community, with its limited resources, made extensive use of the ketch for fishing and coastal trading: during the years 1697–1702, thirty-two ketches were launched at Salem. But in the next six-year period, the high point of Salem shipbuilding, only five ketches were built; and not even one ketch was recorded for the years 1709–14. As ketch construction declined in Salem, the tonnage of another coasting vessel, the sloop, quickly increased, soon surpassing that of the disappearing ketch. Meanwhile, Salem shipwrights also launched more and more larger craft—brigantines and ships. The brief rise of ship construction

in Salem was financed mainly by outside capital. Of twelve ships
built in Salem between 1703 and 1708, eight of more than 100 tons
each were owned by Boston or English merchants. In the last six-
year period, all three ships of over 100 tons were again owned by
Boston or English merchants.[10]

Boston was the only major shipbuilding center in Massachusetts
to maintain its position, even increasing its lead over other centers.
Leaving the four main centers, however, one finds a steady increase
of tonnage production, as in two towns to the northward. Newbury
and Kittery are located on deep rivers with easy access to the extensive timber resources of the hinterland. Few vessels were produced in either port before the late 1690s. Then, in six years, Newbury shipwrights built twenty-three small vessels. At the same
time Kittery launched three ships, two of which were owned by
Boston merchants. During the years 1703–8 Newbury builders
launched five large ships for Boston and London merchants. But
Newbury continued to produce a variety of vessels, while Kittery
concentrated on ships. Boston and English merchants owned all
but one of the ten ships launched at Kittery.[11]

During the years 1703 to 1708, ships in the two small towns were
larger than any others built in Massachusetts. Between 1709 and
1714, Newbury launched almost twice as much tonnage as it had
in the previous six years, continuing to build both coastal and
oceangoing vessels. Four large ships were launched for English and
Boston merchants, and seven small ships were also built. Kittery
began to launch some coasting vessels during this period, but its
main effort was still directed to ship construction. Of the five large
Kittery ships, British merchants had shares in one, and Bostonians
owned the rest. Only three small ships were built in Kittery during
this period.[12]

Cheap construction rates probably explain the increase in building in these towns and the larger size of the ships. According to
Thomas Moffat, shipwrights in the area charged 5–10 shillings
per ton less than those of the Boston region.[13] Newbury and Kittery shipbuilders had less initial expense because timber was more
plentiful there than in Boston. Moffat noted that cordage, fittings,
and sails were more expensive than in Boston. Even so, enough
Boston merchants were willing to invest their capital and that of

English correspondents to ensure the gradual expansion of ship-building in Newbury and Kittery.

With Englishmen now purchasing American vessels on a larger scale, it was logical that someone should attempt to eliminate the expense of a middleman—the colonial merchant. Led by Thomas Hunt, a group of London merchants sought a colonial correspon-dent who could combine the hitherto separate functions of ship-builder and factor. They sent the London shipwright Thomas Coram to Boston in charge of a party of English ship carpenters. Little is known about Coram's work in Boston. Presumably, he received the necessary equipment for his ships from the London merchants, who then sent over captains to navigate the completed vessels to England. Like anyone building in Boston, Coram paid more for timber than did builders in the outlying areas. In the late 1690s, when some Boston merchants began to invest in ship construction at new sites offering abundant timber, such as New-bury and Kittery, Coram searched for a similar location. He chose a site along the Taunton River, flowing into Narragansett Bay. Writing thirty years later, Coram explained, "The convenience of the vast great planks of oak and fir timber, and iron oar which I found abounding at a place call'd Taunton ... encouraged me to take some of my English shipwrights from Boston." The site of Coram's yard, at the village of Dighton, remained part of the town of Taunton until 1712. At Dighton, the Taunton River had sufficient depth to launch a large ship, but above it the river be-came too narrow and shallow for any except the smallest boat. There had been little or no shipbuilding along the Taunton River or in neighboring settlements until Coram established his yard in 1697.[14]

Thomas Coram's efforts to produce cheaper tonnage for his London correspondents initiated a sudden rise of shipbuilding in the Taunton area. Like Kittery, Taunton specialized in the con-struction of ships, launching seven between 1697 and 1702. During this and the following six-year period, Taunton-built ships aver-aged 10 tons less than those of Boston. A local smith, Robert Cross-man, used ore from around Taunton to forge the ironwork for Coram's ships. Though the large ships were sold to London mer-chants, the Massachusetts register shows Boston merchants owning several smaller ships.[15] Coram may have been building for Bostonians also, but more likely other builders had already been attracted to the area.

A forthright individual and staunch Anglican, Thomas Coram was not popular with the Congregationalists of Taunton. They held up construction by refusing to deliver timber or by leaving it in the wrong place and allowing the river to wash it away. This petty persecution led to numerous legal suits in which the county court condemned Coram and the superior court supported him. By 1704 Coram had had enough of Massachusetts and returned to London. He conveyed his land in Taunton to the vestrymen of King's Chapel Church in Boston with the provision that the property would be given to the inhabitants of Taunton if they agreed to build an Anglican church. Whatever his relationship with the Taunton populace, Coram continued to advocate plans for the encouragement of colonial shipbuilding and the production of naval stores in the colonies. After some success as a merchant, he became a trustee of Georgia in 1732 and established several settlements in Maine, Nova Scotia, and the Bahamas.[16]

Even after Coram's departure, interest in building vessels continued to spread throughout the Taunton area. Ship production decreased slightly in both size and number; but whereas only one sloop and one brigantine had been built by 1702, four sloops and five brigantines were launched between 1703 and 1708. As before, Boston and London merchants financed all ship construction. In the next six-year period, 1709–14, Taunton builders returned to working on ships and launched only two sloops and one brigantine.[17]

In 1710 Taunton carpenters launched two of the largest merchant ships of the entire colonial period, the 400-ton *Sea Nymph* and the 600-ton *Thomas and Elizabeth*. English merchants occasionally employed such ships in the trans-Atlantic trade or more commonly used them as East Indiamen. But even Englishmen engaged in long-distance trade considered a 600-ton vessel an awkward giant. After all, such ships were proportionally more expensive to build, were difficult to fill to capacity with cargo, and represented a considerable risk to their investors. In fact, to diminish risk, ownership of the Taunton leviathans was divided among forty-two Bostonians and one London merchant.[18] Except for brief entries in the Massachusetts register, nothing is known about these vessels and their subsequent careers. Two other ships, average-sized vessels owned by Boston merchants, were also built at Taunton in 1710. In the following year, when the building sites were listed under Dighton, only one small ship was launched. Two years later shipwrights constructed another small ship. But Taunton never again repeated the great effort of 1710.

The register not only offers valuable facts on varying production levels of shipbuilding areas in Massachusetts and the relation of those areas to the investments of colonial and British merchants, but also reveals important changes from the seventeenth century in types of vessels produced. For example, the tables contain two new vessel categories—sloop and brig—and older types, the shallop and the pinnace, are not included. The summaries of Massachusetts vessels for each period show a steady decline in the number of ketches and barks produced.

The sloop, a single-mast vessel of Dutch origin that came to New England via New Netherland and via England, where shipbuilders also copied the Dutch model, was, by the mid-1690s, displacing other types as the principal coasting craft. Even the pinnace, a popular exploring and trading vessel in the seventeenth century, was abandoned for lightly built sloops. However, the replacement of the shallop and the ketch by the sloop was gradual enough so that several vessels of the era would be difficult to categorize. In general, varied hull forms and a fore-and-aft mainsail suspended from a short gaff made the sloop more attractive to sailors than its seventeenth-century counterparts; the spritsail on the latter, if a larger vessel, often became awkward. But shallops could be built with a variety of sail arrangements and occasionally appear throughout the eighteenth century.

The bark, with its two masts and square-sail rig, was replaced by the brigantine, commonly referred to as brig. The brigantine carried a combination rig with square sails on the foremast and a fore-and-aft sail on the main. Sometimes square sails were also set on the mainmast. Thus the brig had some characteristics of the bark but boasted a more complicated and versatile rig. The tables reveal a rapid increase in the number and size of brigantines built from 1697 to 1708.

Definite changes to more adaptable rigs and hull forms explain the demise of the pinnace, the shallop, the bark, and the ketch. But it must be emphasized that differences between seventeenth- and eighteenth-century vessel types during the periods covered by the register are often so technical and vague as to suggest that they also reflect a change in preferences for terminology. Nevertheless, by 1714 the sloop for coastal work and the ship for ocean trade, with the brig a common alternative, constituted the major portion of the Massachusetts merchant fleet[19] (see Figs. 3, 4).

More vessels were built in Massachusetts than in any other colony. Massachusetts launched 83.5 percent of the recorded colonial tonnage built between 1674 and 1696, and about 91 percent from 1697 to 1714. Almost all the residual tonnage was from New Hampshire and Connecticut.[20] However, tonnage built in England and prizes captured from the French and Spanish are absent from these statistics. According to the Bailyns' thorough analysis of the register, only 1,430 tons of British-built shipping were registered in Massachusetts. The number of prizes was greater, amounting to about 6,000 tons of shipping. There were less than 500 tons from the West Indies or elsewhere listed under the vague categories of "plantation-" or "foreign-built."[21] Adding up these figures, the resulting 8,000 or so tons hardly compares with the colonial-built total of 85,409. If one subtracts the prizes of war, there remains less than 2,000 tons of shipping built outside the colonies. Obviously, Massachusetts was on its way to becoming a shipbuilding center for the entire British Empire.

The same factors that contributed to the success of Bay Colony vessels abroad were responsible for the small amount of British tonnage in the Massachusetts merchant fleet. Low initial cost made New England–built ships attractive to British merchants willing to accept American tonnage as a form of remittance for goods exported to colonial merchants. Pressed for shipping, the English merchant wanted to acquire tonnage, not to sell it. In 1700 London was at the height of its commercial power, with a merchant fleet larger than that of all other English ports combined.[22] Ships constructed along the Thames had the finest reputation and were called "river-built." But the appellation "river-built" meant little to New England merchants. If new and in good condition, the

London vessel would command a higher price than a similar colonial one because of higher building costs as well as reputation. On the other hand, by contracting with a good carpenter and occasionally viewing the construction, the colonial merchant could expect a vessel of fine quality. Careful supervision was easiest in the merchant's own town, hence the concentration of shipwrights in Boston. An older British vessel might sell in the colonies at a competitive price, after it had been severely damaged in a storm, or when the owners or their factor in Boston decided the ship was not worth the cost of repairing. A colonial merchant might purchase such a vessel, but he too would probably prefer a new sound vessel to a repaired one no matter where it had been built. Thus colonial merchants saw little reason to purchase British-built tonnage, and this attitude persisted throughout the colonial era.

The Massachusetts shipbuilding industry owed much of its growth to the efforts of the energetic Boston merchant community. The Bailyns' ownership analysis of the register emphasizes investments by Bostonians. But a 100-ton vessel, ample for ocean trade, would most likely be purchased by British merchants. Out of a total of 181 ships 100 tons or larger built between 1674 and 1714, 52 were owned entirely by Massachusetts merchants, most of whom lived in Boston and the others in Charlestown and Salem. British merchants owned 40 ships; some owners came from the West Indies, Scotland, and Bristol, but the majority were London merchants. Syndicates of Massachusetts and English merchants owned 89 ships. Altogether, British merchants had investments in 129 of the 181 large Massachusetts ships. The ratio might even be higher, for the register fails to include the licenses of vessels later registered outside Massachusetts. It was common practice for colonial merchants to give the masters of their ships the power to sell them anywhere if offered a suitable price, and a ship on a normal trading voyage might be quickly sold if the opportunity arose to make a good profit. Whatever the actual number of Massachusetts-built vessels sold to British merchants, the investment pattern revealed in these 181 large ships shows strong English interests. British capital subsidized roughly two out of every three Massachusetts ships averaging 100 tons or more, a significant ratio considering 100 tons was slightly less than average for Massachusetts-built ships. Even more im-

portant, in each of the three periods from 1697 to 1714, ships accounted for more than 55 percent of all Massachusetts-built tonnage. The Bailyns note only 84 British investors listed in the register
as compared with 322 from Massachusetts.[23] But British investment
was concentrated in ships, while colonial capital was divided among
all types and sizes of vessels. In addition to British merchants who
gave immediate cash and credit for Massachusetts ships, English
holders of shares in colonial ships provided both money and vital
business connections. They knew British markets and could make
the best arrangements possible for vessels arriving in England.
Thus, the impetus for the sudden expansion of Massachusetts shipbuilding was in fact British capital; and the attempts of British
investors to strengthen and extend the colonial ocean trade encouraged the industry's growth.

This is not meant to belittle the work of colonial merchants. In
1702 Boston was one of ten leading ports in the empire. The tonnage of Boston may be figured as second, third, or eighth to that of
London, depending upon the adjustments different observers
make.[24] Even the position of eighth behind London (the calcula-
tion made by Ralph Davis) is remarkable considering Boston was
the only port outside England to rate among the top ten—no Scottish, Irish, or other colonial port qualified.

Since the register carries no reports after 1714, tonnage figures
must be secured from other government records. The Surveyor of
Customs at Boston, Archibald Cumings, recorded the construction
of 160 vessels in Massachusetts for the year 1716, 12 more than in
1715. He estimated the tonnage at 8,000. According to a 1721 survey, Massachusetts builders "have annually launched 140 to 160
vessels, of all sorts . . . [of which] the greatest part are built for account of, or sold to the merchants of this Kingdom, and in the
plantations." The survey shows an annual production of 6,000 tons.
In both the number of vessels and total tonnage, the production
levels of 1716 and 1721 were higher than any between 1697 and
1714. But the average size of the vessels decreased from 67 tons for
the years 1709 to 1714, to 50 tons in 1716, and finally to 40 tons
in 1721. The decrease in ship production after 1714 resulted from
the peace of the preceding year. With wartime demand for shipping

at an end, British investment in colonial vessels declined.[25] Massachusetts shipbuilders now had to produce smaller vessels to comply with the more limited finances of colonial merchants.

## New Hampshire

Like Massachusetts, New Hampshire offered excellent opportunities for shipbuilding. Famous for its timber, especially white pines used to make masts, the colony could also boast of several iron mines. Portsmouth, New Hampshire's major town, possessed one of the finest harbors in New England, with sufficient depth for the largest warships. A small but active merchant community in Portsmouth thrived on the export of lumber and masts to West Indian and European ports; and, though less important than the timber trade, fisheries provided an additional source of specie. Local builders who supplied the open boats and small coasting vessels for fishermen could also construct the large ships required by the timber trade. In fact, New Hampshire shipwrights must have earned a good reputation, because in the 1690s they launched the first colonial-built warships.[26] Yet despite the colony's resources and reputation, New Hampshire shipbuilding enjoyed only a limited increase during the first third of the eighteenth century.

According to the Earl of Bellomont, governor of New England, New Hampshire merchants owned eleven ships and thirteen smaller vessels in 1700. Nine years later, Gov. Joseph Dudley of Massachusetts reported ten New Hampshire ships and twenty other vessels. The high proportion of ships reflects the concentration of New Hampshire merchants in the timber trade. Both governors remarked on the colony's shipbuilding potential. But as the Earl of Bellomont warned, unless merchants were diverted from the profitable timber trade, neither shipbuilding nor the fisheries would flourish. A government survey of 1721 reached similar conclusions, also noting that New Hampshire shipwrights were building fewer vessels since the conclusion of the war.[27]

Portsmouth's trading activity was modest, so the majority of New Hampshire–built ships had to be sold to merchants outside the colony. Few New Hampshire vessels were recorded in the Massachusetts shipping register before 1703. Then between 1703 and 1708 New Hampshire tonnage increased threefold over the total for the previous six years. Shipbuilding grew even more dramatically in Kittery, across the Piscataqua River from Portsmouth, during the same period. The increased wartime demand and low building costs which spurred shipbuilding in Kittery also caused a burst of activity in New Hampshire. But whereas Kittery builders concentrated almost exclusively on ships between 1703 and 1708, New Hampshire shipwrights launched various types of vessels. The pattern reversed itself in the next six years, when Kittery yards produced a variety of vessels and Portsmouth turned to ship production. The difference between the shipbuilding investors of both towns, however, eventually decided their future economies: the ownership of Kittery-built vessels changed dramatically, from partnerships of Boston and British merchants between 1703 and 1708 to almost exclusively Massachusetts merchants after 1708, while across the river in Portsmouth, New Hampshire ships continued to be purchased by British and Boston merchants. Only one of the ten large ships built in Portsmouth between 1703 and 1714 had any New Hampshire investors among its owners.[28] Because of its continued dependence upon British merchants, New Hampshire shipbuilding suffered more than that of Massachusetts when the peace of 1713 ended the great wartime demand for colonial vessels in England.

A few items from the early 1720s record the construction of New Hampshire ships for sale outside the colony. In 1722 the Boston *News-Letter* advertised a new Portsmouth ship for sale. Apparently two merchants, one from Portsmouth and the other from Boston, had financed the vessel and were now trying to sell it. A Boston merchant in 1723 similarly offered to sell a ship that had recently been launched at Portsmouth. Some British merchants also purchased New Hampshire ships. A Bristol merchant named Isaac Hobhouse, for example, sent one of his captains to Portsmouth in 1723 to supervise the construction of a ship. When completed, the captain found a cargo and sailed for Antigua.[29]

During the 1720s and early 1730s a Portsmouth timber merchant, Joshua Peirce, built vessels for his own trade. Whenever possible, he tried to sell shares in the vessels to his correspondents in Pennsylvania and England. Once, in partnership with a Philadelphia merchant, Peirce built a large schooner for the coastal and West Indian trade. The Philadelphian paid for part of his share by supplying cordage, sails, and iron for the vessel. In 1730, Peirce asked an English correspondent to take a one-quarter to one-third share in a proposed timber ship. Two years later, Peirce asked another English merchant to become a partner in a nearly completed ship designed for the Mediterranean fish trade.[30] Unfortunately, his letter book omits the replies of the English merchants to his proposed ventures.

In summary, New Hampshire shipbuilding increased with the pressure of wartime demand and the inflow of capital from both Boston and British merchants. After peace, construction returned to the prewar pattern of building primarily for the New Hampshire trade and for an occasional sale outside the colony. New Hampshire's building resources had been recognized; but although employed in time of need, they were not fully exploited. Secure investments in timber and fish satisfied local merchants. Timber, after all, was a raw commodity in demand in a variety of markets. On the other hand, the time, money, and effort required to construct a ship did not guarantee a desirable return. The risk of a sustained shipbuilding program kept local merchants generally unresponsive to the colony's building potential.

## Rhode Island

After decades of inactivity, Rhode Island shipbuilding began to rise dramatically in the late 1690s. Between 1698 and 1707, Rhode Island shipwrights launched nearly seventy-five vessels for merchants outside the colony. The number of Rhode Island–owned craft rose from five in 1690 to twenty-nine in 1708.[31] The rapid growth of Rhode Island shipbuilding was a response to demands of merchants both within and without the colony.

Although this growth coincided with the rise of Newport to com-

mercial prominence, the impetus behind Rhode Island shipbuilding was in fact investment from outside the colony. At first Rhode
Island followed the pattern set by Scituate and Taunton in Massachusetts: the timber resources along the eastern shore of Narragansett Bay attracted shipwrights, and the prospect of cheap
building rates attracted outside capital. The travels of shipwright
Ralph Chapman illustrate the spread of shipbuilding to several
regions. After working in Scituate, Chapman moved to Swansey,
near the Taunton River area. There, in 1696 he built two large
ships for merchants in Boston and Bristol, England. Settled in Newport by 1702, Chapman sold extra land for a shipyard to another
builder from Scituate. Besides filling orders from Boston and England, Rhode Island shipwrights also built vessels for West Indian
merchants. As early as 1696, Barbados merchants purchased large
ships from Newport builders. The Massachusetts shipping register
records only nine Rhode Island vessels for the years 1697 to 1708.
Yet Gov. Samuel Cranston reported the sale of about seventy-five
vessels to merchants outside the colony during the same years.[32]

Once established, Rhode Island shipbuilding diverged from the
pattern of Scituate and Taunton because Newport had a strong
merchant community. Besides requiring tonnage for their own
coastal and West Indian trade, Newport merchants ensured the
expansion of Rhode Island shipbuilding by using new vessels to
pay for British imports. This process is well documented in the
papers of an early Newport merchant, Thomas Richardson.

After leaving Boston in 1712, Richardson settled in Newport.
The town, he observed, had too long been dependent upon Boston
merchants for British imports. He urged British merchants to trade
directly with Newport, arguing that profitable returns could be
made in vessels because construction prices were less in Rhode
Island than in Boston. During 1712 and 1713 Richardson had three
ships and one brigantine built for a London correspondent. No
suitable Rhode Island exports could be found for the English
market, so Richardson arranged for the new vessels to secure freight
in Virginia, South Carolina, and the West Indies before sailing to
London. Richardson also had several large sloops constructed for
correspondents in Barbados and Jamaica.[33]

Rhode Island shipbuilding centered around Newport in the

early eighteenth century. By 1712 at least a dozen shipwrights lived in the town. Other builders worked in nearby Jamestown, Portsmouth, and Bristol. Providence, the future rival of Newport, had only two shipbuilders at this time.[34]

Because most of their trade was coastal and West Indian, Newport merchants seldom employed vessels larger than sloops. Out of thirty merchant vessels in one painting of Newport, twenty-five were sloops. Rhode Island shipwrights appear to have concentrated on sloop production, building larger vessels only for sale outside the colony, as when Richardson filled the orders of his London correspondents and in the 1720s when Newport builders constructed several ships for a Bristol merchant. Despite the market for such craft, carpenters were often reluctant to build ships. Specializing in sloops, Rhode Island builders were unable to obtain local materials for larger craft and had to seek the more expensive ship timber from outside sources. If a British correspondent canceled his order, the Newport merchant and builder were then burdened with a vessel too large for their own use. They could try to sell the ship to a Boston merchant, but prospects were uncertain and often unprofitable. In one instance, a Newport merchant advertised a new ship in the Boston *News-Letter* for more than seven months without success.[35]

Although it had begun in war, Rhode Island shipbuilding continued to prosper in peace. To English correspondents, Newport was more than a source of cheap shipping: the town was the commercial center of southern New England. British merchants found Newport to be a good market for their exports, and gladly accepted vessels as a means of payment. The value of Newport as an outlet for British imports was heightened by the expanding coastal and West Indian trade of local merchants. From twenty-nine in 1708, the number of Rhode Island-owned vessels increased to sixty in 1721. In terms of tonnage, Rhode Island merchants had 3,500, or two-fifths that of Massachusetts. Ten years later, Rhode Island tonnage had increased to nearly 5,000.[36] Newport's expanding merchant community, encouraged by British correspondents, accounts for the rapid growth of the local shipbuilding industry at this time. Its concentration on sloops rather than ships was in response to the availability of material for local builders, the demand for smaller vessels in the West Indian trade, and the local merchants' desire to limit risk in case of loss or forced sale.

## Connecticut

Several unusual situations emerged during the expansion of Connecticut shipbuilding in the first third of the eighteenth century. Shipbuilding in Connecticut, in contrast to that in the rest of New England, remained unaffected by the great wartime demand and began to expand only in the 1720s, long after peace had come. This late growth of shipbuilding was unaccompanied by any increases or alteration in Connecticut's maritime trade; nearly all the tonnage built during the decade of expansion, the 1720s, was immediately sold outside the colony.[37]

English capital was drawn to Connecticut during the 1720s just as it had been drawn to the Piscataqua, Taunton, and Narragansett areas twenty years before. Low construction costs are what probably attracted the investors. Good natural resources were available, and the number of shipwrights in the colony had increased steadily since the end of the seventeenth century. Connecticut merchants, like those of Rhode Island, had used sloops almost exclusively, because most of their trade was limited to coastal and West Indian ports. Naturally, Connecticut builders specialized in sloop constructon. But the influx of outside capital in the 1720s inspired shipwrights to produce much larger vessels. British merchants particularly those of Bristol, purchased the majority of vessels, and the remainder were sold in other colonies or in the West Indies.[38] Considering the small amount of tonnage needed for local commerce, Connecticut carpenters must have welcomed the opportunity to build large vessels for merchants outside the colony.

Centered in the New London area, Connecticut builders earned a reputation for heavy ships. In fact, the largest merchant ship of colonial America, a 720-ton vessel built by John Jeffery over a period of two years, was launched at New London in 1725. Jeffery launched another giant in 1733—the 570-ton *Don Carlos*. Both ships sailed to Portugal and apparently were sold to English merchants in Lisbon.[39]

## New York

After Massachusetts, New York possessed the largest colonial merchant fleet in 1700. But numbering less than half of the Massachusetts total, and with small sloops accounting for two-thirds of the
vessels, the New York fleet was a distant second. New York merchants owned only fourteen ships, a poor comparison to the sixty-
four of Massachusetts. As in the cases of Rhode Island and Connecticut, the large proportion of sloops reflects the interest of New York
merchants in the coastal and West Indian trades and the domination by British merchants of the limited trans-Atlantic trade.
Fifteen years later, in 1715, the New York fleet was half of its former
number. Robert Hunter blamed the sharp decrease on a general
decline of trade following the Treaty of Utrecht and the closing of
the Spanish West Indies to colonial vessels. Throughout the 1720s,
New York's mercantile activity remained unchanged.[40]

During the first third of the eighteenth century, the New York
merchant fleet consisted almost entirely of sloops built within the
colony. New York sloops averaged half the tonnage of New England
sloops. A 1717 engraving of New York by William Burgis shows
two types of sloops used in the colony (see Figs. 6, 7). The first and
more numerous class consists of very small vessels suitable for coastal
trade; in the second class are large armed sloops appropriate for
West Indian voyages and capable of defense against pirates. But
New York builders, like those of Connecticut and Rhode Island,
did not limit themselves to sloop production. In one of the five
shipyards shown in the Burgis engraving, two large ships are under
construction. Yet there is no other evidence of either sustained production or sale of ships to English merchants.[41] Obviously, New
York is an example of a colony where pictorial evidence suggests
more activity than surviving documents indicate.

## Pennsylvania

In order to take advantage of the excellent timber and iron resources of his colony, William Penn followed the example John

Winthrop had set fifty years earlier by recruiting shipwrights to accompany the first settlers to Philadelphia. Penn financed the construction of the first Pennsylvania-built ship shortly after his arrival in America. Like the Bay Colony, Pennsylvania was without a product valuable to British merchants, and any profits the colonists could earn depended upon their own ingenuity in shipping. They did not wait for a depression to compel them to try shipbuilding; the Quaker merchants at once appreciated their opportunity to purchase British imports with credit from a West Indian trade. During the second year of settlement, in 1683, two Pennsylvania ships sailed to Barbados with pipe staves and horses. By 1689 ten vessels were leaving annually for the West Indies with provisions, wood, and horses. Quaker merchants also experimented with the sale of tobacco and fur. Widespread trading ventures created a demand for Philadelphia-built ships. In 1685 William Penn wrote: "some Vessels have been here Built, and many Boats and by that means a ready Conveniency for Passage of people and Goods." Penn noted that the colony had all the tradesmen necessary for shipbuilding—ropemakers, sailmakers, smiths, and blockmakers, as well as carpenters. With the establishment of shipbuilding, Quaker merchants could offer low-cost tonnage to English correspondents in exchange for their exports to Pennsylvania. "We are Rarely without ten or twelve Vessels on ye Stocks—Ships, Brigantines and Sloops," Jonathan Dickenson wrote in 1692, "haveing orders from Bristol and London to Build for Merchants there."[42]

A period of slow but steady growth, as Massachusetts experienced after the initial development of a shipbuilding industry, never came to Pennsylvania. Instead, Philadelphia shipbuilding boomed with the wartime demand of English merchants for colonial tonnage. According to one observer, Philadelphia builders launched ships of 200 and 300 tons each. Another visitor claimed that nearly 300 ships had been built in Philadelphia by 1710. In any event, by the second decade of the eighteenth century, Philadelphia tonnage exceeded that of New York, and the Quaker port was second in shipbuilding to Boston.[43] But the growth of shipbuilding represented only one part of the general expansion of Pennsylvania commerce.

With the coming of peace in 1713, Pennsylvania shipbuilding

shared the brief decline suffered by all the colonies when suddenly limited to the demands of local merchants. Philadelphia shipwrights had to sacrifice variety and concentrate on sloop and brigantine construction through the early 1720s. Adequate for Pennsylvania's trade, the sloops and brigantines might also be sold to West Indian merchants. Although now working on smaller vessels, Philadelphia carpenters were far from idle. In 1719, Philadelphia had fifteen active shipyards—as many as Boston had in 1722.[44]

During the mid-1720s, British merchants began to reinvest in Pennsylvania shipbuilding, purchasing shares in seven of the fifteen Pennsylvania-built ships listed in the Philadelphia shipping register for the years 1726 to 1730. According to the register, Philadelphia builders were once more launching the variety of vessels characteristic of the war years and required by English purchasers. The John Reynell Papers for the years 1730 to 1733 record a typical shipbuilding pattern. A Quaker merchant, John Reynell had vessels built for correspondents in England who sent rigging, sails, and often a captain to Philadelphia for the new vessel. On other occasions, Reynell tried to draw English partners into the construction and operation of a vessel designed for a new trading venture. By 1731 Philadelphia merchants frequently used shipbuilding as a profitable method of making returns for their imports from England.[45]

Philadelphia, the colony's financial center, controlled Pennsylvania shipbuilding. Philadelphia shipwrights built at least 80 percent of all Pennsylvania tonnage launched between 1726 and 1736. The concentration of shipbuilding in Philadelphia was so complete that the town never faced even the slight competition Charlestown, Salem, and other Massachusetts ports offered Boston. But the rise of Pennsylvania shipbuilding also stimulated activity in neighboring New Jersey and Delaware, where shipwrights specialized mainly in small craft suited to the resources of their owners and sufficient for a commerce limited to the Delaware River and an occasional voyage to New York. Between 1726 and 1736, New Jersey and Delaware builders supplied almost 10 percent each of the total tonnage registered in Philadelphia.[46] No other colonial region was as completely dominated by one shipbuilding center as the Delaware Valley was by Philadelphia.

## The Southern Colonies

Large ships occasionally were constructed in the Chesapeake colonies. In 1697, for example, Bristol merchants had several ships built in Virginia. Similarly, in 1698 Maryland sheriffs recorded the sale of two locally built ships, including one of 450 tons, to British purchasers. Other ships were launched during the same period, with production centered in Talbot County, on Maryland's Eastern Shore. During the first decade of the eighteenth century alone, English merchants financed the construction of a dozen Maryland vessels, including two 400-ton ships. But this spurt of activity, probably caused by the war, did not survive the peace of 1713. On the whole, in fact, Chesapeake governors reported little shipbuilding in their colonies, and as late as 1720 the Maryland merchant fleet consisted of only four small brigantines and twenty sloops.[47]

In 1720 most of North Carolina's trade consisted of coastal exchanges conducted by New England sloops. Out of 229 vessels built between 1710 and 1739 and trading with North Carolina, only 38 were launched within that colony. And of the 38, all but 5 were small sloops and schooners. South Carolina colonists likewise devoted their energies to agriculture and ignored shipping. British ships were allowed to carry the profitable cargoes of South Carolina rice and deerskins to England. The twenty small vessels owned by South Carolinians in 1720 were all employed in coastal trading.[48]

Between the southern passion for agriculture and the plentiful supply of ships from British merchants, shipbuilding in the southern colonies remained stagnant through 1730 despite the presence of excellent natural resources and skillful shipwrights. Although there probably were unrecorded scattered local building projects, the available evidence suggests that southern shipwrights concentrated on ship repairs and that no general organized building program existed at this time.

## English Reaction

The expansion of colonial shipbuilding attracted some attention in England—especially among shipbuilders. In 1724 the master shipwrights of the River Thames petitioned the Board of Trade to restrict shipbuilding in the colonies. They claimed that half the shipwrights in Great Britain had left the country since 1710, most of them headed for New England. Although ostensibly concerned about the consequences of the emigration of workers from British shipyards, the petitioners actually were worried about the increasing number of cheap colonial vessels purchased by English merchants. A tax upon colonial vessels sold in England, the master shipwrights suggested, would balance the difference in construction costs. The petition received only a brief review. Aside from the legal status of colonial-built vessels as English tonnage under the Navigation Act of 1660, the petition was blocked by several practical considerations. The Board of Trade noted that the low cost of shipbuilding in the colonies, by the petitioners' own admission, was not the only cause of emigration of shipwrights, for many had gone to Russia and Sweden. Since 1710 the pace of building had slowed because the navy had ended all contracts with private yards and had restricted warship construction to naval dockyards. The carpenters suffered a second blow when peace in 1713 caused a decline in merchant ship construction. The Jacobite rebellion, a dispute with the Baltic nations, war with Spain, and the financial crisis of 1720 all limited the opportunities open to shipbuilders in England until the mid-1720s. Such conditions encouraged the craftsmen to travel to any country where work might be found. The petitioners' case was further weakened by the powerful influence of the merchants who purchased colonial shipping. But, more important than current economic conditions or political influences, from the early 1720s the Board of Trade viewed colonial shipbuilding as a desirable alternative to a colonial woolen industry that would compete with that of England. Gov. Joseph Dudley predicted a decline in the manufacture of woolens in New England as the growth of shipbuilding enabled colonists to purchase English cloth. One colonial merchant warned that New England would turn to other manufactures in addition to woolens if unable to exchange shipping for British imports. Therefore, the colonial shipbuilding industry continued to expand with the blessing of British officials and the support of English merchants. By 1730 one-sixth of the English merchant fleet was built in America.[49]

CHAPTER IV

# Colonial Shipwrights

## The English Tradition

SHIPWRIGHTS learned their craft in the government and private shipyards of Great Britain. Government-financed, or "royal," dockyards specialized in the construction and maintenance of warships; private yards produced primarily merchant vessels and an occasional naval ship. Although only six royal dockyards existed during the seventeenth and eighteenth centuries, the government actually employed the highest number of shipwrights, for in contrast to the hundreds of workers in each royal dockyard, an average private yard usually employed one or two dozen men. Even the largest private establishment seldom hired as many as one hundred hands.[1]

The undisputed center of English shipbuilding lay on the river Thames, where four of the six royal dockyards and the largest of the private yards had their works. Renowned for their East Indiamen, the largest and finest merchant ships in England, the Thames private yards were reluctant to seek improvements. At the beginning of the eighteenth century, northeast coast builders in a region centered about Whitby began to compete with shipwrights of the Thames and neighboring East Anglia by launching large inexpensive bulk carriers based on the Dutch flyboat design. Further competition came from shipwrights scattered throughout coastal villages who produced mostly small vessels for coastal needs but who could also build ships when required.[2] Most craftsmen traveled from yard to yard in search of work, for employment was haphazard and production never at a steady rate. Consequently, many ship carpenters gained experience at several yards in both merchant and warship construction.

Burdened with the corrupt practices of government officials as well as laborers, royal dockyards were notorious for their slow construction and high cost, while private shipyards, competing with each other for building contracts, were forced to work efficiently and economically or go out of business. A ship of the line that required three years of work in a royal dockyard could be built by a private yard in half the time. On the other hand, government builders usually launched better-designed and -constructed vessels than private shipwrights because they were better acquainted with naval architecture, a well-developed art by the eighteenth century.[3]

Because of its financial resources, a government yard could afford elaborate and costly facilities consisting of half a dozen building slips, wet and dry docks, large reserves of seasoned timber, mast ponds, storehouses and ropewalks.[4] With few exceptions, private yards had simple facilities—a building slip or two; a small stock of timber, often unseasoned; and a storehouse or shed. Docks, ropewalks, and mast ponds constituted separate enterprises. The government shipwrights knew more about building various types of vessels from plans than private ship carpenters, who usually limited themselves to merchant ships of standard form and size.

Despite these differences, organization of work was similar in royal and private shipyards. A master shipwright supervised all construction. In government yards, run by a port admiral and naval commissioner, the master shipwright was the foreman. In private yards, one man usually served as both owner and foreman except in those instances in which the yard was leased from a merchant. An artist, the eighteenth-century term for naval architect, might prepare plans, but normally the master shipwright drew his own plans or else relied upon his memory and worked by "eye" in producing a traditional hull of the desired size.[5] Sometimes used as a supplement to plans, models were really more a decorative than a building device.

A shipyard required the skills of a variety of tradesmen, working under the master shipwright, to build and complete a vessel. Other shipwrights did the main construction. Then joiners smoothed the rough outside planking, built rails along the upper decks, and finished the cabins. Caulkers filled every seam in the ship, from outside planking to the topmost deck, and even around the treenails, with oakum (unraveled hemp).[6] When the basic hull was complete, even more craftsmen were needed to finish the vessel. Painters, carvers, glaziers, plumbers, and coopers were all part of the naval dockyard establishment, but a private yard had to hire them for each individual task. The masts, blocks, and cordage had to be prepared before the vessel could be rigged. The boat-builder made one or two boats for a merchant vessel and about half a dozen for a naval ship. An oarmaker supplied the sweeps for each boat. Smiths forged anchors in addition to supplying the ironwork already in the hull. Finally, sailmakers finished the suits of sails and bent the canvas to the yards.

Shipyards employed two more kinds of workers. Sawyers cut all plank and many parts of the ship's frame by hand, as sawmills were rare in England until the end of the eighteenth century.[7] Because of the large amount of sawed timber and plank used in construction, plus the slow nature of their work, sawyers had to be employed in both government and private yards throughout the building process. Common laborers were also hired to do odd jobs such as hauling wood about the yard. Royal dockyards seem to have used such unskilled workers more frequently than private yards.

English craftsmen were trained in the apprentice-journeyman tradition. Since the apprentice soon gained sufficient skill to earn money for his master, the premium for an apprenticeship in the shipbuilding trade was relatively small, about £5 or £10. The master might train an apprentice for two years, send him to sea as a carpenter's mate, and collect the boy's wages for the remaining five years of the apprenticeship. The amount of instruction an apprentice received, especially in the art of ship design, depended upon the skill and interest of his master, the specific terms in his articles of apprenticeship, and the watchfulness of his parent or guardian. After his apprenticeship, the young shipwright became a journeyman, seeking employment and eventual admission to the local guild. Without completing their formal training, and to the considerable annoyance of those who did, many apprentices and journeymen went to places where they were unknown and established themselves as shipwrights.[8]

If fortunate, the new shipwright quickly found work and could then increase his income by taking on several apprentices. Otherwise, he had to seek employment in distant yards—a search that took some East Anglia builders to the Whitby area and others to the colonies or to foreign nations. The rise from shipyard worker to owner was long and difficult. While private yards required simple facilities, land was expensive; and if he hoped to receive any building orders, the shipwright needed good mercantile connections as well as an adequate reputation.

Most shipwrights, without the financial resources to build for future sale, found it safer and cheaper to wait for an order. Building usually began only after the master shipwright signed a detailed contract with a purchaser. Then the builder hired various tradesmen, paying them by the day or for a specific piece of work. The master shipwright received payment in installments, specified by the contract, as the building progressed. Work usually went slowly. Even the largest private yards seldom turned out a ship a year.[9] A large ship ideally could be built in less than a year, sometimes in only four to six months, but negotiations over the contract or labor and timber problems caused incessant delays in construction.

Few master shipwrights ever became wealthy. The exceptions, like Thomas Coram, made their fortunes only after they ceased shipbuilding to become merchants. At best, even famous builders had only a modest income, limited by the low production rate of a shipyard, dependence upon merchant contracts, and the competition of other builders. Perhaps these poor financial prospects explain the absence of shipbuilding dynasties in England. An occasional family produced two generations of shipwrights, but in all cases the third generation entered other trades. Dependent upon the master shipwright, but lacking his resources, the ordinary shipyard craftsman was in an even more precarious position. Both builder and yard workers, even though skilled, socially were considered tradesmen.[10] The few who gained high social position did so only after they left the shipyard for the countinghouse.

## Apprentices in Colonial America

In the colonies, the demand for skilled labor and the absence of guilds to enforce work standards and limit competition produced an apprenticeship system far more flexible than its English model. Colonial apprentices served anywhere between four and seven years or, in some cases, until they were twenty-one. Public wards, or "poor boys," the lowest type of shipbuilding apprentices, were indentured to local tradesmen by town officials in order to eliminate the expense of supporting the boys and to provide their future usefulness for the community. In the small shipbuilding center of Newbury, Massachusetts, for example, town selectmen often indentured "poor boys" to local shipwrights. The apprentices were bound until their twenty-first birthday, a term varying from two to eleven years with six as an average. In exchange for the boy's service, the master instructed him in the "art and mystery of a shipwright." With the lack of specie in the colonies, most financial transactions were conducted by the transfer of credit and recorded in the account books of merchants and tradesmen. Hence the master was required to teach his apprentice "to Read, write & cypher so far as to keep a tradesman Book."[11] Upon completion of his service, the apprentice received from his master two suits, one for workdays and another for Sunday.

Limited evidence suggests that most shipbuilding apprentices were sons bound out by artisan or yeoman parents. Indentures for the sons of shipbuilding families have not been found; the recorded occupations of the apprentices' parents have always been in other fields, especially farming, and occasionally in a related trade such as that of ship joiner. Indentures within this group vary considerably: the length of service might be anywhere from three to eight years; some apprentices received freedom clothing and others received nothing; three of the four New Hampshire and Massachusetts masters gave their apprentices tools upon completion of the term, while those of Philadelphia did not. One surprising feature of all these indentures is the absence of the apprentice premium. The general demand for apprentices in the colonies eliminated this traditional fee. Masters suffered little loss, however, since the labor shortage also increased the value of the apprentice's work. One Newbury shipwright, Joseph Cottle, received 25 shillings per day in local currency for the work of his apprentice, a substantial addition to Cottle's own 30-shilling-per-day wage.[12] While a master would follow the profitable English custom of collecting wages for apprentice labor, the colonial apprentice worked in local shipyards and was never sent to sea, for better wages were available ashore than aboard a small merchant ship.

Three sons of West Indian merchants served as apprentices. Their training was more thorough than that of other apprentices, especially in the field of ship design, as they were bound to leading colonial shipwrights. After one young man had been sent to New York for schooling, his father died and his mother remarried. When the boy was neglected, merchant friends of his deceased father apprenticed him to a shipwright for seven years. The other two boys, both from Barbados, were bound to a well-known Philadelphia shipbuilding family.[18] One indenture, for seven years, held the father responsible for all the boy's clothing and required the master to allow the apprentice to attend night school at the parent's expense. The other indenture, for four years, also required the parent to provide his son's clothing and particularly emphasized the boy's thorough preparation in ship design. This last apprentice left after three years, having paid his master £50 for copies of ship plans and extra written instructions.

Probably none of these boys intended to remain in shipbuilding, for training a merchant's son in shipbuilding was not meant to limit him to a tradesman's life. In the first instance, friends were providing a neglected child with a trade from which in time he might advance into the countinghouse. After training under a famous shipwright, the two Barbados lads could promote better building methods on their own island. Then they might follow their fathers and become merchants. As in England, colonial shipwrights seldom became wealthy, but builders who became merchants could.

Apprentice indentures were occasionally violated and sometimes completely broken. On one side, the master might fail to instruct the apprentice. An angry parent wrote Gov. John Winthrop in 1647 that the master of his son neglected the boy and tried to sell him first to a Scot bound for Barbados and then to a local brewer. Above all, the parent complained, the boy was in danger of losing his trade and becoming incapable of earning a living. In a similar case, a shipwright lent his apprentice to a tavern keeper. Charging neglect and poor training, several young shipwrights initiated unsuccessful legal suits against their former masters. On the other hand, after investing both time and money, the master could lose his apprentice before the indenture expired. In an unusual incident, a father delayed signing his son's indenture for two and a half years and finally took the boy away from his master. Lacking a signed indenture, the shipbuilder was without legal claim to the apprentice he had clothed, fed, and instructed. Runaway apprentices were supposed to have been common in colonial America, yet five major newspapers advertised a total of only seven runaway shipwright apprentices during the entire colonial period. The *Virginia Gazette, Maryland Gazette* and *South Carolina Gazette* reported one each; the *Pennsylvania Gazette* listed four, all in the 1760s; and the Boston *News-Letter* did not mention a single runaway.[14] The low number of advertisements cannot be attributed to the reluctance of shipbuilders to purchase newspaper space, since the same journals carried many notices for slaves and bond servants absent from shipyards. It might support the theory that the apprentice held a privileged position, with all his necessities provided for him and the promise of a valuable skill in the future. Or it might simply indicate that a youth was more ready to serve out his time than an older man in bondage. One could also conclude that this only reflects a low number of apprentices in general for a trade where untrained workers might try their hands at skilled jobs. Masters also lost the services of apprentices through shipyard accidents, which were common and occasionally resulted in death.

If his master died, the apprentice was left in a precarious position: the time he had to serve was valued along with the rest of the master's possessions. Under such circumstances, the heirs were supposed to sell the boy's remaining time to another shipwright. In one instance, a Massachusetts apprentice was allowed to choose his own master.[15] Parents and guardians were of particular value in such cases to ensure the boy's continued training, because a lad without influence might be sold into an entirely different trade.

Most masters and apprentices survived their mutual ordeals without incident. A colonial shipwright probably trained no more than a couple of apprentices at one time. When his indenture expired, the lad became a journeyman. Only lack of money hindered his rise to master craftsman in America, because there were no guild requirements to meet. Opportunities might have been limited in England, but in the colonies high wages and a chronic labor shortage encouraged the energetic journeyman to establish his own business as soon as possible.[16] Land was relatively cheap, so with just a small amount of capital the journeyman could open his own shipyard much sooner than his counterpart in England.

Since the few records of apprenticeship indentures that have been found are from the major shipbuilding centers of Massachusetts and Philadelphia, a picture emerges of a greatly varying degree of formal training, especially from rural areas to towns. It is my guess that professionalism also varied greatly. In view of the pressures on shipyard owners to build quickly while the climate and markets remained favorable, hiring practices could not have been consistently strict. Scant records on apprenticeships might merely reflect the flexible standards of a rapidly expanding industry faced with a short labor supply.

## Slaves and Servants

Colonists responded to the labor shortage by purchasing individuals bound to a temporary or permanent servile status. Shipbuilders throughout the colonies used slaves, while white servants were popular in Virginia, Maryland, and Pennsylvania yards. South Carolina favored slave to indentured labor. New England colonists distrusted and therefore discouraged importation of servant labor, preferring to do their own work or occasionally using slaves.[17] Ropemakers and sailmakers were more likely than shipwrights to employ servants or slaves. A ropemaker owned his own ropewalk, a sailmaker his sail loft, and both required a steady number of laborers to maintain their trade. But not all shipwrights owned their own yards or could guarantee steady employment. No system was entirely successful, but labor was often so scarce that colonial craftsmen were compelled to use bound workmen throughout the colonial period.

Extreme care must be used when considering bound labor, because not all records distinguish between servants and slaves. In general, however, there were two kinds of white servants: (1) indentured servants serving a four- or five-year term to pay for debts and for transportation to the colonies, and redemptioners, with a smaller debt, serving only one or two years, and (2) convicts or political prisoners bound to a seven- to fourteen-year term of labor.

Maryland and Virginia received large numbers of both indentured servants and convicts. Pennsylvania, on the other hand, welcomed indentured servants but accepted few convicts.[18]

The best evidence of indentured servitude exists for Philadelphia before 1750. In 1746, four servants, all Irishmen, were bound to Philadelphia shipwrights; three were indentured for four years and the fourth bound to a term of three and a half years of labor. Upon completion of their service, the Irishmen received the customary freedom clothes due apprentices, but they did not get free tools. The number of Philadelphia shipyard servants, however, declined in the thirty years before the Revolution. There is no mention of them in the *Pennsylvania Gazette* after 1750, and only a few of the more than thirty Philadelphia shipwrights in the various town tax lists from 1767 to 1775 had servants.[19]

As Chesapeake Bay shipbuilding expanded in the late 1740s and early 1750s, Virginia and Maryland sought cheap labor by importing skilled workers serving prison sentences. During that time, eleven trained shipwrights, two joiners, a carver, a caulker, and a sailmaker were reported as escaping from Maryland or Virginia yards. Only one of seventeen runaways did not have a trade. Servants advertised for sale in the Chesapeake area from newly arrived vessels included one shipwright with his own chest of tools and another who claimed seven years of experience in the royal dockyard at Deptford.[20] Whether debtors or criminals, there can be no doubt that these skilled craftsmen helped ambitious local merchants to increase their shipping and expand their trade.

In 1754 Charles Carroll, an Annapolis merchant, decided to supplement his iron and tobacco trade with shipbuilding. He bought a yard site and then purchased servants and slaves as shipwrights and other workers. Samuel Galloway was another Maryland merchant who used servant labor in his shipyard. But three of his yard servants, a shipwright, a joiner, and a carver, ran away in 1755. The carver, incidentally, later completed his service and opened his own shop at Annapolis in 1760. Patrick Creagh also depended upon servant labor in his Annapolis shipyard and, like other merchant-builders, suffered from runaway servants.[21]

The runaway servant problem seems to have been severe in Maryland and Pennslyvania, the two colonies with the most servants. Builders knew, however, that eventually they would lose the cheap labor of servants when they completed their term of service. Some servants without a skill received sufficient training to become tradesmen by the time their indentures expired.[22] In such cases the departure of the servant meant a particularly significant loss for the shipbuilder.

Shipbuilders found slaves to constitute a more permanent and therefore more attractive labor force. The first record of slave labor in a shipyard comes from Massachusetts. While building a brigantine for a local merchant in 1713, the end of peak wartime production during Queen Anne's War, Jonathan Bowers of Boston hired three slaves. Because their length of employment and high wages indicate that they were skilled workers, slave labor in the shipyard must date from an earlier period—perhaps the 1690s, when the pressure of wartime building demands first began. However, the fact that each slave had a different owner suggests such workers were few in number and scattered throughout the area.[23]

Shipyard slaves next appear in Charleston, South Carolina, during the 1730s. Without wartime demands or even an active shipbuilding industry, the presence of black labor in South Carolina shipyards must be attributed to the general expansion of slavery in that colony. At first, South Carolina shipyard slaves were often employed as sawyers; but many were also trained as shipwrights.[24] Builders must have quickly appreciated that a slave could earn more money with an advanced skill, for after the 1730s slaves worked mostly in the more skilled positions of shipwright and caulker.

By the end of the 1740s, builders from New Hampshire southward employed skilled and unskilled slave labor. Slaves, like free men, were trained under the apprenticeship system. Although no indenture for a slave shipwright has yet been found, the indenture of a slave apprentice to a carpenter is revealing. A Maryland gentleman bound his slave to a carpenter for a four-year apprenticeship. The tradesman was to instruct, feed, shelter, and clothe the slave; but if the latter became ill, the owner had to care for him. That the carpenter did not receive an apprenticeship fee suggests that he was most grateful for the extra pair of hands in his shop. Two slaves advertised for sale in Virginia were described as ship carpenter apprentices with three more years to serve. Occasionally,

an owner without shipbuilding interests apprenticed young slaves
to a local shipwright in order to increase their value. After the
apprenticeship, the owner might sell the slave or rent him to a
shipwright by the day, month, or year. From the builder's point
of view, it was obviously better to purchase a young slave himself
and then raise him as a shipwright. One Newbury, Massachusetts,
slave was born into the household of a builder and raised to be a
shipwright. Several slaves were raised to be ship carpenters in a
similar manner.[25]

At least thirteen of the twenty South Carolina shipwrights working in the 1730s and 1740s used slave carpenters. Their principal
motive was probably economy: it was cheaper to use slaves than to
hire whites. Builders could afford only a few slaves at first, but
when successful they might possess up to a dozen slave shipwrights.
In fact, widespread use of skilled slave labor put South Carolina
shipbuilders without slaves at a disadvantage. Perhaps at first they
tried to follow the example of Peter Birot, a cooper who advertised
in 1736 that all his work was "done by white People, and not by
Negroes, [and] as cheap as anywhere else." But claims for the superiority of white workmanship and low wages were eventually
abandoned. In 1744 the non-slave-owning builders petitioned the
Commons House of Assembly to limit the number of Negroes in
South Carolina shipyards. Free white shipwrights, the petitioners
complained, could not compete with slaves. In turn, the slave-
owning shipwrights, including all the more successful and well-
known builders in South Carolina, explained that only through
hard work and frugal living had they been able to save money and
purchase slaves. They cited the expense of training the slaves and
recalled numerous instances when the shipwrights without slaves
had refused work or else charged outrageous prices.[26]

A committee hastily appointed by the Assembly to consider the
affair reported "that the Number of Negroes hired out . . . to do
the Business of shipwrights . . . is a Discouragement to white Men
of that Business." In an apparent effort to calm both sides, the
legislature immediately recommended for consideration a bill "for
limiting the Number of Negroes that may be hired out to work of
the shipwrights' Trade . . . , and for ascertaining the Wages of
shipwrights, as well white Men as Negroes." This public display of

concern and action satisfied the legislature, and they quickly buried the bill. Probably ready to make an effort to protect free white labor from slave competition, the legislators were unwilling to give either group an economic advantage they did not already possess or any new opportunities to overcharge the public. There must have been further and stronger demands for protection against black competition. Several months later, the legislature defeated a more extreme measure forbidding the training of slaves as trades-men.[27] By the 1760s, the use of slaves in every large South Carolina shipyard, as well as their ownership by nearly all white shipwrights, made the question of free versus slave labor academic.

This controversy does not prove South Carolina employed the largest number of shipyard slaves, however, for South Carolina was among the lowest-ranking colonies in ship construction. Of the fifteen Norfolk residents between 1742 and 1752 who have been identified as shipwrights and caulkers, the nine who appear on a list of tithables for 1751 all owned slaves. The exact number of slaves they used in the shipyard is unknown, but wills and inventories support the picture of extensive slave-ownership by Virginia builders. For example, shipwright William Ashley left fourteen slaves to his family; John Whiddon left ten; and Thomas Herbert more than thirty. Only one Norfolk shipwright, in fact, had no slaves to bequeath in his will. In addition, at least two Virginia planters owned some shipwright slaves.[28]

Shipyard slaves were a common sight in Philadelphia as well. According to the 1767 and 1772 tax assessors' reports, about 20 percent of the shipwrights in Southwark, the town's shipbuilding center, owned slaves.[29] Although a few shipwrights reported three slaves, the average was one or two. The almost total absence of servants bound to shipwrights in the same tax records suggests that builders seeking bound labor preferred to use slaves when they became more available.

Three of the slaveholders in the 1767 assessor's report were the Penrose brothers. They had inherited two shipyard slaves from their father in 1757 and had acquired four more slaves within ten years. A total of six slaves for one of Philadelphia's leading shipbuilding families seems rather meager when compared with the holdings of southerners. Quakers of good reputation, the Penroses kept their slaves through the Revolution. Only one member of the rival ship-building family, the Wests, owned a slave shipwright. And Quaker James West requested in his will that his slave be freed providing he pay the estate £10 annually for six years and "behave himself well." Similarly, another Philadelphia shipwright left his "Two Negro Men free to Serve No Body after My Decease," provided they each paid the estate £ 8 yearly.[30] These are the only known instances of shipwrights freeing their skilled slaves. Significantly, both ship-wrights waited until death to free their slaves, and both assured their families of some continued income from the freed men.

Slaves were a common sight in New England also and yet re-mained beyond the reach of the average builder. Most shipwrights with slaves owned only one or two. Benjamin Hallowell, like sev-eral other leading shipwrights, used slave labor in his yard, but owned only two slaves between 1730 and 1740, one a trained ship-wright. His equally famous son, who continued building through 1773, also reported owning two slaves in a valuation of Boston's in-habitants. Two other shipwrights in that valuation were listed with only one and two slaves respectively. Samuel Hood likewise left two slaves, both adult males, to his family in 1733. The construction accounts of New England ships from the 1730s on seldom record more than two shipyard slaves belonging to the same individual.[31]

Whenever possible, New England slave-owners charged the same daily wage for both their own labor and that of the slaves; this was in sharp contrast to South Carolina, where the daily wages of a free shipwright were approximately one-third greater than those of a slave. Of course, the shipbuilder might receive a small dis-count in the daily rate when he hired a slave by the month instead of by the day. In exchange for the lower rate, the owner was guaranteed a longer period of income. For example, one Newport merchant paid 10 shillings per day for a shipyard slave instead of the 12 shillings required by a slave rented on a daily basis. In times of shipyard labor shortages, slave-owners could refuse to give monthly discounts. The wages of a slave also varied, like those of a white tradesman, according to the type of work he performed. Thus, when Black Joseph did common labor in a Salem shipyard, his master received only 7 shillings a day instead of the usual 10 he earned as a caulker.[32]

The market value of shipyard slaves also varied greatly. In South Carolina, slave shipwrights were worth £300 to £800 in local currency according to the degree of skill. Caulkers brought only £300 to £350, because their trade was easier to learn and consequently less valuable. In terms of pounds sterling, slave shipwrights sold for £100 in the 1770s, in contrast to £60 for a field hand. Because of their high value, only eight slave shipwrights were ever advertised for sale in the *South Carolina Gazette*. Two of these slaves were sold by their original masters, but the rest were sold by estates. Whether or not he was a shipbuilder, an owner could always profit more from renting his skilled slaves than from selling them. During the 1750s and 1760s, South Carolina builders rented black shipwrights at £20 per month in local currency. Thus Robin, trained by shipbuilder John Daniel and valued at £450 in local currency, brought the widow Mary Daniel a monthly wage equal to almost one-twentieth his total value.[33]

Influenced by the large number of slaves in the colony and their high value when trained, South Carolinians invested heavily in slave shipwrights; the difference between South Carolinian and northern builders is striking. Of the total wealth listed in the inventories of nine slave-owning New England shipwrights, an average of 5 percent was tied up in slaves. On the other hand, nine South Carolina shipwrights had an average of 57 percent of their total wealth invested in slaves.[34] This contrast may be further demonstrated by comparing Rhode Island builder Roger Kinnicut with southerner Thomas Middleton. Kinnicut's 11 percent ratio of slave to total property value was the largest of any New Englander, but it was still far below Middleton's 20 percent, the smallest ratio among the South Carolina builders.

Mention of a total of only thirteen runaway shipyard slaves has been found so far in colonial newspapers. Two slaves described as being able to read and write were among the six single runaways. In most cases the advertisements indicate that the slave's position had changed or was about to change when he disappeared. For example, one Massachusetts slave shipwright left before his master could sell him to a West Indian. He found refuge and work in his hometown; his master advertised for him only after having seen the slave several times—nearly two years after he had first run away.

In 1765 another slave shipwright, Billy, ran off with two other slaves, making his way to Charleston, South Carolina, where he worked for several years before being identified and returned to Virginia. He promptly ran away again, this time alone.[35]

That at least two runaway slaves found work and shelter suggests that colonial shipyards employed free black workers, but unfortunately there is little information available about the free black shipwright. In Rhode Island, a free black caulker, rigger, and shipwright are known to have received wages equal to those of free white workers. The work of Prince Miller, the caulker, was frequently requested by the same merchant family, and the rigger, Daniel Beard of Newport, had an excellent reputation in his own colony as well as in neighboring Massachusetts towns.[36]

Both slaves and servants seem to have been beyond the means of most builders. Large numbers of servants in Maryland and slaves in South Carolina and Virginia provided shipwrights with a source of cheap labor; but in the rest of the colonies only a small portion of the wealthier builders, plus some ropemakers and sailmakers, could afford slaves or servants. Even a smaller number actually employed them.

## The Shipyard

As land was cheap, and sometimes given to him free, the colonial shipwright had better opportunities than a builder in England to acquire his own yard site. A small waterfront lot with flat or gently sloping land could easily be found and secured anywhere except in the major cities of Boston, New York, and Philadelphia. If a shipwright constructed only small coasting vessels with the aid of a few helpers, or else built larger vessels using bound labor, the shipyard could be located in an isolated area. But most builders had yards in communities where they could hire the various tradesmen necessary to finish the ships.

Once he had purchased land, the colonial shipwright could begin building vessels without any shipyard equipment beyond his own tools. Engravings of New York and Boston in the 1750s show shipyards without any facilities beyond an occasional toolshed.

However, Thomas Coram, the Englishman who brought shipbuilding to Taunton, Massachusetts, constructed a large double saw-pit "covered with a house to work in all weathers." Such a structure appears in a painting of a rural Maryland shipyard of 1770.[37] Other builders were probably content with a simple open sawpit or the even simpler pair of trestles that could be moved conveniently about the yard. With few exceptions, colonial builders also avoided permanent launching ways, preferring instead to construct temporary ones for each vessel. In time the shipwright might build a small wharf, which, besides its usefulness as a landing place for boats, would provide workmen with easy access to a newly launched vessel.

Shipwrights in the smaller communities of Salem, Massachusetts, and Portsmouth, New Hampshire, could usually secure enough land to live in their yards. But in major cities, where land was in great demand, the shipwright was more likely to live near rather than in his shipyard. Likewise, shipyards in major towns tended to be grouped together along the main waterfront areas, while those in smaller towns were usually in coves away from the central cluster of wharves. Most Boston shipyards and wharves were crowded along the town's northeast shore. New York shipyards were grouped around the East River; but since there was more available land and less shipbuilding activity in New York than in Boston, shipyards were not as pressed for space (see Figs. 6, 7). Philadelphia shipwrights remained on the town's original waterfront, eight blocks long, until the mid-eighteenth century, when crowded conditions finally forced shipbuilders to an independent borough just south of the city line. Southwark, named after the shipbuilding suburb of London, remained the center of Philadelphia's shipbuilding through the nineteenth century and, eventually, most of the city's maritime tradesmen moved there. At the time Southwark was established, a number of shipwrights settled in Northern Liberties, an area just north of the city line.[38]

Shipwrights in smaller towns often grouped together also, as in Ruck's Village, Salem. Newport shipwrights lived and worked in an area called the Cove.[39] Both these building centers were located in small coves, separated from the main shipping anchorage and well protected from storms. In Portsmouth, New Hampshire, yards were scattered about the town without any particular center. Yet the Portsmouth builders also favored coves, especially the well-sheltered North and South Mill Ponds. Likewise, southern ship-wrights in Annapolis and Charleston tended to locate their yards in coves away from the settled areas of the towns.

The organization of work within the shipyard, like the equip-ment, was simple but effective. When outside the shipyard and con-tracting with a purchaser, the builder was formal and precise. Within the shipyard, he relied on oral agreements. When builders sublet part of the hull construction to other shipwrights, such oral agreements would include sums from 3 or 4 shillings for daily wages to, in one case, over £600 sterling for building half a ship. The builder hired workers as he required them. Throughout most of the construction process, however, each shipyard employed one or two pairs of sawyers to cut timbers and planks into special shapes that sawmills could not fashion.[40]

The number of shipwrights helping the builder of a vessel varied from one to half a dozen or more. Usually during the major stage of construction, the builder employed between four and six ship-wrights paid either by the day or for specific tasks. Working on the same vessel, a shipwright might collect a daily wage for several weeks and later do piece work, such as planking part of the hull, for an agreed price.[41] The piecework method allowed the shipwright to work in several different yards at the same time. Also, he could bargain for more money than under the daily wage system. Either way, the builder always increased and decreased his labor force according to the progress of the work.

The colonial workday was from sunrise to sunset. In the Westons' shipyard at Duxbury, Massachusetts, at the end of the eighteenth century, work began at 4:30 A.M. during the summer and lasted until 7:15 P.M. Besides half an hour for breakfast and an hour for dinner, the men received breaks at 11:00 A.M. and 4:00 P.M. for grog. But whether the shipwrights worked a six-day week is open to question. Out of a total of 100 weeks, the work record of a New-bury shipwright shows 26 six-day weeks, 30 five-day weeks, 17 four-day weeks and 27 weeks of three days or less.[42] According to mer-chants' accounts, shipwrights often worked a half day, especially when doing repairs.

Knowing that the number of workers varied with the progress of the vessel, shipwrights did not expect steady employment in one yard and sought simultaneous work in several yards. They also faced seasonal layoffs. Northern shipwrights, for example, had less work in the open shipyards during the winter months. To avoid the numerous delays involved in winter construction, most shipwrights preferred building in the spring and summer. Between building schedules, weather, and personal situations, some colonial shipwrights had very irregular employment. One Newbury ship carpenter worked only 296 out of 710 consecutive days.[43]

Working in a small, almost barren yard with a constantly changing labor force, the colonial shipwright could build a large merchant ship in four months. But few ships mentioned in the papers of Boston and Philadelphia merchants were launched on schedule. As in England, at least a year was considered necessary for the entire process of building a ship—from the selection of a shipwright to the finding of a cargo for the completed vessel. While delays plagued both colonial and British shipyards, the colonial builder frequently launched more than one vessel from his yard per year. One ambitious Annapolis shipwright simultaneously built a sloop, a brigantine, and a ship. The very active builders along the Merrimack River occasionally constructed two ships at the same time in one yard.[44] Given good contracts, a steady labor supply, and favorable weather, the energetic colonial builder could produce two ships a year, in comparison with the one launched by the English counterpart.

The only pattern discernible from the records is one of minimal organization in the shipyards for both equipment and the labor force. Purchasing supplies and hiring workers when required encouraged a great variety in appearance and procedure from yard to yard. Professionalism probably also varied. The simplicity of organization did not ensure a steady or reliable work situation. The builder and his employees were at the mercy of weather, markets that changed with political as well as economic developments, and the availability of supplies, labor, and even financial backing. Timing and luck were, of course, influential. Actually, the deceptively simple appearance of the colonial shipyard belied its constantly changing nature.

## The Builders and the Community

Because of the unstable and often unprofitable nature of ship-building, most colonial merchants stayed out of the shipyard. Notable exceptions included Charles Carroll, Samuel Galloway, and Patrick Creagh, all of Maryland. These merchant-builders had been forced to establish their own yards when shipbuilding in their colony was still quite limited. Another merchant made shipbuilding his primary interest. George Boyd, a former ropewalk foreman of Portsmouth, New Hampshire, found some treasure, married an English girl with mercantile connections, and eventually purchased the shipyard of the town's leading builder. By expanding his own shipyard and ordering ships from other local yards, Boyd supplied as many as fourteen vessels to British correspondents in a single year. A few builders in small communities became local merchants thanks to the goods they received from merchants in larger towns in exchange for ships. Like Gideon Woodwell of Newbury, a shipwright could use part of the same goods to pay his workers.[45] Prospects were limited without established business connections. While Gideon Woodwell had to build ships for Massachusetts merchants who in turn might sell the vessels in England, George Boyd was able to secure direct orders from British merchants. Interestingly, no merchant-builders lived in Boston or Philadelphia. The availability of skilled labor in the two major shipbuilding centers allowed for a specialization in responsibility that the Maryland merchants could not afford.

Except for the few merchant-builders, shipwrights were members of the respectable unpretentious class in colonial society, the trades-men. Because they produced the most complicated and expensive product of colonial America, shipbuilders have often been depicted as the most respected and wealthy of tradesmen. But in fact their wealth appears to have been less than average. The seasonal nature of shipbuilding, after all, offered only irregular employment to its laborers and uncertain profits to its employers. Tax lists do not distinguish between the builders who owned their own yards and those who sought employment; all were simply listed as ship-wrights. The Philadelphia tax assessment ledger of 1775 shows shipwrights paying slightly lower taxes than average for tradesmen.

The average assessment for hatters, bricklayers, bakers, carpenters, and tailors ranged from £25 6s. to £15 8s. At £13 8s., shipwrights were rated £5 less than house carpenters. After shipwrights followed smiths, joiners, saddlers, and painters. Last on the list, barbers, assessed on the average at £9 8s., were still well above the £6 minimum of any individual tradesman. Rates for tradesmen compared favorably with those for other occupations. Captains, sailors, and schoolmasters, for example, had smaller assessment averages than shipwrights. Tavernkeepers were assessed at the same rate as shipwrights, and shopkeepers averaged only £3 more. Even ministers exceeded the rate for shipwrights by no more than £4. With an average assessment of £100, doctors had the highest occupational rating, followed by the £70 average for merchants. Thus, while not occupying a high economic position, Philadelphia shipwrights earned a comfortable livelihood in respect to the general community. A recent study of Boston reports similar relationships.[46]

Inventories confirm the impression of general prosperity for shipwrights throughout the colonies, their financial position being part of the modest affluence enjoyed by most colonial tradesmen. Successful shipbuilders in Newbury (Massachusetts), New London (Connecticut), and Charleston (South Carolina), reported greater wealth than those in the major building areas of Boston and Philadelphia. Energetic builders in Newbury and New London, it seems, were able to acquire more land, while leading Boston and Philadelphia shipwrights invested their smaller wealth in elaborate household furnishings. Although South Carolina shipbuilding did not even begin to expand until after 1760, Charleston claimed the wealthiest colonial shipbuilders—tradesmen who made their fortunes by taking advantage of the cheap land and slave labor available in that southern colony. One Charleston builder, John Rose, eventually left the shipyard and became a planter with a capital of £45,000 sterling in 1775. The slaves of one minor Charleston shipbuilder accounted for nearly two-thirds of his entire estate. His property included three shipwright slaves and a schooner on the stocks, but the most valuable item listed was a "Mustee house Wench Molley."[47]

Some shipwrights achieved local prominence, although such ad-

vancement usually occurred only in small towns. Jonathan Greenleaf, a poor boy bound to a Newbury shipwright, completed his
apprenticeship and then married his former master's daughter. The
young shipwright established his own yard by 1750 and became one
of Newbury's leading builders during the 1760s and 1770s. Greenleaf's success was not limited to the shipyard. From 1769 to 1791
he represented his town at the Massachusetts General Court. During the Revolution, Greenleaf served on the local committee of
correspondence, was a member of the Massachusetts Provincial
Congress of 1775, and attended the state Constitutional Conven-
tion in 1780. A Portsmouth, New Hampshire, shipwright, Nathaniel Meserve, won fame as a militia colonel at the siege of
Louisbourg in 1745, and for his services under the Earl of Loudoun
in 1756 and 1757. Meserve's excellent military reputation and his
marriage into a leading Portsmouth family might have enabled him
to enter politics. But while in charge of 100 carpenters at the second
siege of Louisburg, in 1758, Meserve and his oldest son died of
smallpox.[48]

Though able to gain minor political and social positions unat-
tainable in England, the colonial shipwright, like his English
cousin, won high prestige only after he left the shipyard. The first
governor of Massachusetts appointed by the king under the 1691
charter was Sir William Phips, a former shipbuilder. One of twenty-
six children of a blacksmith in a tiny settlement along the Kennebec
River in Maine, William Phips's prospects for wealth and a royal
governorship were most unlikely. His social rise began when he
stopped herding sheep to become a shipwright's apprentice at the
age of eighteen. Completing his apprenticeship in four years, Phips
left Maine to work in Boston shipyards. Within a year he owned
his own yard. This rapid advance was due to a fortunate marriage,
for Phips wed the young widow of a prosperous Boston merchant.
Thanks to her wealth and mercantile connections, Phips soon had
several building contracts with local merchants. He worked in
the shipyard for the next ten years. But ambitious for more wealth
and a higher social position, Phips began his famous treasure-
hunting expeditions. Thirty-two tons of silver plus gold and jewels
naturally pleased Phips' noble backers, and they had him knighted
in 1687. Much to his own advantage, Phips became a close friend

of Increase Mather and joined his church after the imprisonment of Sir Edmund Andros, in 1689. Backed by Increase Mather and acceptable to the crown, the former shipbuilder became governor of Massachusetts in 1691.[49]

William Partridge of Portsmouth, New Hampshire, was another builder who became a royal governor, but Partridge followed a more conventional road to success. He first established himself as a shipbuilder and then left the shipyard for the countinghouse. His success as a merchant was soon equaled by political achievements. Appointed to the Royal Council, he became treasurer of the colony and then served as governor from 1697 to 1703.[50] Both Phips and Partridge tried to promote the construction of British warships in their respective colonies.

Probably because of the general prosperity, colonial shipbuilding families of two or more generations were quite common. Among the Salem families discussed in earlier chapters were two generations of Gedneys, three of Bacons, and seven of Beckets. Similar patterns are found in other New England towns. Three generations of Woodwells built ships at Newbury. Several generations of Jacksons and Meserves operated shipyards in Portsmouth. In Scituate, Massachusetts, five generations of Barstows and six of Briggses launched ships into the North River. Shipbuilding dynasties also grew up in the building centers of Boston and Philadelphia. Hoods and Hallowells, for example, ranked among Boston's leading shipwrights throughout the eighteenth century. In Philadelphia, four generations of Penroses worked as shipbuilders. Besides several generations of Wests, Philadelphia shipbuilding families also included the Lynns from 1717 to 1860, and the Cramps from 1760 to 1927.[51] Shipbuilding families have not been found in the southern colonies. Their absence may be explained partly by the lack of documents; but in South Carolina, which has good records, it seems that sons of shipbuilders did not continue in their fathers' trade.

## Conclusion

Although training and construction methods remained almost unchanged across the Atlantic, colonial shipwrights did modify some traditions familiar to builders in England. Most important, the colonial shipwright worked faster. He introduced slave labor throughout the colonies and even became dependent upon it in South Carolina. Unlike English builders, a few Americans became wealthy. And in towns outside the major building centers of Boston and Philadelphia, shipwrights who advanced themselves economically could also seek higher social or political status not open to tradesmen in England. Within the limits of the trade, the general prosperity of most colonial shipbuilders was remarkable. In turn, that prosperity fostered a tradition of shipbuilding families unknown in Great Britain. But, it must be remembered, the changes that shipbuilding traditions underwent in America are not unique. They merely exemplify the abundant opportunities that characterized colonial society.

# CHAPTER V

# Ship Construction in Eighteenth-Century America

## Colonial Vessels

NAVAL architecture changed gradually in the eighteenth century. Of five classes of seventeenth-century vessels, only the ship continued to be built after the early 1700s. The others were replaced by four new types: sloop, schooner, brigantine, and snow. Likewise, the criteria for judging classes changed. Both hull form and sail arrangement had previously determined class; but the new vessels were typed simply by their rigs, while hull forms began to vary greatly within each class of vessel. Though square sails remained, fore-and-aft sails were now suspended from a short spar, called the gaff, instead of being supported and extended by the sprit, a long spar which crossed diagonally from the tack to the peak of the sail. The elimination of the awkward sprit allowed room for larger sails, which in turn meant larger vessels with fore-and-aft sails. Offering only an occasional modification, colonial shipbuilders followed the European developments in hull design and rigging.[1] Given the constant emigration of shipwrights from England and the limited advances in technology, it is not surprising that eighteenth-century Americans were usually familiar with trends abroad.

There were two types of sloops in the eighteenth century: small coasters averaging 20 to 40 tons, and West Indian traders of 50 or more tons burden. The coaster retained the basic fore-and-aft rig of mainsail, staysail, and jib; the larger sloop added square main- and topsails for ocean passages. Plans of a 100-ton sloop built in Virginia about 1741 show a moderately fast hull with good cargo capacity.[2] Her huge sails, required by the single-mast rig on a 60-foot hull, would have been difficult to handle without a large crew, meaning greater expenses and consequently less profit for the owners.

An alternative was found in a two-mast rig, which divided the sail area into more numerous and easily manageable units. This new vessel, appearing in the colonies during the second decade of the eighteenth century, was destined to become the most distinctive American sailing craft, the schooner, proud descendant of the ketch (see Fig. 5). The schooner retained the two-mast fore-and-aft rig of the ketch, but the more modern vessel also had gaffs instead of sprits, one or more headsails on a bowsprit, and a different division of sail area on the masts. Contrary to legend, the schooner was not invented at Gloucester in 1713[3]. Pictorial evidence shows schooners in England by 1700 and in Holland at least fifty years earlier.

As soon as the schooner was introduced into American waters, it began to threaten the sloop's position as most popular colonial vessel. Like sloops, schooners were divided into a coasting class averaging 20 to 40 tons and a larger West Indian class with square topsails. Because they engaged in the same trade, most schooners and sloops were about the same size.[4] But the schooner had two important advantages over the sloop—sailing ability and economy. The schooner could quickly alter and balance its sail area to meet a variety of weather conditions, while the sloop was severely handicapped by having all sails centered about one mast. Furthermore, with its sail area divided into smaller units, a schooner was more manageable and could operate with fewer men. Smaller sails meant lighter masts and rigging, which in turn reduced expenses for the owners.

The plans of five vessels typify the various models of schooners built by colonial shipwrights. The earliest and most interesting plans are those of the *St. Ann.* Employed by the Portuguese as a government dispatch boat, the American-built *St. Ann* had her lines taken off during a visit to England in 1736. She was capable of high speed in moderate weather, and her unusually narrow and shallow hull reflected the work of a highly competent designer-builder. The *St. Ann* is believed to have been designed as a yacht because she had little cargo capacity. At the other extreme was the New England schooner *Hallifax*, built in the 1760s. The same length as the *St. Ann*, the *Hallifax* was designed as a cargo carrier with little concern for speed. She was 83 tons burden in comparison with the *St. Ann*'s 36. A compromise between these two types, the *Chaleur,* was a full-built schooner with excellent cargo capacity and a fair turn of speed. Another fine vessel, the *Sultana,* a small but sharp schooner built by Benjamin Hallowell of Boston in 1767, was purchased by the British navy for coastal work. A last set of plans shows how the Marblehead model was used to build two patrol boats for the British navy. The large Marblehead offshore fishing schooners, designed to bring profitable cargo home quickly, soon acquired an excellent reputation for speed and good cargo capacity. Even a merchant from South Carolina, where fine schooners were built, preferred to purchase the Marblehead version.[5]

The relative popularity of sloops and schooners differed from colony to colony. In the Massachusetts coasting fleet, schooners became slightly more popular than sloops after the first third of the eighteenth century. According to one New York merchant, by 1750 the Massachusetts fishing fleet was composed almost entirely of schooners. New Hampshire builders also favored schooners over sloops. But in southern New England, Rhode Island and Connecticut shipwrights concentrated on sloop construction and built only a few schooners. Pennsylvania sloops were almost twice as numerous as schooners until the last decade of the colonial period, when schooners began to outnumber sloops by just a narrow margin. Following Massachusetts and Pennsylvania, in Maryland the sloop gradually gave way to the schooner, and, by the late 1760s, Maryland builders were launching three times as many schooners as sloops. The same pattern repeated itself in North Carolina. In South Carolina, however, there was no transition from sloop to schooner. Instead, South Carolina shipwrights built schooners almost exclusively from 1735.[6] Because there had been little shipbuilding in the colony before that date, the sloop never had a chance to become popular. Thus, eighty-three schooners and only four sloops were built in South Carolina during the 1740s. And between 1760 and 1774, South Carolina schooners outnumbered sloops one hundred to one.

At the beginning of the eighteenth century, the brigantine replaced the bark for West Indian and other foreign trade. Developed by English builders, the brigantine had two or more square sails on the foremast and a fore-and-aft sail on the mainmast. Often the mainmast also carried a square topsail. Brigantines averaged from half again to more than double the tonnage of coasting sloops and

schooners. One merchant advised against owning brigantines because the long boom of the fore-and-aft mainsail occasionally
caught wave tops when sailing downwind and damaged the vessel.
He preferred the snow, which had square sails on both masts plus
a small fore-and-aft sail set on a pole about a foot behind the mainmast. Snows averaged 10 to 30 tons larger than brigantines. In
general, however, brigantines were far more popular than snows,
sometimes by ratios greater than five to one.[7]

The eighteenth-century ship was more varied and refined than
its predecessors. English builders abandoned their warship models
and began to launch merchant ships with high cargo capacity and
low operating costs. Additional square sails on each mast made
rigging more complicated but also increased the ship's sailing
ability. Colonial shipwrights kept up with all the changes. Most
colonial ships averaged twice the tonnage of brigantines. The plans
of two ships built between 1770 and 1773 illustrate two basic hull
forms. The *London*, built in New York, had a moderately sharp
hull, which achieved the difficult combination of good speed and
cargo capacity. It was also a well-finished vessel with a beautiful
and elaborate stern. The second ship, the *Codrington* of Newbury,
was a slow, full-built cargo carrier similar to British vessels of the
same size and class. Designed for low-cost operation, the *Codrington*
had no frills whatsoever. Both ships had a feature seldom found in
European vessels—the upper deck fell in a gradual curve from the
foremast to the bow. Because the hawseholes for anchor cables
were usually mounted level with a ship's upper deck, the drop reduced the angle of the cables and enabled the anchors to hold better. This same odd-looking but practical feature was employed by
a Rhode Island builder as early as 1767.[8]

Just as sloops and schooners were divided into two sizes, colonial
builders launched two types of brigantines, snows and ships. The
smaller vessels were employed in colonial trade and usually were
owned in part or wholly by colonists. These were the vessels recorded in all the port records and shipping registers included in
the tables. Shipping listed in *Lloyd's Register*, mostly British-
owned, was used in American, African, and Mediterranean trade.
With their greater financial resources and need for long-distance
carriers, British merchants ordered American vessels of a much

larger tonnage than those purchased by colonists. The tonnages in *Lloyd's Register* for Pennsylvania-built brigantines, snows, and ships were 140.4, 156.7, and 235.8, respectively, far above the tonnages of 62.2, 83.3, and 145.9 listed in the Philadelphia shipping register for the same period. This pattern held true for all the colonies. Massachusetts and North Carolina brigantines in *Lloyd's Register* were nearly twice the size of those used in the coasting and West Indian trade.[9]

Besides differences in class and size, colonial vessels frequently had hull form and construction details peculiar to a region or even to a particular province. A knowledge of these characteristics enabled sailors to identify vessels found abandoned at sea—such as a New England schooner or a Philadelphia sloop. Once common knowledge, the unique features of each region are now unknown except for a rough distinction between the New England and Chesapeake hull forms. New England sloops had a reputation throughout the colonies for their large cargo capacity and shallow draft. They were full built with little deadrise (the amount of rise or angle of rise in the bottom timbers of the vessels). Plans for New England craft generally show less draft and deadrise than those of Chesapeake vessels. Also, while Chesapeake sloops had a slight outward flare to their topsides, New England vessels had their sides tumbled home—that is, the beam was narrowed at the deck line, which gave them a more rounded midsection. Even the swift Marblehead schooner, with many features similar to the Chesapeake craft, had shallow draft and sides markedly tumbled home. According to contracts and orders, New England shipwrights used this "fair, round side" throughout the eighteenth century.[10]

"Proof" can be found for the superiority or inferiority of vessels from any colony by sifting through the numerous and conflicting statements of contemporary writers. But, fortunately, one unbiased record does exist. All vessels listed in *Lloyd's Register* were inspected and rated according to the condition of their hull and rigging. Most American vessels built in the 1770s received the highest hull rating, A, and most built in the preceding decade had only a slightly lower grade, E. Exceptions have nothing to do with the colony or region in which the vessels were built. The ratings of the remaining 6.6 percent of colonial vessels, built before 1760, varied from a high of E to the lowest grade of U, without favor or prejudice for any area.[11] Of course, it is doubtful that colonial shipwrights always practiced the same degree of workmanship reported by *Lloyd's Register*. American merchants must have given much attention to the construction of ships destined for the British market.

## Contracts

Most shipwrights built vessels under contract from a merchant who provided sufficient capital and the necessary market outlet as well as vital supplies, such as iron and pitch. At times, the merchant even recruited the various tradesmen needed to complete the vessel. Receiving building orders from correspondents in other colonies and in Great Britain, a merchant would often serve as an inspector to ensure the quality of the shipwrights' work. Two exceptions were the carpenter who launched a small coasting vessel for a local sailor and the merchant-builder who occasionally speculated in ships. Otherwise, shipwrights and merchants, working closely together, sought to reduce risks and increase mutual profits through the use of carefully prepared contracts.

According to the correspondence of Joshua Coffin, Daniel Flexney, John Hunt, and a Mr. Greenleafe, the colonial merchant first had to define his own requirements. He established the basic dimensions of keel length, breadth, and depth of hold through a combination of the approximate tonnage of the vessel, local custom, and his own preference. His choice of sailing rig varied according to the vessel's size and trade, as well as local practice. Finally, the merchant decided whether to have a plain or elaborate finish on his vessel. He usually left hull design and construction detail to the shipwright. Building orders from English correspondents included the vessel's rig and dimensions and left the rest to the discretion of the colonial merchant. Occasionally, however, English merchants sent over plans for the vessel with extremely detailed building instructions listing the size of each timber and plank.[12]

Agreeing to hull specifications with relative ease, the merchant often had difficulty with the questions of how to pay a builder and where to secure naval stores and iron for the vessel. Some merchants viewed shipbuilding as a convenient means of getting rid of unsold goods by forcing the shipwright to accept them at inflated prices for his work. But when paid in unwanted goods instead of valuable merchandise or cash, shipwrights might take longer to build a vessel and do inferior work. Most merchants speculating in the sale of colonial ships or having them built for British correspondents found delays and bad workmanship unprofitable and therefore intolerable. The colonial merchant had to strike a balance between the type of payment he wished to offer and what the builder would accept. The matter resolved itself quickly if the merchant assumed the debts of an insolvent shipwright in exchange for his labor.[13]

The introduction of a third party, the English correspondent, made decisions more complicated. Rarely did the correspondent send along with a ship order a parcel of goods whose sale could pay for building costs. Usually, the English merchant promised to send commodities at an indefinite future date. He, like the colonial merchant, occasionally tried to pay his debts with inferior goods. The English correspondent might also order a West Indian partner to send molasses in payment, and the shipment would be delayed for several months. The colonial merchant's response would be to demand prompt delivery of goods and the use of cash instead of overpriced merchandise.[14]

Regarding iron and naval stores, the merchant had to decide first whether to import or to use local products. Although much colonial iron was used in American vessels, some builders preferred Spanish, Swedish, or English ore. The merchant could secure good tar, pitch, and turpentine from North Carolina, but he usually imported cordage and sailcloth from England. As with any imported items, the merchant had to expect late shipments, which in turn could delay construction and increase expenses.[15] However, if he was indefinite about the type of payment or the manner in which he would supply naval stores and iron, the colonial merchant would forfeit part of his advantage when bargaining with a shipwright. The latter might refuse to negotiate, especially during a shipbuilding boom, if the merchant's terms appeared uncertain or unfavorable.

Frequently the merchant or correspondent wanted a particular shipwright to build the vessel. Some builders, such as Benjamin Hallowell and Thomas Taylor of Boston, or Thomas Wells and James West of Philadelphia, had excellent reputations, and their work was sought by merchants throughout the colonies and Great Britain. Kinship rather than reputation occasionally affected the choice of builder. In one instance, a Philadelphia merchant contracted with his shipbuilder son-in-law, and in another a West Indian correspondent asked a Newport merchant to employ the brother of a friend.[16]

Success in drawing up a contract often depended on local market conditions. When their yards were full, carpenters readily refused offers they would have accepted in duller times. The cost and delivery date of a vessel also varied according to the amount of shipbuilding activity. But cost was mostly related to size and hull design, for as the dimensions of a vessel increased, the shipwright had to use heavier, more expensive timber and plank, which were harder to work. Similarly, because a full-built vessel needed more wood than a sharp one of the same length, builders demanded, and received, a higher price per ton for the heavier ship. The type of payment the merchant offered, again a matter related to local market conditions, also affected prices. After agreeing to a certain price per ton, the builder might permit the merchant to subtract between 1 and 4 feet from the rake of the stem and add it to the keel without charge. This increase in length could give a couple of extra tons to a small vessel and 10 tons to a large one. Of course, the carpenter's willingness to allow the merchant free tonnage changed accordingly with business. While those anxious for contracts were generous, shipwrights with plenty of work gave merchants little or no free tonnage.[17]

After establishing a mutually satisfactory price and form of payment, the merchant and shipwright still had to settle a few details. If he thought the vessel might not be seaworthy, the builder would insist on altering the dimensions. Disputed dimensions were usually proposed by inexperienced merchants who promptly acquiesced to the shipwright's alterations. As a rule, the merchant would agree to furnish naval stores and iron, and the builder would supply the wood. Sometimes the two men set a delivery date which allowed between three and nine months to complete the vessel.

However, most builders encountered unexpected delays and were late with ship deliveries. Some merchants requested particular construction features, such as lumber and ballast ports or a gallery and quarter pieces, which the shipwright could provide without difficulty; these were minor items. Occasionally, a merchant wanted the builder to allow the completed hull to season all winter on the stocks.[18] While seasoning might benefit the ship, it left the builder responsible for any damages to the vessel, for which he could forfeit the unpaid balance owed him. Considering the low number of requests, most shipwrights must have refused to season a vessel on the stocks.

Once they had reached a verbal agreement, the merchant and the shipwright were ready to sign a formal contract. Shipbuilding contracts were simple and usually brief. The document first listed the basic dimensions of the vessel and any special features the merchant desired. The builder promised to construct the vessel and complete all the customary work "to a cleat." "In consideration whereof," the merchant agreed to furnish the naval stores and iron, and to pay the builder a certain amount of money for each ton the vessel measured. Because few merchants paid the entire sum in currency, the contract listed the proportion of cash to goods and frequently specified the type of commodities. For example, some merchants divided the cost of the vessel into thirds, paying one part in cash, one in West Indian rum and sugar, and the last in British goods. The contract required the merchant to make payments as the building progressed. At the signing of the contract, the merchant made the first payment in cash, which enabled the shipwright to purchase the necessary timber and planks. The builder received further payments after completing the frame and planking the hull. When the vessel was safely launched and delivered to the merchant, the shipwright received the final payment. Sometimes, the contract included a definite delivery date for the vessel. Most contracts concluded with a bond by both builder and merchant to forfeit a specific amount of money if either failed to perform the requirements placed upon him.[19]

The colonial propensity for lawsuits is reflected in disputed shipbuilding contracts. For example, two shipwrights and a merchant, all of Boston, met in a tavern to sign a contract. The merchant was supposed to exchange the cash down payment for the signed contract, but he left quickly with both money and contract while the builders were busy drinking. Because he refused to give them any payments, even after they had purchased timber on their own credit, the shipwrights eventually refused to do any further work on the vessel. In retaliation, the merchant brought an unsuccessful suit against them for a broken covenant. Considering the delivery dates included in some contracts and the frequent delays in construction, the absence of more lawsuits is most surprising. In one instance, when shipyard workers threatened to leave unless they received higher wages, a merchant allowed the shipwright to increase his building price beyond contract specifications to meet the new labor costs.[20] In that case, both the merchant and the builder exercised sufficient flexibility and mutual consideration to make recourse to legal action unnecessary.


Construction

The builder's first task was to draw plans or drafts based upon the dimensions specified in the contract and appropriate for the purposes of the vessel.[21] If he launched craft of the same form and size year after year, the shipwright could simply build by "eye." The numerous 20-ton coasting schooners of Massachusetts and South Carolina were probably produced in this rough yet effective fashion. Shipwrights who launched a variety of vessels had to plan different hull forms and construction details best suited to each trade plus whatever particular features the merchant desired. Howard I. Chapelle suggests that by the end of the seventeenth century, builders commonly used drafts to design their vessels. The degree of sophistication of the plans or drafts would, of course, vary greatly, but certainly some sort of plan was a necessity for the larger vessels.

Although all methods of shipbuilding required a similar degree of skill, the use of drafts permitted a degree of flexibility in the building process. Shipwrights could study the art of drafting from the dozen or so seventeenth- and eighteenth-century English shipbuilding books and a wide variety of volumes from other European presses. Some colonial builders owned the more famous of the English works and probably allowed apprentices to copy them. A few colonists acquired reputations for skillful drafting and occasionally provided plans for other builders.[22] Most shipwrights made their own drafts.

Shipwrights needed three drafts to build a vessel, each representing a different view. The sheer plan, or side view, showed the keel, stem, stern, and deck profiles, and the location of the mold stations. On the floor plan the builder drew the waterline, underwater planes parallel to it, and the decks. The body plan was a cross-sectional view of the hull outlining the mold stations, which were perpendicular to the plane of the waterline and spaced along the keel at every third or fourth frame. The sheer and floor plans were drawn within the basic dimensions of the contract and according to the particular shape the builder favored.[23]

The shipwright used either the sweep or whole molding method to design the body plan. In the sweep method, each section, such as the midship frame, was formed by arcs of circles, called sweeps and usually four in number, with varying radii. A builder employing the whole molding method would also begin by drawing the midship frame with sweeps and would then make two patterns, or molds, which reproduced the curves of that frame. By altering the relative positions of the bend, or upper mold, and the hollow or lower mold, the shipwright shaped the remaining mold stations. Both methods varied with the art and skill of the designer. Modern observers' analysis of surviving drafts, though, confirm the ability of colonial shipwrights to produce excellent designs.[24]

After completing the drafts, the shipwright who had employed the sweep method of design enlarged the mold stations to the body plan and then cut out a full-size wooden pattern of each. If he had used the whole molding method, he simply made two full-scale bend and hollow molds and utilized the same design method to reproduce the shape of any station. The shipwright then used the molds as guides to find frame timbers with the necessary curvature.[25]

It must be emphasized that the shipwright was not bound by mathematical formulas or textbook methods for building. In fact, strict adherence to regulations could not guarantee a smooth symmetrical hull at all. As with many maritime problems, the skilled craftsman knew when and how to adjust the rules. The ship he launched, not plans or books, was the testament of his workmanship. Thus the colonial shipwright leaves modern historians puzzling over the literature of his trade, without substantial records to settle the issue of how his craft was actually practiced.

The next task was to get timber and plank. Ephraim Robinson, a New Hampshire merchant, supplied timber to Portsmouth builders by purchasing trees along the upper reaches of the Piscataqua River, converting the logs into boards at his own sawmills, and then transporting timber and plank downstream to the shipyards. Usually, shipwrights found it cheaper and less time-consuming to purchase wood from timber merchants. On occasion the timber merchant tried to reduce costs by cutting trees without paying the owners. Sometimes the shipwright used the down payment on his contract to settle with the timber merchants. Such early payment was practical, since the price of timber could increase a third or more during a drought when low water level hindered mill operation and downstream transportation. Sometimes a shipwright contracted with a local farmer who promised to deliver timber rather than plank to the shipyard. This method was, understandably, more common in smaller settlements without timber merchants than in the more populous shipbuilding centers. Customarily, shipwrights had their timber cut during the fall and used it in construction the following summer.[26]

The shipwright began work on the body of the vessel by laying the keel upon a number of timber blocks. Next he fastened the stem and the stern post to the ends of the keel. Each frame, or rib, of the ship consisted of one floor timber, four or more overlapping futtocks, and a pair of top timbers. The builder bolted the middle of each floor timber, which he had shaped with his molds, to the keel. Then the keelson, a timber similar in size to the keel, was laid atop the centers of the floors and bolted through them to the keel. Now the shipwright had the difficult task of cutting and fastening the remaining frame timbers. First, he ran two long narrow wooden strips called ribbands from the stem to the sternpost beneath the ends of the floor timbers on either side. Then, working at the mold stations, at every third or fourth frame, the shipwright shaped each frame member according to his molds and attached all the lower futtocks to the floors, then the middle and upper futtocks, and finally the top timbers. He ran more ribbands along the ends of each set of timbers as he erected them. Using the ribbands as guides, the shipwright shaped and raised the remaining frames into place. After building staging about the hull, workmen began planking both the interior and the exterior of the hull. As the inside planking, or ceiling, rose to the level of a deck, the shipwrights added deck beams and fastened them to the frames with large wooden knees (see Fig. 7). In the nineteenth century, instead of building a frame up piecemeal, shipwrights assembled the entire unit and then hoisted it into position on the keel. It is quite possible that the later method was employed earlier than written sources indicate, especially on smaller vessels. Workmen also framed ports and hatchways, made gratings, cleats, and a windlass, and installed pumps and scuppers.[27]

While the shipwrights were busy with these details, nearly twenty additional craftsmen were also at work on the ship. Joiners smoothed the outside planking, built rails and did interior cabin work. Caulkers filled seams with oakum to make the ship watertight. With iron more plentiful in the colonies than in England, colonial builders often used more iron on masts, blocks, and deckware than British shipwrights did; occasionally they even went to the trouble of bolting the butt, or end, of every plank instead of using only treenails. Responsible for all the iron work on the vessel, smiths also had the task of forging anchors. A mason laid bricks to support the galley, a tinman lined the scuppers, and a glazier installed glass ports. Mastmakers, sailmakers, blockmakers, and ropemakers supplied their respective products. Other tradesmen included painters, riggers, boatmakers, coopers, tanners, and carvers. Before sailing, the ship required the services of instrument makers, chairmakers and upholsterers to complete the officers' quarters, and brewers, bakers, and butchers to supply provisions.[28]

The work of these tradesmen varied according to the merchant's tastes. Those who wanted plain, inexpensive ships limited carved work, joinery, painting, and ironwork to a minimum. One very effective way to reduce the cost of both constructing and operating a vessel was to under-rig her, that is, furnish her with the masts, sails, and cordage of a smaller craft. At the opposite extreme, some merchants ordered fancy ships with extensive carvings, an elaborate figurehead, excellent paintwork, and a fine cabin decorated with wallpaper and beautiful furniture. While Thomas Hancock had ships built in a "most frugal manner," his nephew John did the opposite. But when colonial merchants sent their ships to Great Britain in hopes of a sale, a fancy finish made little difference to prospective buyers, for most purchasers were unwilling to pay more for an elaborate vessel.[29]

When the vessel was near completion, the shipwrights often sheathed the underwater surface of the hull before allowing the painters to begin their work. Sheathing gave the ship some protection against the sea worms and was especially useful to vessels sailing to the West Indies or other tropical climates. The builders coated the surface with a mixture of tar and hair and then covered it with half-inch fir boards nailed to the planking. Because sheathing hid part of the hull and thus might tempt caulkers to do careless work, some merchants waited until the caulking had been completed and inspected before asking the builder to sheath the vessel. Such delayed requests gave the shipwright little trouble, since he could sheath a vessel in only four days.[30]

Painting was the last important task to be done before launching. Even a merchant anxious to save money could give his vessel a handsome appearance at little cost. A common inexpensive method was to cover the upper sides of the hull with turpentine, which weathered to a dark yellow, and to relieve it with several bands of tar and lampblack. The underbody was painted with a mixture of tallow and sulphur, which gave an off-white color. Owners such as John Hancock, who favored fancy ships, had them decorated with various combinations of shades of red, yellow, green, blue, and white paint imported from England.[31]

To prepare for launching, the shipwrights had to lay two parallel tracks of timber, called ways, on either side of the keel and extend them, at a gentle grade, down into the water. Then the carpenters could build a cradle, with its upper part conforming to the underbody of the vessel and its lower section matching the ways beneath. After greasing the ways and cradle and attaching the latter to the hull with temporary lashings, the ship was at last ready for launching.[32] Descriptions of launchings do not always specify the use of a cradle, so other methods may have been used.

Launching was a time for celebration. The builders had completed months of labor and would now receive the last payment. The merchant was finally getting the vessel, probably after some delay, and could at last put her to work to earn a return for his sizable investment. The launching provided a spectacle to observers and the new owner would supply free dinner and drink for all. Launchings were even used occasionally to celebrate a special day. Members of the Society for Ancient Britons, for example, commemorated the simultaneous birthdays of their patron, Saint David, and Queen Caroline by launching a ship. With typical flair, John Hancock launched a ship to climax Boston's anniversary of Guy Fawkes Day in 1770. To reduce the chances of an accident, shipwrights launched the vessel at the beginning of the celebration. The carpenters split the keel blocks supporting the vessel. If all went well, the cradle, with the vessel atop it, gradually settled onto the ways and slid down them into the water. Then everyone present attended to the food and rum which the merchant customarily provided. Carpenters attacked one merchant who refused to give them rum at the launching of his ship. If especially pleased with a ship, the merchant presented the builder with a porcelain or silver bowl during the launching dinner[33] (see Fig. 8).

The newly launched ship was christened with a simple toast that most people probably missed amidst the revelry. Merchants selected an interesting variety of names. Women's names were, and still are, the most popular. According to a name analysis of vessels in the North Carolina port records, 1767 to 1775, Sally was the most popular girl's name in the late colonial period, and 33 of the 566 vessels were so named. Betsy was second with 27, and Nancy third with 15. When a London merchant ordering a colonial ship forgot to specify a name, the Rhode Island correspondent prudently christened the vessel after the Englishman's wife. Vessels' names also included the political heroes of the colonists. A Rhode Island sloop was named William Pitt, after the Englishman who had saved the colonies from the French in the recent war and from Parliament in 1766. The Corsican Pasquoli Paoli was popular in the colonies, and in 1768 the owners of a Boston schooner named their vessel after him. John Hancock, the colonists' own patriot, was represented among the ships' names. In 1774 Hancock himself named a brigantine *Undutied Tea*.[34]

Aside from the active categories of women and politics, names were drawn from place names. A sloop built in Providence, Rhode Island, was named *Providence*. Some schooners launched in other colonies but trading with North Carolina were listed as the *Carolina Packet* or the *Cape Fear Packet*. A North Carolina–built brigantine registered in Greenock, Scotland, appropriately became the *Greenock*. In a society based on hard work, *Industry* and *Endeavour* were common names for small sloops and schooners. Some names reflected a literary interest, such as the New Hampshire brigantine *Roderick Random*. In an unusual and generous gesture, one Annapolis merchant named his ship after her two builders.[35]

With the launching and delivery of the vessel, the shipwright had fulfilled his contract. The merchant supervised the remaining tradesmen who had to finish their respective tasks. Masts were stepped and rigged. Joiners, carvers, and painters added their final touches. Anchor smiths, boatbuilders, and furniture-makers delivered their wares to the vessel. During this rush to furnish the ship, the merchant also had to find a cargo, crew, and provisions. When all was aboard, sails were bent to the yards, and the ship was ready for her maiden voyage.

Any description of ship construction would be incomplete without a discussion of the unexpected problems that might confront both shipwright and merchant. The builder's main worry was shipyard accidents, which could happen at any stage of construction. Falling timber caused many deaths. Most accidents occurred when shipwrights were at work on the staging about the ship. Although such accidents usually involved a fall of 15 feet or less, they were often serious, even causing death, because the person would fall on the massive timbers scattered on the ground about the ship.[36]

Launchings could cause tragic accidents. On one occasion the cradle settled on the ways but refused to slide. When the shipwrights used a long boom to lever the vessel down the ways, the lever suddenly swung about and killed several spectators. If a ship began its slide too soon, men could be caught and crushed beneath the cradle. When someone was killed at a launching, the vessel was said to be "launched in blood" and therefore unlucky. Superstition aside, accidents were more common to the careless builder, and merchants were wise to avoid any association with an unlucky ship. At a Maryland launching, a cable aboard the ship caught the ways and swung them into a large crowd of spectators, killing two and seriously injuring eight. Another man was killed when the masts were raised aboard the same vessel. Finally, the ship overturned during her first trial sail.[37] Obviously the ship suffered from more than just bad luck. A vessel that fell out of the cradle was costly to the builder, who had to repair the ship at his own expense before receiving final payment from the merchant.

Though seldom destructive of life, weather damaged ships and impeded construction. A hurricane entered the lower portion of the Merrimack River valley in August 1773, and carried two vessels 20 feet from their stocks, leaving the builders with the burdensome task of repairing and reblocking the ships. Boston shipyards lost hundreds of tons of timber when a winter storm flooded these low areas and floated the wood off to sea. Although shipwrights preferred to work in spring and summer, many would build in the fall and winter months if contracts were available. Because the builders had to work in the open, low temperatures caused numerous delays in winter construction. Frozen rivers, such as the Taunton and the Delaware, delayed launchings for months on end. Illness in the builder's family could cause further delay. Ironically, a shipbuilding boom could not only delay construction but might ruin the shipwright. Workmen demanded and usually got higher wages. As a result, the higher price per ton the builder charged during a boom could still barely meet the increased wages, and the scarcity of labor meant a longer construction time for each vessel. Financially pressed by high wages and a labor shortage, one builder was unable to complete his ship, which then became the property of the merchant.[38]

Ships built in the winter were supposed to be ready by late spring, and summer-built vessels by the fall. Because destinations and freights varied according to the season, any delay in the delivery of a ship could ruin the merchant's careful preparations for her first voyage. Thus the builder became the merchant's main problem. He did his best to keep the builder on schedule despite shipyard accidents and bad weather. In one instance when workers demanded higher wages and a shipwright became recalcitrant, the merchant offered encouragement in the form of extra money. "I tip the builder often," another merchant explained, "so that he [will] work, and he sucks in the money; but I am content since we get along well."[39]

In general the merchant had little difficulty with the finishers and provisioners of ships. On the other hand, the merchant had frequent trouble in getting naval stores from English correspondents. When sails and cordage arrived late, as they often did, the ship was prevented from sailing just as effectively as if she was still on the stocks. Such delays and overcharges provoked strong American replies, but time and money were already lost. These correspondence and remittance problems were typical of all eighteenth-century commerce.

## Building Costs

The price of a vessel varied according to its tonnage, design, sailing rig, builder, and local market conditions. Comparison of building costs in different colonies introduces a sixth factor, the numerous and fluctuating currencies of eighteenth-century America. In Massachusetts alone during the late colonial period, merchants used three local currencies—old tenor, new tenor, and lawful money —besides pounds sterling and foreign specie. Despite attempts to peg exchange rates by law, the relative value of these bills and coins continued to change. So instead of conclusive statements about the precise cost per ton of colonial vessels, one can offer only a relative comparison of prices.

Philadelphia ships, an English merchant once complained, were much more expensive than those of New England. Yet because he found it easier to secure remittances from that town, he continued to order vessels from that city. However, New England shipbuilding was not necessarily synonymous with Boston. Shipyard wages and general construction costs were higher in Boston than in other New England towns. The pattern of lower costs outside the main shipbuilding centers of Boston and Philadelphia was identical to the situation in Great Britain, where shipyard wages and other expenses were much higher in London than in the countryside.[40]

An analysis of the accounts of fourteen colonial vessels shows the builder receiving approximately 45 percent of the merchant's total expenditure. Cordage was the second-largest expense, receiving 21 percent, and iron was third, receiving 16 percent. Because some merchants had old sails on hand while others imported new ones from England, the percent figure for sails varied between 2 and 14. Remaining costs break down into numerous small accounts. The joiner's bill accounted for 2 per cent of the merchant's expenses. Carved work, at 1.6 percent, was a slightly larger expense than was painting. About 2 percent went for boats, and between 1 and 2 percent for blocks. The other accounts received less than 1 percent.[41]

The low cost of colonial shipping was its major attraction for British merchants. According to contemporary observers, the building price per ton for a colonial vessel was often £2 to £4 less than a British-built one. On occasion, however, colonial tonnage became as expensive as or even more expensive than British shipping when a shipbuilding boom or a general inflation throughout the colonies raised the cost of construction. In wartime, both the price of English naval stores and their freight to the colonies increased. One colonial merchant even advised his British correspondent to build in England rather than in America. But, generally, American ability to produce adequate shipping at reasonable cost helped shipbuilding develop in the colonies during the eighteenth century.

CHAPTER VI

# The Markets for
# Colonial-built Vessels

## Local Markets

EXTENSIVE business connections enabled many merchants to sell their newly acquired vessels in other colonies, in England, or even in foreign countries. Shipbuilders, on the other hand, had to work within the local market through contracts with merchants in their area. Merchants within the same community purchased new tonnage directly from builders, not from each other. The abundant, detailed records of contracts and correspondence between merchants and shipbuilders indicate that most vessels were built to order. The death of a builder or the inability of a merchant to fulfill a contract sometimes caused the appearance of an incomplete or newly launched vessel upon the local market. But otherwise one finds few newspaper advertisements for new colonial vessels[1] (see Fig. 9).

## Intercolonial Markets

The intercolonial shipbuilding market consisted of American sales to the British continental and West Indian colonies as part of the coastal and West Indian trade. Throughout the colonial period, Massachusetts merchants and their vessels dominated coastal commerce. Pennsylvania and Rhode Island also had active coasting fleets by the middle of the eighteenth century, but both merchants' correspondence and port records emphasize the unchallenged role of New England as the builder of coasting craft for other colonies. Even Philadelphia merchants occasionally ignored local builders to purchase coasters from New England correspondents. Such purchases must have become common: during the last decade before the Revolution almost 20 percent of Philadelphia's merchant fleet was New England–built.[2]

The New England coasting fleet made the major contribution to North Carolina's maritime activity during the eighteenth century. Approximately 70 percent of all colonial tonnage trading to North Carolina and more than 30 percent of the colony's own merchant fleet came from New England shipyards. New England tonnage registered in North Carolina was concentrated in coasting sloops. South Carolina also favored New England coasters, and roughly 25 percent of all colonial tonnage owned in South Carolina between 1745 and 1775 was New England–built. Philadelphia merchants conducting coastal trade with South Carolina at the same time sold few Pennsylvania-built vessels to the southern colony. Despite Maryland's large coastal trade with New England, however, an average of only 6 percent of the tonnage registered in Annapolis was built in New England. Annapolis, as one of the colony's two major ports until the end of the colonial period, was probably representative of Maryland's disinterest in outside builders during an era of great shipbuilding expansion on the Chesapeake.[3]

Availability alone fails to explain the general popularity of New England–built tonnage in other colonies. Cost may have been the decisive factor. After all, among the American colonies, New England shipyards produced the most tonnage and often had the lowest building rates.[4] Convenience must have been an important attraction also. Surplus goods and ships could be exchanged for mutual benefit.

Merchants seem to have been more interested in the method of payment for the vessels, in fact, than in the price per ton. The intercolonial shipbuilding market gave New England merchants an opportunity to secure both colonial produce and European imports. Philadelphia merchants offered flour and iron for New England shipping. When Jonathan Scott, Jr., a Charleston merchant, wanted a New England schooner, he asked his Rhode Island correspondent what South Carolina produce would be most acceptable, "as it will be better than sending cash." While having a vessel constructed for a New York merchant, Thomas Richardson of Newport requested that the correspondent send some goods to help pay the builders. Unable to maintain a direct trade with England until the late colonial period, Newport merchants had to import British goods through Boston and New York. Aaron Lopez opened a small direct trade with Bristol in the late 1760s, but he also secured some European goods from New York in payment for building a vessel. One-half of the construction price, Lopez specified, was to be paid for in English dry goods, one-quarter in tea and Russian duck, and the remainder in credit on his accounts with Bristol merchants.[5]

In several instances new vessels were supplied when merchants established business relations; for example, when two Baltimore merchants opened a correspondence with one from Boston, the latter sold the former two a coastal schooner so that they could send him flour on a regular basis. Similarly, two other Baltimore merchants began a flour trade with Aaron Lopez in 1773, arguing that they could supply it at less cost than Philadelphia shippers. Christopher Starbuck of Nantucket asked Thomas Wharton to purchase a new sloop that would specialize in a Nantucket and Philadelphia trade. But sensing that greater profits were to be made in whaling, Wharton accepted Starbuck's proposal with the provision that the sloop make one whaling voyage each summer. One Connecticut merchant, Seth Osborn, tried to pay his debts to Thomas Hancock of Boston with a new vessel. "When you Rite a gain," Hancock replied, "let it be on half a sheet of paper which will cost less. . . . I Expect my money when it's Due according to agreement, and as to being Concerned in Vessels of any Sort I do not Incline."[6] While Osborn's request was denied, some shipwrights did build to pay debts, and there are even instances of colonial merchants using ships to repay their English correspondents.

New England merchants owned the bulk of colonial shipping engaged in the West Indian trade and provided much of the tonnage sold to West Indian merchants. In fact, one finds only an occasional reference to the sale of vessels in the West Indies by anyone except New England merchants. Whereas the sale of tonnage between the continental colonies was conducted by special order, the West Indian shipbuilding market included vessels constructed as speculative ventures as well as those built to order. New England merchants made speculative ship sales to supplement their normal West Indian commerce. They would load provisions and lumber in their West Indian–bound shipping and give masters the power to sell the vessels if stated minimum prices were met.[7]

In return for tonnage sold, New England merchants received West Indian goods, cash, and credit. While building a vessel for a Jamaica merchant, for example, Peter Faneuil of Boston requested payment in rum, sugar, and molasses. Similarly, Thomas Richardson of Newport secured West Indian goods as payment for vessels sold to Barbados and Jamaica merchants. When Samuel and William Vernon of Newport built a sloop for a Barbados merchant, they received partial payment in sugar and molasses and the remainder in credit upon a Charlestown, Massachusetts, merchant who could offer them valuable European goods. Payment varied with individual tastes. Daniel Rindge of Portsmouth instructed a master to accept only cash in payment for a vessel. Two other Portsmouth merchants wanted the proceeds of any ship sale to be forwarded to their London correspondents as credit for future purchases.[8] But whether paid in goods, cash, or credit, energetic merchants successfully turned New England into an important economic center by increasing their shipping sales as they gained control of most intercolonial commerce.

## British Markets

The sale of colonial ships on the British market enabled English merchants to secure cheap tonnage and gave American merchants an important source of income to pay for their imports (see Fig. 10). All the colonies exported shipping, but, once again, New England was the chief contributor. Specifically, New England shipyards supplied about half of the American-built tonnage in Great Britain at the end of the colonial period. Within New England, Massachusetts and New Hampshire were the leading producers; Pennsylvania, followed by Virginia and Maryland, launched most of the remaining tonnage.[9]

Colonial merchants built vessels for the British market on speculation and order. When speculating in the British market, a merchant either gave his captain the authority to sell the vessel or, more commonly, consigned it to an English merchant. Unless particularly desperate for funds, the merchant set a minimum price upon his ship. If unable to fetch the desired price, the vessel was returned to the colonial merchant with some freight aboard to help cover the expenses of the return voyage. Speculation in ships was very chancy and required a good rapport between the colonial merchant and his British agent. George Boyd, one of the few merchant-builders, enjoyed fruitful relations with his agents, Messrs. Lane, Son, and Fraser of London and Henry Cruger, Jr., of Bristol.[10] But Aaron Lopez had difficulty with the same Henry Cruger, Jr.

In 1765 Aaron Lopez began a regular trade between Newport and Bristol. In order to overcome the problem of direct remittances to England, he purchased new Rhode Island vessels, loaded them with lumber, and consigned the ships and cargoes to Cruger. Agreeing that a steady Newport to Bristol commerce could support only one partnership, both men were determined to discourage any competition from other merchants in their respective ports. "I need not observe to you," Lopez emphasized, "how Essential it will be in our Correspondence your furnishing me regularly with the Variations of your Market." Having just ended a similar arrangement with a London merchant, Lopez was most anxious for the new partnership to prosper. Although there was little demand for colonial tonnage at that time, Lopez and other American merchants continuously speculated in ships, thereby flooding the British market. Tension increased between the two men as Lopez overestimated the market value of his ships and his credit. By the beginning of 1769, the Newport merchant owed Cruger more than £8,000. Relations improved slightly in 1769 as Lopez managed to pay most of his debt. When the demand for shipping increased in 1772, Cruger saw an opportunity for Lopez to pay the balance of the debt and urged him to send over some ships. With the slow communication of the eighteenth century and the necessary delays to secure suitable tonnage, the shipping arrived too late for Lopez to benefit from the high market. While Lopez and Cruger maintained their partnership despite such frequent strains, John Hancock broke a twenty-year association with John Barnard and Jonathan Harrison of London when the excitable Hancock disagreed with his London partners over credit, oil shipments, and ships.[11]

A few colonial merchants avoided the hazards of speculation by securing orders for new American-built vessels while visiting England. John Barrell, a Boston merchant, spent the year 1738 in

London establishing trade connections and getting shipping orders. We are to build, he wrote his partner, four ships and three brigs. A unique combination of merchant, master, and naval architect, Joseph Harrison went to England in 1743. He sold one ship owned with his partner, John Banister of Newport, and got orders for several more vessels. In turn, when in England during 1745, John Banister secured orders for three ships and forwarded them to Harrison in Newport.[12]

After building twelve ships and two brigs in 1773 on speculation for the British market, George Boyd embarked for England in the spring of 1774. Boyd wanted to visit his agents in Bristol and London and personally handle the sale of several ships left over from the previous year's speculation. He also hoped to get some orders for new vessels and to establish social connections. If all went well, he could clear £5,000 from his voyage to England. Soon after his arrival at Plymouth in June 1774, he received orders to build two ships. Boyd dined with the master of the King's Dock (navy yard) at Plymouth, who placed a ship order with the colonial merchant on behalf of his son. A brief side trip to Dartmouth earned Boyd an additional contract for a small ship. At Bristol he sold one of his vessels built on speculation and sent some shipbuilding stores to New Hampshire. A Scottish nobleman, James Boyd, the Lord Erroll, recognized the New Hampshire Boyd as a kinsman and took him about London introducing him to "Lord North, Lord Dartmouth, and several other great people." Boyd's friendly reception by London society bore fruit. As the finishing touch to his successful trip, he was appointed to the Royal Council of New Hampshire.[13] Unfortunately for Boyd's contracts and new political position, the Revolution began shortly before his return to New Hampshire.

Considering the hazards of speculation and the expense of visits abroad, most colonial merchants found it safer to refrain from building vessels for the British market until they received an order for a ship from an English correspondent. When ordering, the British merchant might simply list the general dimensions of the desired vessel or else send specific instructions covering the sizes of the various timbers and other construction details. John Radburne of London sent a brief note to John Banister of Newport for a ship of a certain keel length, beam, and hull depth to be built as soon as possible. Radburne promised to forward canvas and cordage to complete the ship, to send other goods to help cover expenses while building, and to pay the remainder in credit upon delivery. In contrast, a Liverpool merchant, Joseph Manesty, included extremely detailed directions about hull form, construction, and finishing work in an order to John Banister for two slave ships. Although he specified a launching date for his ships and promised to send the necessary cordage, canvas, and other fittings for them, Manesty failed to mention anything about payments. He placed an order for two ships the following year, this time listing only the main dimensions of the vessels and requesting that they be finished like the two previous ones. To avoid errors arising from any misinterpretation of written instructions, a few British merchants sent their colonial correspondents building plans for the new vessels.[14]

In a few cases, British merchants canceled their orders. After contracting with a local builder for a ship ordered by a London correspondent, John Erving of Boston received a note canceling the order. Erving forfeited a small down payment he had given the builder and charged it to the London merchant's account. Although Peter Faneuil received a cancellation note, he decided to continue with the contract in hope that the London merchants would change their minds and accept the vessel. His faith was rewarded, and the London correspondents finally accepted the ship. Thomas Hancock was less fortunate. His British correspondents canceled a ship contract when they learned he was unwilling to purchase a share in the vessel. As a matter of fact, several letters suggest that British merchants occasionally wanted a new ship only if the colonial correspondent held a share, since the presence of a colonist among the owners would assure better attention to the ship and its freight when in a colonial port.[15] Yet with few exceptions, colonial merchants did not hold shares in vessels they built on order for British correspondents.

An examination of one ship built on order for the British market illustrates the role of the colonial merchant. John Reynell, a leading Philadelphia Quaker merchant, received an order from Elias Bland of London. He sent detailed building instructions for a large ship destined for the West Indian and London trade. Bland gave Reynell £500 immediate credit to cover initial expenses and asked him to collect a lumber cargo for the ship's first voyage to Jamaica. There the vessel would exchange the wood for sugar from the merchant house of one of Bland's two London partners and then would continue to England. Before receiving the ship order, Reynell doubted Bland's business ability. Nine years earlier, Reynell had accepted Bland, son of a Quaker goldsmith in London, for a five-year apprenticeship and had thoroughly trained him. Bland did not fulfill his master's hopes of becoming an efficient agent for Philadelphia Quaker merchants, but Reynell was still happy to undertake the ship order from his former apprentice. On the whole. the ship order encountered surprisingly little difficulty, although the vessel was completed several months behind schedule. A Jamaica agent for one of Bland's partners contacted Reynell to advise him about a cargo for the new ship.[16]

The late arrival of cordage, canvas, and other fittings was a frequent cause of delay in the delivery of colonial ships to the British buyer. The difficulty of assembling a cargo for the new ship could also delay her departure. Because their own areas lacked valuable produce, New England and Pennsylvania merchants often sent new ships to the southern and West Indian colonies in order to secure freight for the British market. George Boyd delayed the sailing of three or four new ships because he could not assemble cargoes owing to a scarcity of lumber during a drought. Similarly, a drought in the Philadelphia area delayed many ships because mills could not produce flour for export. When John Radburne of London ordered a colonial ship, he instructed John Banister of Newport to load the vessel with masts and other products suitable for the West Indies. The idea was not a new one. More than thirty years before, one of Newport's leading merchants, Thomas Richardson, had written a London correspondent that because of the difficulty in getting any freight in Rhode Island for vessels bound for England, it was better to send new ones via the West Indies, where they could load cargoes. Robert Ellis of Philadelphia sent his new ships to Charleston for cargoes of rice and tar before crossing to England. To avoid delays in Charleston, Ellis notified his South

Carolina correspondent several months in advance. John Reynell, another Philadelphia merchant, sent a newly completed ship to Maryland to take on tobacco for the British Market.[17]

Although the colonial merchant visited the building yard, ordered cordage, canvas, and other fittings, and made arrangements for a freight for the new ship, he could not devote his full time to a ship order. He had, after all, other business ventures that demanded his attention. As a result, British merchants frequently sent over representatives, the masters of the proposed vessels, to supervise construction and attend to the merchants' interests. In a unique instance, a British captain arrived in Pennsylvania with "pieces of good English oak" for a new ship's stem, sternpost, and transom because the London owners insisted upon only the finest materials for their vessel. This extravagance was of doubtful value, since the rest of the ship's frame and all her planking was, of course, from American forests. Colonial merchants had only occasional praise for British masters. "Captain Stephens will have a very good Ship," Thomas Moffat wrote a Bristol merchant, "& he's very carefull in seeing her built that no bad Timber or Planks is put into her." A Newport merchant bragged to a London correspondent that "your Ship is Actually the finest built vessel ever fitted out in this Part of the World and in a great Measure owing to the Superior knowledge of your Captn. Mudie has in the finishing of a Vessel." Yet the same Newport merchant advised against sending masters from England to supervise colonial shipbuilding because they were an unnecessary expense. "I have thought thou has been at very great expence of sending [a] Master . . . from England for thy Vessels formerly," a Philadelphia merchant wrote, "which may be as well supplied here at most times, without any expence of passage over or wages going on till the vessel is launched." John Reynell had particular difficulty with one English master whose arrival in Philadelphia was so late that Reynell had already hired a local captain for the ship. After replacing the temporary master appointed by Reynell, the English captain quit just before the vessel's departure. Once again Reynell had to find a local master to take the ship to England.[18] Disagreements between colonial and British merchants over the usefulness of the English master was natural, given their respective standpoints. Americans tended to consider the English captain only as a master for a vessel, while British merchants treated him as both a master and a representative of their interests.

The colonial merchant charged a 5-percent commission on the total cost, including fittings sent from England, of a vessel built on order for a British correspondent. Richard Deeble, a Portsmouth merchant, protested the commission that John Reynell charged for completing a ship order. The 5-percent commission, Reynell replied, is customary in Philadelphia, "as thou will find if thou will give thy Self the trouble to Inquire of Other Merchants who have had Vessels Built here." The English merchant threatened to remove all his goods from Reynell and "to end all accounts with thee until thee hast made me satisfaction for that unjust Commission." The dispute was settled, but Deeble continued to be so troublesome that Reynell avoided doing business with him again.[19]

British merchants sometimes used exports to pay for colonial ship orders, and occasionally English cargoes failed to bring as much as expected in the colonial markets. Under these circumstances, the colonial merchant had to use credit drawn upon the British correspondent to help cover the expenses of his ship order. In one instance the trouble was not a low colonial market. After ordering a Philadelphia vessel, Robert Wheatle of London sent some cordage to Samuel Powell, Jr., part of the cordage for rigging the new ship and the remainder to be sold to help pay building costs. However, West Indian goods shipped by Wheatle's Jamaica agent to Philadelphia were also to help finance the vessel. Despite frequent requests from both Wheatle and Powell, the Jamaica merchant failed to send any molasses or rum to Philadelphia, and Powell had to draw upon Wheatle's credit to pay the builders.[20]

New England merchants sent shipping to England on both contract and speculation, while those of Philadelphia restricted themselves to orders only. Two Maryland merchants favored speculation. Whatever the preferences of buyers or sellers, the proportion of American- to British-built vessels owned by English merchants rose from one in six around 1730 to one in four by 1760. Colonial shipbuilding offered more to British merchants than simply a means of payment for their exports to America. Along with England's northeast coast, America became an important source of cheap shipping and a reliable alternative to the expensive vessels of London and the Thames. Less expensive tonnage, by reducing shipping costs, enabled British merchants to compete more successfully with other European carriers.[21]

## Foreign Markets

Foreign purchasers provided colonial merchants with a fourth ship-building market. Writing to the Council of Trade and Plantations, Col. David Dunbar, surveyor general of His Majesty's Woods in America, reported that "there are very large ships built and frequently building in this country [New England], many of them from 20 to 40 guns, . . . and built more for sailing than burthen, they are all for French and Spaniards, and purchased with French rum and molasses." Most of these vessels, Dunbar continued, are loaded with lumber and fish, and delivered to the French and Spanish West Indies. From his description, the ships were probably built for privateering. As an agent for Massachusetts, Jeremiah Dunbar appeared before the House of Commons in 1730 to answer questions concerning his colony. When asked about shipbuilding, Dunbar replied that the year before in Massachusetts he had seen two new 300-ton ships filled with lumber and ready to sail for the French West Indies, where both ships and cargoes were to be sold. He further explained that colonial merchants often acted as agents for French buyers. A merchant would contract for a ship, register it under his own name, and later hand the vessel over to a master sent by the French to give payment. For example, writing to two Boston agents, a French merchant in Haiti ordered a large ship to be built and armed with ten cannon. Although there is no mention of payment, the letter indicates that the Boston correspondents had built other ships for the French merchant.[22]

Most of the colonial vessels sold in the foreign West Indies were small traders, identical to those going to the British islands, rather than the large ships discussed by the Dunbars. These small vessels carried provisions and lumber to foreign colonies and were often sold along with their cargoes. The merchants usually received cash for their sales and then remitted the money to Great Britain to help pay for imports.[23]

The West Indies was not the only foreign market, as colonial shipping was also sold in Europe, especially in Spain and Portugal. New England captains sent their fish- and lumber-laden vessels to Cádiz and Lisbon, where they tried to sell both ship and cargo. As with all speculation, the vessels often failed to find a market. William Pepperrell sent several vessels to Cádiz to be sold with their cargoes of staves and fish. The cargoes sold; but when no purchasers appeared for the vessels, the captains loaded them with salt and returned to New England. Pennsylvania merchants exported wheat to Spain and Portugal, where both vessels and cargoes were sold and the profits forwarded to England to purchase British goods. Robert Ellis, a Philadelphia merchant, sent vessels to his agents in Cádiz and Lisbon, asking them to sell both ships and cargoes. None of the vessels had been ordered. Ellis simply gave agents and masters authority to sell if minimum prices were met. If sold, the proceeds were to be deposited with an agent in London. Similarly, another Philadelphia merchant sent a captain to Lisbon to sell his ship if offered a minimum price and to forward the money to a London correspondent. Only one other letter has been located in merchants' correspondence about the foreign shipbuilding market. Two Boston merchants sent a brig to England with staves. After selling the staves through a London agent, the captain was to find freight and sail to Amsterdam. There, with the aid of a local merchant, the captain was to sell the vessel and remit the proceeds to the London correspondent.[24]

Foreign ship sales, it seems, tended to follow the pattern of other established trade. On ordinary trading voyages, captains often sold their vessels if they found a favorable market. Such speculative sales were most common in the Spanish and Portuguese trade, while New England merchants supplied foreign correspondents in the West Indies with ships built to order. Colonial merchants forwarded their proceeds from foreign ship sales to British correspondents.

CHAPTER VII

# Colonial Warships

TWO administrative boards conducted the affairs of the British navy. Composed of the Lords of the Admiralty, the Admiralty Board primarily concerned itself with the formation and execution of naval policy. The Navy Board regulated the supply and maintenance of the fleet. Leading naval officers with powerful political connections formed the Admiralty Board, while the Navy Board, whose members were called Commissioners of the Navy, united civilian dockyard officials with a few inactive captains. Technically responsible for all naval matters, the prestigious members of the Admiralty Board could assert their higher authority by overruling the Navy Board. Only an occasional dispute arose between the two groups, however, as the Commissioners of the Navy usually operated without interference.[1]

The Navy Board's chief responsibility was management of the royal dockyards. Requirements of armament, speed, strength, and seaworthiness made warships more difficult to design and construct than merchant vessels. Naval dockyards offered the facilities and experienced labor necessary for building British warships, and, as a rule, the navy accepted warships built in private yards only in wartime when demand for ships surpassed the production capacity of the royal dockyards. With no threat of competition, the Commissioners of the Navy remained conservative about dockyard matters. They gained a wide reputation for corruption and inefficiency during the eighteenth century.[2]

Attracted by low construction rates and the chance to preserve England's diminishing timber reserve, the Admiralty Board considered suggestions from colonial officials that warships be built in America. The Commissioners of the Navy consistently opposed the idea. Warships should never be constructed outside Great Britain, the Navy Board argued, lest the nation become dependent upon a source that could be cut off in wartime. Furthermore, the commissioners considered American oak greatly inferior to British oak.[3] Despite opposition, on several occasions the Lords of the Admiralty did order construction of warships in the colonies.

During the War of the League of Augsburg, for example, the need for warships at least equaled the need for merchant vessels. Sir William Phips, governor of Massachusetts, advocated construction of warships in New England for the mutual benefit of the colonists and the navy. Willing to make a trial, the Admiralty Board ordered one warship. The *Falkland*, a forty-gun ship, was launched near Portsmouth, New Hampshire, about 1694. As her successful rebuilding in 1720 indicates, the *Falkland* was originally a well-constructed vessel able to survive well beyond the ten years average life for a warship of the time.[4]

Shortly after the completion of the *Falkland*, an English merchant named John Taylor proposed to build a second warship at the same site. In 1695 the Lords of the Admiralty had agreed to accept the ship if it passed a rigorous examination by the Navy Board. Taylor had to finance the construction with his own resources. Following the Admiralty's orders, the Commissioners of the Navy gave Taylor a set of plans for a thirty-four-gun ship. When Taylor presented the *Bedford Galley* for inspection two years later, the Navy Board found "her fitly qualified for a man of war . . . and to be well wrought and . . . she sails very well." The Navy Board's approval of the *Bedford Galley* may be puzzling until one considers John Taylor's position in the 1690s as the major mast contractor for the government with a near monopoly on all Baltic and New England masts sold to the navy. Taylor doubtless used his influence to encourage the Commissioners of the Navy to accept his ship. Whatever the reasons for the Navy Board's approval, the subsequent career of the *Bedford Galley* justified her purchase. She remained in active service for nearly twenty years, and in 1716, when no longer suitable as a regular warship, she was converted to a fireship. The vessel was deliberately sunk in 1725 to help form a breakwater.[5]

Despite the success of the *Falkland* and the *Bedford Galley*, the Admiralty Board waited fifty years before ordering construction of more warships in the colonies. The Treaty of Ryswick, signed less than six months after the purchase of the *Bedford Galley*, eliminated immediate pressure for more naval vessels. When war resumed in 1702, there was no discussion about building warships in America. This time the Lords of the Admiralty yielded to the adamant opposition of the Navy Board to colonial-built vessels and did not press the issue.

A Virginia-built sloop was the next colonial vessel to enter the Royal Navy. Unlike the *Falkland* and the *Bedford Galley*, the sloop was not designed as a warship; she was built in 1741 as a West Indian trader. A naval officer on the West Indian station purchased the sloop in 1745 and sent her to England. After a survey, the Admiralty Board approved the purchase and registered the vessel, named the *Mediator*, in May 1745. A large and well-armed craft, the *Mediator* was probably intended to serve as a dispatch boat, but she sank soon afterward. Although there may have been others before, the *Mediator* is the earliest known colonial merchant vessel purchased for naval service. In the 1760s and 1770s the conversion of colonial trading vessels into dispatch boats, small cruisers, or supply ships became more common.[6]

In 1746, during the War of the Austrian Succession, the Admiralty Board decided to have four frigates built in New England to help relieve the shortage of warships on American stations and to reward the colonists for their capture of Louisbourg in the preceding year. Admiral Peter Warren, who had commanded the naval forces at Louisbourg, recommended construction of two forty-four-gun frigates in Massachusetts and New Hampshire because those colonies "had the greatest share of any in the reduction of Louisbourg." New York and Connecticut would receive contracts for two twenty-four-gun ships. Warren also suggested that the Admiralty Board send experienced men to the colonies to supervise the building. The Lords of the Admiralty accepted Warren's proposals and then ordered the Navy Board to recommend four qualified persons to inspect construction of the ships. The Commissioners of the Navy protested the decision. "We are of Opinion that it cannot be of any Advantage to his Majesties Service to build Ships or Vessels of War of any Class in any part of America." American timber, they argued, was poor, and colonial builders inexperienced with naval construction. But the commissioners had to obey. They sent plans for the warships to the colonies, but, claiming that building inspectors were reluctant to go to America, they took nearly a year to recruit the four supervisors.[7]

Admiral Warren met with difficulties in the colonies too. New York and Connecticut builders declined the contracts. When Warren awarded a contract to Benjamin Hallowell, one of Boston's leading shipwrights, the Massachusetts builder chose one of the small twenty-four-gun frigates instead of a larger warship. With other markets available, colonial builders apparently did not wish to commit themselves to the long, demanding effort of constructing naval vessels. They may also have been discouraged by the prospect of trying to collect payment from the distant, rather antagonistic, Navy Board. Warren found some success in New Hampshire, however. There he awarded a contract to Sir William Pepperrell, who had led the New England troops at the siege of Louisbourg. In turn, Pepperrell subcontracted with Nathaniel Meserve, another Louisbourg veteran, to build a forty-four-gun frigate.[8]

Hallowell's warship, built in Boston and named after that city, was launched in May 1748. Her fittings came from England, after a supply ship loaded with stores had been delayed five months by bad weather, enemy privateers, and the difficulty of assembling a convoy for America. The *Boston* had a much sharper hull than standard British twenty-four-gun frigates, as Hallowell had modified the original plans, a common practice among English builders who constructed warships in private yards. However well designed, the *Boston* may have been poorly built. Because of improperly seasoned timber, the frigate had to be broken up in 1752.[9]

Nathaniel Meserve launched the large New Hampshire frigate, the *America*, in 1749. Admiral Charles Knowles, the governor of Louisbourg, had persuaded Meserve to give the frigate a longer keel than originally specified, which meant a heavier vessel. Sir William Pepperrell tried to persuade the Navy Board to pay for the extra tonnage. When the Massachusetts frigate was broken up in 1752, the *America* was renamed the *Boston*. But her timbers were no better than her namesake's. In 1757 she was declared unfit for naval service and was sold.[10] The brief, unsuccessful careers of the *Boston* and the *America* discouraged the Admiralty Board from further construction of large warships in the colonies.

In order to enforce trade regulation in the colonies after the Seven Years War, the Admiralty Board had to increase the then limited number of naval vessels patrolling the American coast. The Lords of the Admiralty thought it practical to purchase small, swift colonial vessels to capture American smugglers. Because of the excellent reputation of Marblehead schooners for speed, the Admiralty Board ordered Adm. Alexander Calville, the commander of all naval forces in North America, to purchase six of them. Acquired in 1764, the schooners were soon on patrol. Irate Rhode Islanders burned the *Gaspee* in 1772 as a result of her effective work in Narragansett Bay. The schooners' success encouraged the Admiralty Board to purchase more colonial craft. When the Jamaica station needed several schooners, the Admiralty Board sent a captain to New York to supervise the construction of two Marblehead-type schooners. Built in the same shipyard and according to the same plan, and launched on the same day in 1767, both schooners pleased the officers who inspected them.[11]

The Navy Board did not object to the use of small colonial-built vessels, and during the 1760s and 1770s they even gave favorable inspection reports on some American work. When the Admiralty needed a survey vessel for the western coast of Ireland, the Navy Board recommended a sloop, then in the river Thames, from the yard of Benjamin Hallowell, who had built the ill-fated *Boston*. The Lords of the Admiralty bought the sloop and were probably satisfied, because they purchased another of Hallowell's schooners four years later.[12]

The Admiralty Board bought several large colonial merchant ships as well. In answer to a request by the Admiralty for a survey ship in 1774, the Navy Board examined three New England–built vessels and found two to be "good sound ships." Following the advice of the Navy Board, the Lords of the Admiralty bought the *Codrington*, considered the better ship. Also acting on recommendation of the Navy Board, the Admiralty purchased South Carolina's *Rose Island* as a supply ship in 1769. The vessel had been built three years earlier on Rose Island, near Beaufort, South Carolina, for a London merchant. At the outbreak of the Revolution, the Admiralty secured a number of colonial vessels to meet the severe shortage of supply ships. The Navy Board carefully examined and selected all the ships.[13]

The Navy Board's willingness to accept small craft and merchant ships from the colonies may be explained by the fact that such vessels were auxiliaries rather than regular warships. Supply ships and patrol schooners were simply colonial vessels adapted to naval service; they offered no competition to the royal dockyards. In this context the Navy Board never complained about the quality of American timber.

But American warships were built. When the War of Jenkins' Ear broke out, Spanish privateers threatened commerce off the American coast. Since the British navy could not station enough vessels to protect merchant ships in the English Channel, let alone those across the Atlantic, several colonies decided to build their own warships to patrol local waters. Rhode Island completed its first warship in May 1740, a twelve-gun sloop built by Newport shipwrights in thirty-six working days. While obviously not a regular warship, the sloop resembled small naval vessels of sufficient size to handle most privateers. Benjamin Hallowell built a 180-ton snow in thirty-two days for the defense of the Bay Colony. The snow carried sixteen guns. Connecticut hired James Ward of Middletown, who completed a sloop with the same tonnage and armament as the Rhode Island vessel in less than twenty working days during the summer of 1741. The following year an armed vessel built in Charleston, South Carolina, was stationed near the entrance of that harbor to drive off enemy privateers.[14]

None of these provincial warships was particularly large. In fact, colonial shipwrights launched privateers with greater tonnage and armaments. But the warships, sailing mostly in local waters, sufficed for their limited purpose. Large work gangs must have labored long hours to build the three New England warships so quickly. To speed construction of the Massachusetts snow, Lt. Gov. William Shirley issued warrants to impress six shipwrights into Hallowell's building crew.[15] Rapid building probably forced shipwrights to use some unseasoned timber, but it would have made little difference, since provincial warships were expected to serve for brief periods only.

During the Seven Years War, Massachusetts built a large, twenty-six-gun ship. Otherwise, colonial energy was devoted to privateers. By the time shipwrights had to supervise construction of warships and privateers during the Revolution, Americans had had long experience constructing large privateers. New England shipwrights had supplied several large privateers to the Spanish and French West Indies, and in 1724 Massachusetts builders launched a huge ship, 130 feet long and 1,000 tons displacement, armed with twenty guns, for sale abroad. During the Spanish and French wars of the 1740s, colonial shipwrights built 300- and 400-ton privateers (see Fig. 11). Such craft would be equal in size to sloops of war and small frigates in the Royal Navy. Colonial builders launched similar privateers during the Seven Years War. Benjamin Hallowell constructed the largest known privateer of the war in 1758. Carrying thirty-six guns, the 680-ton ship was comparable to the average Royal Navy frigate.[16]

Privateers were relatively small vessels, simple to design and build, for strength and armament were not needed to attack merchant vessels. Yet some merchants were willing to finance construction of a class of large privateers that were more expensive and difficult to build, equip, and maintain. Perhaps they had caught the privateering fever that had swept every colonial port.[17]

Like all speculative booms, privateering began to wane. A few privateers made fabulous captures, but most gave shareholders little profit on their investments. Thomas Hancock gained some profit from his shares in three privateers operating during the War of the Austrian Succession. However, he lost several of his own vessels to enemy privateers. During the Seven Years War, Hancock did not invest in privateers. In December 1744, Philadelphia was busy building new privateers and supplying old ones returned from cruises. Then, one year later a Philadelphia merchant wrote that "our Privateers are mostly returned home without any prize which discourages that business so much that no new ones are building."[18]

During 1758 more than 150 shipwrights from New Hampshire, Massachusetts, and New York built hundreds of whaleboats for the

1. Map by H. Moll, ca. 1730. (Colonial Williamsburg)

2. Portrait of Thomas Coram, colonial shipwright. Oil painting by William Hogarth, 1740. (Courtesy of the Trustees of the Thomas Coram Foundation for Children, London)

3. A ship and, to the right, a brig, the main carriers of trans-Atlantic cargo in the eighteenth century. Detail of *The Shipyard at Spencer Hall, Kent Island, Maryland.* Unsigned oil painting, ca. 1770. (Maryland Historical Society)

4. Sloops and, in the right background, two schooners. These vessels competed with each other for the coastal and West Indian trade in the eighteenth century. The schooner finally won. Detail of *The Shipyard at Spencer Hall, Kent Island, Maryland.* Unsigned oil painting, ca. 1770. (Maryland Historical Society)

5. Schooners on the stocks. Detail of *A Colonial Shipyard.* Diorama constructed by Harold Hahn, 1969–73. (The Mariners Museum)

6. New York City shipyards, ca. 1717. These two yards were situated at the present intersection of Fulton and Water streets. The workmen have yet to plank the lower part of
the hull of the larger vessel. The smaller vessel to the left, between the two slaughterhouses
on piles, is probably a sloop. Detail of *A South Prospect of Ye Flourishing City of New
York in America.* Engraving by William Burgis. London: Thomas Blakewell, 1746. (New-
York Historical Society)

7. New York City shipyards, ca. 1717. This yard stood at the present intersection of Roosevelt and Water streets, just north of the yards in Fig. 6. To the right is the newly laid keel of a large merchant ship. Workmen have erected her stem and sternpost and are now attaching the floors to the keel—indicating the frames of this vessel will be raised timber by timber and not joined into one unit beforehand. The stern of a large vessel can be seen to the left. The staging has been removed, and the vessel will be ready to launch in a short time. Between these two works is a pair of launching ways. The large vessel in the foreground was probably just launched from that shipyard, and now tradesmen are at work to complete her outfitting. Detail of *A South Prospect of Ye Flourishing City of New York in America*. Engraving by William Burgis. London: Thomas Blakewell, 1746. (New-York Historical Society)

8. Porcelain punch bowl sent by an Edinburgh merchant to Jonathan Greenleaf, a Newbury shipwright, in 1752. (Peabody Museum)

9. Newspaper advertisements from the *Virginia Gazette*, 1766. (Virginia Historical Society)

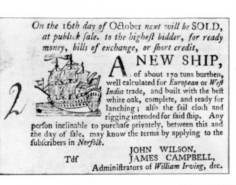

On the 16th day of *October* next will be SOLD, at publick sale. to the highest bidder, for ready money, bills of exchange, or short credit,

A NEW SHIP, of about 170 tuns burthen, well calculated for *European* or *West India* trade, and built with the best white oak, complete, and ready for lanching; also the sail cloth and rigging intended for said ship. Any person inclinable to purchase privately, between this and the day of sale. may know the terms by applying to the subscribers in *Norfolk*.

JOHN WILSON,
Tdf     JAMES CAMPBELL,
Administrators of *William Irving*, dec.

For SALE, A NEW SCHOONER, that will be lanched in *August* next, or sooner if required, burthen 71 tuns, and will carry near 3000 bushels of grain; she is built with the best white oak plank and timber, and will be a very complete vessel when finished. He has also for sale a sloop, burthen 25 tuns, 3 years old, together with her sails, anchors, &c. Any person inclinable to purchase either, or both, may know the terms by applying to the subscriber living on the head of *East* river, in *Gloucester* county.

2     EDWARD HUGHES.

To be SOLD, at NORFOLK, A SHIP on the STOCKS, of the following dimensions, viz. Sixty three feet keel, twenty three feet beam, nine feet eight inches hold, and four feet four inches between decks; together with the rigging, sails, cables, anchors, &c. provided for her. She will be completely finished, and ready to launch by the 20th of next month. For terms apply to the subscriber, who will show the ship and materials.

THOMAS M'CULLOCH.
JUNE 25, 1766.

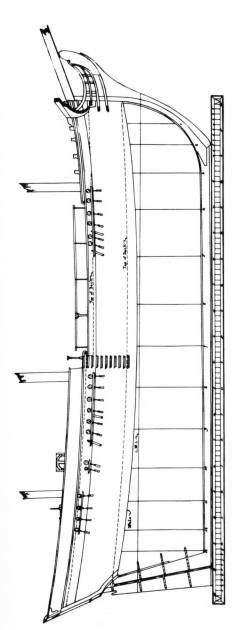

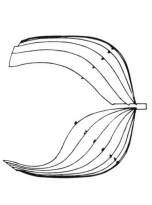

*LORD CAMDEN*

Built at Philadelphia in 1775. Purchased by the Royal Navy in 1778 and fitted out as the fireship *Vulcan*. Sunk at Yorktown 1781.

| | |
|---|---|
| Length on the lower deck | 91'·6" |
| Length of keel for tonnage | 72'·4" |
| Breadth, extreme | 27'·9" |
| Depth in hold | 12'·3½" |
| Burthen in tons | 296 19/94 |

Redrawn from Admiralty Draught Reg. No. 4360, Box 61, by Walter Caswell Cheatham.

10. The ship *Lord Camden*, 1775. This vessel well illustrates the type of full-built cargo carrier produced by Philadelphia shipyards for the British market. (Courtesy of the Trustees of the National Maritime Museum, Greenwich)

11. The ship *Bethel* of Boston. Unsigned oil painting, 1748. The *Bethel's* capture of a Spanish treasure ship was no doubt what caused her owners to commission her portrait. This vessel represents the class of large privateers produced by colonial shipyards in the 1740s. (Peabody Museum)

unsuccessful expedition against Ticonderoga. The carpenters also launched a sloop and a row galley.[19]

Other colonial shipwrights labored at military outposts during the Seven Years War to help the British win control of the Great Lakes. Instead of large privateers and frigates, however, the builders launched whaleboats, sloops, schooners, and brigs. The shipwrights worked under the most trying circumstances to produce even these small vessels.[20] All fittings and supplies had to be transported from Albany to building sites on the lakes, and, since there were no nearby sawmills, the carpenters lost much precious time cutting planks. Furthermore, the men were always subject to enemy attacks.

Shipbuilders worked at Lake George and Lake Champlain, but the best-known building program took place at Oswego, on Lake Ontario. In 1755 the Admiralty Board sent officers and stores to New York for two vessels to be built at Oswego. Gov. William Shirley of Massachusetts, who became commander of all British forces in North America after the death of Gen. Edward Braddock, appreciated the importance of controlling Lake Ontario and ordered the construction of more vessels at Oswego. The governor recruited Massachusetts shipwrights and sent them to the building site. Late in 1755 the frames of two small brigs, prepared in England, disassembled, and shipped to the colonies, arrived at Oswego. More shipbuilders arrived the following spring.[21]

By the summer of 1756, the British had more vessels on Lake Ontario than the French. But while the British continued to build, the French approached Oswego unnoticed and captured it after a brief siege in August. All the work of the shipwrights—two brigs, two sloops, one schooner, one row galley, and a large number of whaleboats—fell into French hands. The number of shipbuilders captured at Oswego is unknown, but there may have been as many as 100, mostly from New England and New Jersey. Newbury, Massachusetts, alone contributed eighteen carpenters. After their capture, the shipwrights were taken to Quebec and then put aboard transports bound for France. According to a petition by Rhode Island shipwrights, the Admiralty Board paid the carpenters full wages from the time of their capture until their eventual return home. Two years after the fall of Oswego, the British captured Fort

Frontenac, the major French base on Lake Ontario. Nine armed vessels, representing the entire French naval force on the lake, surrendered with the fort, and the English regained control of Lake Ontario.[22]

# CHAPTER VIII

# The Development of Shipbuilding in the South

DEPENDENCE on documentation is extremely difficult in a consideration of the development of shipbuilding in the South. Whereas the agricultural activity of each colony is well documented, records of maritime industries are scarce. Yet by the Revolution, southern shipbuilding was widespread and the Chesapeake had become a major construction center for American shipping. To trace the gradual rise of this industry in a step-by-step fashion will require the discovery of more local sources.

It appears that shipbuilding in the South was stagnant through 1730. With the southern preference for agriculture and the annual arrival of English ships to carry tobacco, rice, and naval stores to British markets, there was neither desire nor need to develop an active shipbuilding industry. The demand for small vessels to carry on limited coastal and West Indian trade sufficed to support local shipwrights.

The practice of chartering British ships to transport colonial produce from southern ports to England continued, though not without challenge, up to the Revolution. Writing in 1752, a Norfolk, Virginia, merchant explained that "owners of Vessels are under a necessity of employing them often with almost a Certainty of Loss which those who are not engaged in them are not obliged to, but when there is a prospect of advantage can Charter ... on better terms than to own them." Similarly, a visitor to Charleston, South Carolina, observed that "people here don't incline to be concerned in Navigation because of the great Number of Vessels which comes here ... to take in freight at a very reasonable lay [rate] which suits the Merchants better than to be incumbered with vessels of their own."[1]

Some merchants, however, doubted the advantages of chartering. Both Stephen Bordley of Maryland and Henry Laurens of South Carolina voiced complaints about British-owned ships. English owners often failed to notify colonial correspondents about the number and expected arrival dates of ships; and when the vessels reached the colonies, changes in local market conditions could encourage either the charter party or the owner's representative to seek a different freight rate. Occasionally, disputes over rates plus normal shipping delays caused colonial cargoes to arrive late at British markets and consequently to sell at a lower price. Other merchants shared the doubts of Bordley and Laurens. In the 1740s and 1750s, a number of Maryland and Virginia merchants began to purchase their own ships.[2]

The desire of Chesapeake Bay merchants for their own trans-Atlantic vessels stimulated the local shipbuilding industry. At least four of Maryland's leading merchants opened their own shipyards. Two of the merchants, Charles Carroll and Samuel Galloway, constructed vessels for themselves in addition to ships for sale on order or speculation. Because there were too few builders to meet the new demand for shipping, Chesapeake merchants imported convicts from Great Britain who were skilled in the shipbuilding trades and put them to work in local shipyards.[3]

Of the thirty-seven pre-1748 colonial ships listed in the Annapolis port records, only two were launched by Maryland shipwrights. Three were Pennsylvania-built, and New York and Virginia contributed one each. The remaining thirty ships were built in New England. But the situation changed after 1748. First, the figure for New England–built vessels declined from 80 to 30 percent of all colonial tonnage entering Annapolis. Except for a temporary high of 39 percent in the early 1750s, the New England tonnage percent remained at about 30. Second, Maryland and not New England yards now launched the majority of colonial vessels trading to Annapolis. Third, and equally important, natives of Maryland by this time owned much of the tonnage built in their colony. In terms of Maryland-built ships used primarily for trans-Atlantic voyages, production rose from two such vessels before 1748, to thirty-three between 1748 and 1759, to forty-six from 1760 to 1771, and to twenty-three during the four years preceding the Revolution.[4]

Both pre-1748 Maryland ships listed in the Annapolis records were owned in the colony. With the dramatic rise of ship production in the late 1740s, one might expect to find a large proportion of

Maryland-built ships owned by outsiders. Yet approximately 75 percent of the ship tonnage built between 1748 and 1759 was owned within Maryland. The figure for Maryland-owned ships rose to 80 percent for the years 1760 to 1771 and finally to 95 percent between 1772 and 1775. In all classes of vessels, Maryland-built tonnage increased between 1748 and 1751, declined a bit during the next nine years, and then rose again until the Revolution.[5] Although based on vessels trading to Annapolis only, and therefore offering only an incomplete record of the colony's maritime activity, these statistics do confirm the sudden rise of ship production and ownership in Maryland beginning in the late 1740s and continuing to the Revolution.

Virginia shipbuilding likewise grew up quite suddenly. Newspaper advertisements for the sale of Virginia-built ships began to appear in the 1750s and became more common during the following decade. Much of Virginia's shipbuilding was centered in the Norfolk area. Norfolk merchants, like those of Annapolis, supported the expansion of the local shipbuilding industry as they established for themselves a thriving commerce with the British West Indian colonies to supplement the trans-Atlantic tobacco trade. After purchasing new vessels and loading them with provisions and lumber, the Norfolk merchants tried to sell both ships and cargoes in the West Indies. There is little detailed information about the Virginia shipbuilders, but they were probably as active as those of Maryland.

During the late 1760s and early 1770s, the Chesapeake colonies launched a similar volume of tonnage.[6] Chesapeake Bay builders constructed unusually large ships. Averaging between 150 and 250 tons each, the Maryland and Virginia ships equaled the size of the British-built and -owned tobacco ships that came annually to Chesapeake Bay. Chesapeake builders were also famous for their swift sloops and schooners. In fact, the speed of its sloops and schooners established Chesapeake Bay as one of the two centers for fast vessels in America, its chief rival being Essex County, Massachusetts, where fishing schooners were produced. Builders in both regions combined local variations with a basic hull form derived from English craft. A similar design characterized Jamaica and Bermuda sloops. The Chesapeake sloops of the first half of the eighteenth century were powerful vessels with good cargo capacity. When it replaced the sloop in Chesapeake Bay during the late 1750s, the schooner continued to employ some of the advantageous features of the earlier vessel. Chesapeake builders constructed schooners with as few timbers and the lightest planking possible, further reducing hull weight by lowering the height of superstructures on the deck. Similarly, shipwrights gave schooners masts with a smaller diameter than average and a minimum amount of rigging. The combination of sharp hull lines and light weight made the schooners fast sailers, and during the Revolution they earned an international reputation for speed.[7]

By the end of the colonial period, the Chesapeake area had replaced Philadelphia as the shipbuilding center second in importance after New England. But Maryland and Virginia each produced less tonnage than Pennsylvania.[8] Nevertheless, in less than thirty years, Chesapeake merchants and shipwrights had transformed a minor shipbuilding region into a major one.

North Carolina, on the other hand, launched relatively little tonnage according to the records. Besides sloops and schooners for local use, the colony's tonnage was devoted mostly to brigs to be sold to British and North Carolina merchants. The latter probably used brigs in their limited West Indian trade. North Carolina builders also launched a limited number of average-sized ships, which British merchants purchased.[9]

Until 1760 most South Carolina–built tonnage was in easily constructed schooners averaging 20 tons each. Launching 140 schooners between 1735 and 1760, South Carolina builders constructed only seven ships and twenty-five smaller oceangoing vessels. "We have few or no ships of our Own," Gov. James Glen wrote in 1749. "We depend in great measure upon those sent from Britain, or on such as are built in New England for British merchants, and which generally take in this Country in their way to England to get Freight." But while launching few large vessels, Charleston builders repaired visiting ships. As Henry Laurens wrote in 1764, a South Carolina shipwright could earn more money in repair work than in new construction. When masters were forced to have their vessels repaired for the voyage to England in order to arrive during favorable marketing periods, Charleston shipwrights often charged outrageous rates.[10]

Between 1760 and 1774, however, South Carolina builders suddenly launched seventeen ships registered in the colony. At this time, British merchants began to purchase South Carolina–built ships designed for voyages between Charleston and England. These ships boasted the largest average tonnage of any built in the colonies. Of course, launching one or two ships a year may seem insignificant, but because almost none had been built in South Carolina before 1760, the one or two ships were quite noteworthy. Concentrating on schooner and ship construction, South Carolina builders launched few other types of vessels.[11]

Apparently only a handful of South Carolina merchants promoted ship construction in the early 1760s. Most Charleston merchants avoided owning ships during those years. As late as 1771, Henry Laurens, the town's leading merchant, complained about the uncertainties of depending upon British-owned ships, but he continued to charter them. Earlier, in 1763, when making an attempt at ownership, Laurens had a ship constructed in England because he doubted the skill of local builders. In this only known instance of a colonial merchant having a ship built in England, Laurens encountered the same difficulties British merchants met when ordering American vessels. There were confusions and delays in correspondence, and the ship ended up costing much more than originally expected.[12]

As construction and local ownership of South Carolina ships increased in the early 1770s, Henry Laurens became involved in the shipbuilding program. In 1771 he had a ship built for an English correspondent. Laurens praised South Carolina shipbuilding during a visit to England, thus obtaining another order for a ship. He urged the builder to do an excellent job, "as well as to oblige me as to encourage Ship building in our Province." The increased activity of South Carolina merchants and builders is reflected in the shipping records. Between 1770 and 1774, more ships were built and registered in South Carolina than in the two preceding five-year periods. Moreover, the ships were larger than those of the pre-1770 years.[13]

Immigrant builders seem to have provided much of the skill necessary for the increased ship production, as most native South Carolina carpenters concentrated on schooner construction and

ship repairs. One South Carolina merchant asked a Boston correspondent to secure a shipwright willing to come to Charleston.
Henry Lloyd, the Boston merchant, found only one carpenter
willing to move. When the builder changed his mind at the last
moment and refused to go, Lloyd used threats and the promise of
more money to persuade him to leave for Charleston. Similarly,
when Henry Laurens built a ship for British correspondents, he
recruited a Philadelphia shipwright to come to Charleston to construct the vessel. At least four shipwrights came from Great Britain.
John Imrie, known to have launched at least one large ship, began
working in Charleston in 1761 and achieved a modest success.
Several years later, in 1763, William Begbie and Daniel Manson,
destined to become South Carolina's leading builders, arrived in
America. They moved to Charleston around 1769, opened a shipyard, and were soon launching large ships. William Tweed, another
successful British shipwright, settled in Charleston in 1769.[14]

According to the shipping records, Georgia constructed less tonnage than any other colony except New Jersey. Despite the very
restricted production, Georgia-built ships were larger than those of
any other colony but South Carolina. Of course, Georgia was still
a newly settled colony, and its inhabitants devoted their energy
to rice and indigo.[15]

In summary, shipbuilding in the South at the beginning of the
Revolution was quite different than it had been thirty years before.
Instead of concentrating on small coastal vessels, Chesapeake Bay
builders were launching a number of large ships. Maryland and
Virginia merchants financed the expansion of ship production,
making the Chesapeake Bay region the second center of colonial
shipbuilding. In South Carolina, local merchants were also responsible for the growth of shipbuilding within the colony and the
establishment of the importance of Charleston in the American
shipbuilding industry.

# CHAPTER IX

# Conclusion

THE shipbuilding industry began in America as a necessity. The earliest colonists found that Europe failed to supply a regular source of trans-Atlantic transportation, and that they had to construct their own vessels for local commerce. Later settlements without raw commodities desired by the British were obliged to establish a merchant fleet of their own if they wished to have any trade at all. Southern agricultural communities had ships arriving from England every year, but some merchants in those colonies eventually tried shipbuilding also in an effort to diversify their income. The British did not interfere with the growth of colonial shipbuilding because they feared competition from other colonial industries more and because enemy privateers during the frequent wars severely depleted their merchant fleet. By the time peace prevailed, colonial vessels were so popular with British merchants there was no thought given to suppressing their construction.

Initiating building activity involved risks at every level. Workers were injured and occasionally killed in shipyard accidents. Builders faced labor shortages, adverse weather conditions, delays in obtaining materials, and changes in the general market for their product. For financial backing, they turned to the colonial merchant, who was required to invest substantial amounts in a large commodity whose quality, serviceability and even market value could not be accurately predicted. As middlemen between British correspondents and American shipwrights, colonial merchants were subject to pressures from both sides.

In the 1640s, Massachusetts had the greatest need for shipbuilding and, coincidentally, the merchant community most able to sustain the risk. The colonial government backed the building program by encouraging skilled shipwrights to work and settle in the area. The success of Bay Colony efforts to initiate building demonstrates the close working relationship between merchants and builders, as Boston agents were able to draw capital into their building ventures in a region that otherwise might have faced economic isolation. Patterns of growth in New England show movement to rural areas with good timber and iron supplies, and the subsequent abandonment of these small towns when the natural resources were exhausted. But Boston supplied the money for much of this building activity also, and that city remained a major shipbuilding center even when other places offered lower prices. Obviously, British correspondents liked to know their colonial agents could oversee construction conveniently and frequently.

Massachusetts maintained its dominance of American shipbuilding for most of the colonial era, but by the end of the seventeenth century Philadelphia had its own active building community. From its beginnings, Philadelphia welcomed shipbuilders and suffered little competition within its region. Chesapeake building grew most rapidly in the mid-eighteenth century, and South Carolina followed with a limited program about a decade later. The spread of shipbuilding throughout the colonies can be explained by the search for new resources and opportunities. But mercantile initiative from both British and American sources must have been the prime factor, because business interests in maritime activity preceded a sudden increase of trained shipwrights in each area.

The war years, 1690 to 1713, saw the greatest spurt in ship construction. Large numbers of vessels needed to be replaced quickly for merchants to overcome losses: a greater volume of building and repair work was needed simply to maintain commerce at a consistent level. Furthermore, in the eighteenth century the British merchant community was rapidly expanding its interests to the extent that even in peacetime they required more vessels than private yards in Britain could produce. The question arises here, Did the British buy American shipping only when war losses and widening markets forced them to look beyond the production capacity in England? Or did the colonial vessels have certain desirable features unavailable elsewhere?

Maritime industries usually depend on shortages created by war or sudden increases in commercial ventures to stimulate growth. But economy of design and maintenance was a common American trademark that must have attracted British merchants. Reduced sail area, simple rigging, large cargo capacity, and few frills or decorations characterized many American merchant vessels. A smaller crew was then required to work the finished ship. These colonial simplifications, when added to the availability of natural resources in the New World, resulted in a comparatively inexpensive vessel. Like cheap goods anywhere, American vessels did not enjoy the reputation for quality of their more expensive counterparts. But their ever increasing popularity among British merchants indicates that colonial shipwrights were doing something right.

The speed that distinguished some colonial-built vessels was another advantage, but it probably was not the essential factor in their popularity. In peacetime, the swift vessel could become expensive. Larger sails, wear and tear at greater speeds, and limited cargo space all were cumbersome inconveniences. Nor could rushing guarantee that reportedly favorable markets would prove advantageous on arrival. Furthermore, slower ships could still sail in convoys when threatened with attack, and the speediest merchant vessel in this case had to sail at the same rate as the slowest member of the expedition. More than likely, colonial interest in speed reflects an American idiosyncrasy still prevalent today as much as a need by British merchants for fast ships.

During the colonial period, American builders generally stayed close to European technology. Other than speed, their main innovation was the development of the schooner, a simple flexible craft easily handled by a small crew, which became the principal coasting vessel by the Revolution. The profusion of building activity in the late eighteenth century set the stage for the subsequent rapid advancements in technology and design. But it is impossible to pinpoint leadership for the prerevolutionary era, when simplicity and gradual change were the rule rather than the exception.

Shipbuilding was a well-established industry in the years immediately prior to the Revolution. Intercolonial and local shipping was generally built and owned by colonists. Likewise many West Indian traders were American. Finally, much of the British-owned trans-Atlantic commerce was carried in colonial-built vessels. By the Revolution, at least a third of the British merchant fleet was American-built. Since some of the fleet was also foreign-built, it can easily be concluded that on the eve of war, Britain had grown to rely on the colonies as a major source of shipping.

Shipbuilding provided New Englanders with the means to escape economic depression and achieve important commercial status. It greatly enhanced Philadelphia's role in trade and supplemented the limited business ventures of the Chesapeake. One would expect, therefore, that the colonists held shipwrights in the highest esteem and considered their craft an essential, praiseworthy addition to their society. But what appears obvious in retrospect is not always apparent at the time. Colonists paid ship construcion no more attention than Americans today give to truck manufacture, with the occasional exception of towns building warships for self-defense. Why did the colonists so casually ignore what today may be considered an important part of their economy? First of all, shipwrights were tradesmen, and though they enjoyed greater prosperity and respect in America than in Europe, they were still merely workmen in the eyes of their contemporaries. Second, maritime workers are often outside the mainstream of an agricultural or business community. Finally, the merchant was the key to the success of American shipping, promoting it at home and abroad and then employing it as much as he could; he was unlikely to see the builder's role as being equal in importance to his own.

It must be added that these attitudes can be directly related to the question of the profitability of shipbuilding. Merchants encountered both success and failure in their shipbuilding ventures, and delays or setbacks during the many stages of construction made this a frequently frustrating enterprise. For the shipbuilder, his seasonal trade could not be depended on as a reliable road to wealth. "Shipbuilding," wrote Massachusetts governor Francis Bernard, "is generally a losing trade, but it is a necessary resort to make good the balance due to Great Britain when other branches fail or prove insufficient."[1] Provincial merchants thus had to finance the development of local shipbuilding in order to obtain badly needed cash and credit as well as to acquire their own shipping for coastal and overseas trade. Without the presence of a shipbuilding industry, American commerce could not have attained the level of maturity it did prior to the Revolution. While not a glamorous or promising industry in an isolated context, shipbuilding played an essential role in the development and expansion of colonial commerce and thus in the achievement of the growing economy that characterized the colonies on the eve of the Revolution.

*Appendix*
*Shipping Tables*

The shipping tables have been compiled from three sources: ship registers, port records, and insurance lists. According to an Act of 1698 for Preventing Frauds and Regulating Abuses in the Plantation Trade, the owners of each ship engaged in colonial trade had to register a certificate giving their names and a description of the vessel with the local customs officer. Only fishing craft and small vessels trading within the same colony were exempt from registration. Although all the ship registers sent to London were destroyed by fire during the eighteenth and nineteenth centuries, duplicate registration lists have been preserved for vessels licensed in Massachusetts (1697–1714), Pennsylvania (1722–76), and South Carolina (1735–80). Also, a brief postcolonial register kept by Rhode Island officials contains records of some vessels built before 1776. Port records listing the entry and departure of vessels are available for most colonies. But due to the difficulty of making a complete study, and the limited use made of shipping statistics in the present work, only a few port records have been examined. In terms of ship detail, both registers and port records contain the same basic information. They list the rig, tonnage, and places and dates of construction and registration of each vessel.

Maritime historians have hitherto ignored a third source, Lloyd's of London insurance records. Besides noting the rig, tonnage, and place and date of construction, *Lloyd's Register* rates the condition of each vessel's hull and rigging. Because the first two issues, those of 1764 and 1768, list colonial vessels only under the general categories of plantation- or American-built, the third issue, that of 1776, which usually gives the specific colony of construction, was used for this study. It must be emphasized that *Lloyd's Register* does not list all colonial-built vessels, but only those already owned by or likely to be hired by British merchants.

In the shipping tables which follow, the number of vessels in each of five or six categories is listed with total tonnage in parentheses. Below these two figures is the average tonnage of the vessels in that category. In computing the average tonnage, all quotients were carried out to two decimal places and then rounded off to one. Tables 53–55, which list Lloyd's quality ratings A, E, I, O, and U for colonial-built vessels, differ from the above pattern.


## Sources for Tables


*Further information on the sources can be found in the Bibliography.*

*Tables 1–4*: Massachusetts shipping register, 1697–1714. From Vol. 7, Commercial, 1685–1714, Massachusetts Archives.

*Table 5*: Boston port records, 1753. From Shipping Returns, British Public Record Office.

*Tables 6–8*: New Hampshire port records, 1744–45, 1756–57, 1768. From Shipping Returns, British Public Record Office.

*Table 9*: Rhode Island shipping register, 1776–78. From Rhode Island Archives.

*Tables 10–17*: Philadelphia shipping register, 1726–75. From Ship Register Books of the Province of Pennsylvania, 1722–76, 21 vols., Historical Society of Pennsylvania.

*Tables 18–33*: Annapolis port records, 1747–75. From ships lists in Vaughan W. Brown, *Shipping in the Port of Annapolis, 1748–1775* (Annapolis, 1965).

*Tables 34–37*: Register of vessels trading with North Carolina, 1725–51. From the Treasurer and Comptroller Port Papers, Port of Roanoke, Book of Registers, 1725–51, North Carolina State Archives.

*Tables 38–42*: North Carolina port records, 1767–75. From Records of Port Roanoke, 1771–76, James Iredell Notebooks, Southern Historical Collection, University of North Carolina; and a typed copy of the Brunswick Port Records, 1767–68, 1774–75, Southern Historical Collection.

*Tables 43–50*: South Carolina shipping register, 1735–74. From South Carolina Ship Register, 1734–83, South Carolina Archives.

*Tables 51–55*: *Lloyd's Register of Shipping*, 1776 (reprint; Ridgewood, N.J., 1964).

Table 1. Massachusetts shipping register: Vessels built 1674–96

| Construction site | Sloop | Ketch | Bark | Brig | Ship | Total |
|---|---|---|---|---|---|---|
| Pemaquid | 1(35) | — | — | — | — | 1(35) |
|  | 35.0 |  |  |  |  |  |
| York | — | — | — | 1(60) | 1(60) | 2(120) |
|  |  |  |  | 60.0 | 60.0 |  |
| Kittery | 1(25) | — | — | 1(40) | — | 2(65) |
|  | 25.0 |  |  | 40.0 |  |  |
| Total Maine Province |  |  |  |  |  | 5(220) |
| Amesbury | — | — | — | 1(35) | — | 1(35) |
|  |  |  |  | 35.0 |  |  |
| Salisbury | 1(25) | — | — | — | — | 1(25) |
|  | 25.0 |  |  |  |  |  |
| Newbury | 4(124) | — | 1(20) | 2(55) | — | 7(199) |
|  | 31.0 |  | 20.0 | 27.5 |  |  |
| Total Merrimack River |  |  |  |  |  | 9(259) |
| Ipswich | 1(30) | — | — | 1(30) | — | 2(60) |
|  | 30.0 |  |  | 30.0 |  |  |
| Gloucester | 1(15) | — | — | — | — | 1(15) |
|  | 15.0 |  |  |  |  |  |
| Beverly | 1(30) | 2(59) | 1(40) | — | — | 4(129) |
|  | 30.0 | 29.5 | 40.0 |  |  |  |
| Salem | 9(187) | 10(248) | 3(108) | 3(140) | 4(490) | 29(1,173) |
|  | 20.8 | 24.8 | 36.0 | 46.7 | 122.5 |  |
| Marblehead | — | — | 1(20) | — | — | 1(20) |
|  |  |  | 20.0 |  |  |  |
| Total Salem area |  |  |  |  |  | 37(1,397) |

Table 1 *(cont.)*

| Construction site | Sloop | Ketch | Bark | Brig | Ship | Total |
|---|---|---|---|---|---|---|
| Lynn | 3(40) | — | — | — | — | 3(40) |
| | 13.3 | | | | | |
| Cambridge | — | — | — | 3(110) | — | 3(110) |
| | | | | 36.7 | | |
| Charlestown | 3(60) | — | — | 4(195) | 2(550) | 9(805) |
| | 20.0 | | | 48.8 | 275.0 | |
| Boston | 9(230) | 3(85) | 3(115) | 8(370) | 8(920) | 31(1,720) |
| | 25.6 | 28.3 | 38.3 | 46.3 | 115.0 | |
| Milton | — | — | — | 3(150) | 1(300) | 4(450) |
| | | | | 50.0 | 300.0 | |
| Braintree | — | — | — | 1(35) | — | 1(35) |
| | | | | 35.0 | | |
| Weymouth | — | — | 1(50) | — | — | 1(50) |
| | | | 50.0 | | | |
| Total Boston area | | | | | | 52(3,210) |
| Hingham | 5(100) | — | — | — | — | 5(100) |
| | 20.0 | | | | | |
| Scituate | 12(327) | 1(25) | 3(200) | 6(275) | 5(420) | 27(1,247) |
| | 27.3 | 25.0 | 66.7 | 45.8 | 84.0 | |
| North River | 1(20) | — | — | — | — | 1(20) |
| | 20.0 | | | | | |
| Plymouth | — | — | — | 1(60) | — | 1(60) |
| | | | | 60.0 | | |
| Total Plymouth area | | | | | | 34(1,427) |
| Tiverton | 1(25) | — | — | — | — | 1(25) |
| | 25.0 | | | | | |

Table 1 (cont.)

| Construction site | Sloop | Ketch | Bark | Brig | Ship | Total |
|---|---|---|---|---|---|---|
| Freetown | 1(20) | — | — | — | — | 1(20) |
| | 20.0 | | | | | |
| Swansea | 1(40) | — | — | — | — | 1(40) |
| | 40.0 | | | | | |
| Bristol | 2(40) | — | 1(50) | — | — | 3(90) |
| | 20.0 | | 50.0 | | | |
| Total Bristol County | | | | | | 6(175) |
| Massachusetts (location unspecified) | 1(20) | — | — | — | — | 1(20) |
| | 20.0 | | | | | |
| Total Massachusetts | 58(1,393) | 16(417) | 14(603) | 35(1,555) | 21(2,740) | 144(6,708) |
| | 24.0 | 26.1 | 43.1 | 44.4 | 130.5 | |
| New Hampshire | 1(10) | — | 1(60) | 4(120) | 2(240) | 8(430) |
| | 10.0 | | 60.0 | 30.0 | 120.0 | |
| Rhode Island | 4(77) | — | — | 1(60) | — | 5(137) |
| | 19.3 | | | 60.0 | | |
| Connecticut | 17(359) | 1(30) | — | 4(150) | — | 22(539) |
| | 21.1 | 30.0 | | 37.5 | | |
| New York | 3(80) | — | — | — | — | 3(80) |
| | 26.7 | | | | | |
| Virginia | 3(67) | — | — | — | — | 3(67) |
| | 22.3 | | | | | |
| Other colonies | 4(68) | — | — | — | — | 4(68) |
| | 17.0 | | | | | |
| Total non-Massachusetts | 32(661) | 1(30) | 1(60) | 9(330) | 2(240) | 45(1,321) |
| | 20.7 | 30.0 | 60.0 | 36.7 | 120.0 | |

Table 1 *(cont.)*

| Vessels registered in Massachusetts | | % of tonnage |
|---|---|---|
| Massachusetts-built | 144(6,708) | 83.5 |
| Other colonial-built | 45(1,321) | 16.5 |
| Total | 189(8,029) | 100.0 |
| Vessels built in Massachusetts | | |
| Salem-built | 29(1,173) | 17.5 |
| Charlestown-built | 9(805) | 12.0 |
| Boston-built | 31(1,720) | 25.6 |
| Scituate-built | 27(1,247) | 18.6 |
| Other | 48(1,763) | 26.3 |
| Total | 144(6,708) | 100.0 |

Table 2. Massachusetts shipping register, 1697–1702

| Construction site | Sloop | Ketch | Bark | Brig | Ship | Total |
|---|---|---|---|---|---|---|
| Saco | — | — | — | 2(90) | — | 2(90) |
| | | | | 45.0 | | |
| Kittery | 1(35) | — | — | — | 3(230) | 4(265) |
| | 35.0 | | | | 76.7 | |
| Elsewhere in Maine | 2(90) | — | — | — | 1(50) | 3(140) |
| | 45.0 | | | | 50.0 | |
| Total Maine Province | | | | | | 9(495) |
| Bradford | 1(12) | — | — | — | — | 1(12) |
| | 12.0 | | | | | |
| Amesbury | — | 1(30) | — | — | — | 1(30) |
| | | 30.0 | | | | |
| Salisbury | — | — | — | 1(30) | — | 1(30) |
| | | | | 30.0 | | |
| Newbury | 12(353) | 6(165) | 3(120) | 2(90) | — | 23(728) |
| | 29.4 | 27.5 | 40.0 | 45.0 | | |
| Total Merrimack River | | | | | | 26(800) |
| Ipswich | 3(60) | — | — | 1(30) | — | 4(90) |
| | 20.0 | | | 30.0 | | |
| Gloucester | 4(118) | — | — | 1(60) | 1(230) | 6(408) |
| | 29.5 | | | 60.0 | 230.0 | |
| Manchester | 2(60) | 1(25) | — | — | — | 3(85) |
| | 30.0 | 25.0 | | | | |
| Beverly | — | 1(40) | — | — | — | 1(40) |
| | | 40.0 | | | | |
| Salem | 10(245) | 32(1,003) | 4(138) | 1(35) | 5(590) | 52(201) |
| | 24.5 | 31.3 | 34.5 | 35.0 | 118.0 | |
| Total Salem area | | | | | | 66(2,634) |

Table 2 (*cont.*)

| Construction site | Sloop | Ketch | Bark | Brig | Ship | Total |
|---|---|---|---|---|---|---|
| Lynn | — | 2(60) | — | 1(35) | — | 3(95) |
| | | 30.0 | | 35.0 | | |
| Medford | — | — | — | 1(40) | — | 1(40) |
| | | | | 40.0 | | |
| Cambridge | 1(18) | — | — | — | — | 1(18) |
| | 18.0 | | | | | |
| Charlestown | 7(261) | 1(80) | 3(140) | 2(90) | 19(2,527) | 32(3,098) |
| | 37.3 | 80.0 | 46.7 | 45.0 | 133.0 | |
| Boston | 19(612) | 8(305) | 8(470) | 13(600) | 34(3,850) | 82(5,837) |
| | 32.2 | 38.1 | 58.8 | 46.2 | 113.2 | |
| Milton | — | — | — | 1(50) | 2(140) | 3(190) |
| | | | | 50.0 | 70.0 | |
| Weymouth | — | — | — | 3(150) | 5(470) | 8(620) |
| | | | | 50.0 | 94.0 | |
| Total Boston area | | | | | | 130(9,898) |
| Hingham | 3(93) | — | — | — | — | 3(93) |
| | 31.0 | | | | | |
| Cohasset | 1(30) | — | — | — | — | 1(30) |
| | 30.0 | | | | | |
| Scituate | 19(540) | 3(100) | 4(250) | 19(830) | 16(1,330) | 61(3,050) |
| | 28.4 | 33.3 | 62.5 | 43.7 | 83.1 | |
| Duxbury | 1(30) | — | — | — | — | 1(30) |
| | 30.0 | | | | | |
| Plymouth | 5(109) | 3(91) | — | — | — | 8(200) |
| | 21.8 | 30.3 | | | | |
| Total Plymouth area | | | | | | 74(3,403) |

Table 2 (*cont.*)

| Construction site | Sloop | Ketch | Bark | Brig | Ship | Total |
|---|---|---|---|---|---|---|
| Manamoit | 1(20) | — | — | — | — | 1(20) |
| | 20.0 | | | | | |
| Total Cape Cod area | | | | | | 1(20) |
| Rochester | — | — | — | 1(60) | — | 1(60) |
| | | | | 60.0 | | |
| Taunton | 1(30) | — | — | 1(60) | 7(714) | 9(804) |
| | 30.0 | | | 60.0 | 102.0 | |
| Swansea | 1(22) | — | — | — | 1(78) | 2(100) |
| | 22.0 | | | | 78.0 | |
| Bristol | 1(30) | — | — | — | — | 1(30) |
| | 30.0 | | | | | |
| Rehoboth | — | — | — | 2(85) | — | 2(85) |
| | | | | 42.5 | | |
| Total Rochester and Bristol County | | | | | | 15(1,079) |
| Total Massachusetts | 95(2,768) | 58(1,899) | 22(1,118) | 52(2,335) | 94(10,209) | 321(18,329) |
| | 29.1 | 32.7 | 50.8 | 44.9 | 108.6 | |
| New Hampshire | 7(170) | — | — | 1(30) | 2(224) | 10(424) |
| | 24.3 | | | 30.0 | 112.0 | |
| Rhode Island | 4(130) | — | — | — | — | 4(130) |
| | 32.5 | | | | | |
| Connecticut | 42(1,046) | — | 1(70) | 4(210) | 2(190) | 49(1,516) |
| | 24.9 | | 70.0 | 52.5 | 95.0 | |
| New York | 2(32) | — | 1(80) | — | — | 3(112) |
| | 16.0 | | 80.0 | | | |

Table 2 (*cont.*)

| Construction site | Sloop | Ketch | Bark | Brig | Ship | Total |
|---|---|---|---|---|---|---|
| Other colonies | 2(47) | — | — | — | — | 2(47) |
| | 23.5 | | | | | |
| Total non-Massachusetts | 57(1,425) | — | 2(150) | 5(240) | 4(414) | 68(2,229) |
| | 25.0 | | 75.0 | 48.0 | 103.5 | |

| Vessels registered in Massachusetts | | % of tonnage |
|---|---|---|
| Massachusetts-built | 321(18,329) | 89.2 |
| Connecticut-built | 49(1,516) | 7.4 |
| Other colonial-built | 19(713) | 3.5 |
| Total | 389(20,558) | 100.0 |

| Vessels built in Massachusetts | | |
|---|---|---|
| Salem-built | 52(2,011) | 11.0 |
| Charlestown-built | 32(3,098) | 16.9 |
| Boston-built | 82(5,837) | 31.8 |
| Scituate-built | 61(3,050) | 16.6 |
| Other | 94(4,333) | 23.7 |
| Total | 321(18,329) | 100.0 |

Table 3. Massachusetts shipping register, 1703–8

| Construction site | Sloop | Ketch | Bark | Brig | Ship | Total |
|---|---|---|---|---|---|---|
| York | 3(100) | — | — | — | — | 3(100) |
| | 33.3 | | | | | |
| Kittery | 1(30) | — | — | 1(40) | 10(1,690) | 12(1,760) |
| | 30.0 | | | 40.0 | 169.0 | |
| **Total Maine Province** | | | | | | 15(1,860) |
| Merrimack River | 1(30) | — | — | — | — | 1(30) |
| | 30.0 | | | | | |
| Haverhill | — | — | — | 1(30) | — | 1(30) |
| | | | | 30.0 | | |
| Amesbury | — | — | — | 2(80) | — | 2(80) |
| | | | | 40.0 | | |
| Newbury | 11(340) | 1(50) | — | 6(330) | 5(790) | 23(1,510) |
| | 30.9 | 50.0 | | 55.0 | 158.0 | |
| **Total Merrimack River** | | | | | | 27(1,650) |
| Rowley | 1(25) | — | — | — | — | 1(25) |
| | 25.0 | | | | | |
| Ipswich | 2(60) | — | — | 1(50) | — | 3(110) |
| | 30.0 | | | 50.0 | | |
| Gloucester | 15(488) | — | 1(60) | 14(825) | 2(155) | 32(1,528) |
| | 32.5 | | 60.0 | 58.9 | 77.5 | |
| Manchester | 1(35) | — | — | — | 2(175) | 3(210) |
| | 35.0 | | | | 87.5 | |
| Salem | 8(283) | 5(117) | 1(60) | 6(285) | 12(1,770) | 32(2,515) |
| | 35.4 | 23.4 | 60.0 | 47.5 | 147.5 | |
| **Total Salem area** | | | | | | 71(4,388) |

Table 3 *(cont.)*

| Construction site | Sloop | Ketch | Bark | Brig | Ship | Total |
|---|---|---|---|---|---|---|
| Lynn | — | — | — | 1(40) | — | 1(40) |
| | | | | 40.0 | | |
| Medford | — | — | — | — | 1(60) | 1(60) |
| | | | | | 60.0 | |
| Charlestown | 4(120) | — | — | 4(245) | 19(2,175) | 27(2,540) |
| | 30.0 | | | 61.3 | 114.5 | |
| Boston | 39(1,237) | — | 5(290) | 34(1,765) | 50(4,956) | 128(8,248) |
| | 31.7 | | 58.0 | 51.9 | 99.1 | |
| Weymouth | 1(40) | — | — | — | 3(350) | 4(390) |
| | 40.0 | | | | 116.7 | |
| Total Boston area | | | | | | 161(11,278) |
| Hingham | 2(65) | — | — | 1(40) | 1(160) | 4(265) |
| | 32.5 | | | 40.0 | 160.0 | |
| Scituate | 18(511) | — | — | 21(1,192) | 4(250) | 43(1,953) |
| | 28.4 | | | 56.8 | 62.5 | |
| Marshfield | 1(40) | — | — | — | — | 1(40) |
| | 40.0 | | | | | |
| Duxbury | 6(170) | — | — | 3(120) | 1(75) | 10(365) |
| | 28.3 | | | 40.0 | 75.0 | |
| Plymouth | 3(85) | — | — | 1(50) | — | 4(135) |
| | 28.3 | | | 50.0 | | |
| Total Plymouth area | | | | | | 62(2,758) |
| Rochester | — | — | — | 1(75) | — | 1(75) |
| | | | | 75.0 | | |
| Tiverton | 1(40) | — | — | 1(45) | — | 2(85) |
| | 40.0 | | | 45.0 | | |

Table 3 (cont.)

| Construction site | Sloop | Ketch | Bark | Brig | Ship | Total |
|---|---|---|---|---|---|---|
| Taunton | 4(130) | — | 1(60) | 5(305) | 6(535) | 16(1,030) |
|  | 32.5 |  | 60.0 | 61.0 | 89.2 |  |
| Freetown | — | — | — | — | 1(120) | 1(120) |
|  |  |  |  |  | 120.0 |  |
| Swansea | — | — | — | 1(50) | 2(290) | 3(340) |
|  |  |  |  | 50.0 | 145.0 |  |
| Bristol | 5(180) | — | — | 4(250) | 1(80) | 10(510) |
|  | 36.0 |  |  | 62.5 | 80.0 |  |
| Rehoboth | — | — | — | 1(60) | — | 1(60) |
|  |  |  |  | 60.0 |  |  |
| Total Rochester and Bristol County |  |  |  |  |  | 34(2,220) |
| Massachusetts (location unspecified) | 3(90) | — | — | — | 1(50) | 4(140) |
|  | 30.0 |  |  |  | 50.0 |  |
| Total Massachusetts | 130(4,099) | 6(167) | 8(470) | 109(5,877) | 121(13,681) | 374(24,294) |
|  | 31.5 | 27.8 | 58.8 | 53.9 | 113.1 |  |
| New Hampshire | 4(84) | — | 2(140) | 6(238) | 9(825) | 21(1,287) |
|  | 21.0 |  | 70.0 | 39.7 | 91.7 |  |
| Rhode Island | 4(145) | — | — | 1(60) | — | 5(205) |
|  | 36.3 |  |  | 60.0 |  |  |
| Connecticut | 17(588) | — | 1(70) | 3(165) | — | 21(823) |
|  | 34.6 |  | 70.0 | 55.0 |  |  |
| New York | 2(27) | — | — | — | — | 2(27) |
|  | 13.5 |  |  |  |  |  |

Table 3 (*cont.*)

| Construction site | Sloop | Ketch | Bark | Brig | Ship | Total |
|---|---|---|---|---|---|---|
| Other colonies | 2(70) | — | — | — | — | 2(70) |
|  | 35.0 |  |  |  |  |  |
| Total non-Massachusetts | 29(914) | — | 3(210) | 10(463) | 9(825) | 51(2,412) |
|  | 31.5 |  | 70.0 | 46.3 | 91.7 |  |

| Vessels registered in Massachusetts |  | % of tonnage |
|---|---|---|
| Massachusetts-built | 374(24,294) | 91.0 |
| New Hampshire–built | 21(1,287) | 4.8 |
| Other colonial-built | 30(1,125) | 4.2 |
| Total | 425(26,706) | 100.0 |

| Vessels built in Massachusetts |  |  |
|---|---|---|
| Kittery-built | 12(1,760) | 7.2 |
| Newbury-built | 23(1,510) | 6.2 |
| Gloucester-built | 32(1,528) | 6.3 |
| Salem-built | 32(2,515) | 10.4 |
| Charlestown-built | 27(2,540) | 10.5 |
| Boston-built | 128(8,248) | 34.0 |
| Scituate-built | 43(1,953) | 8.0 |
| Other | 77(4,240) | 17.4 |
| Total | 374(24,294) | 100.0 |

Table 4. Massachusetts shipping register, 1709–14

| Construction site | Sloop | Ketch | Bark | Brig | Ship | Total |
|---|---|---|---|---|---|---|
| York | 3(120) | — | — | — | — | 3(120) |
| | 40.0 | | | | | |
| Kittery | 5(170) | — | — | 5(265) | 8(1,200) | 18(1,635) |
| | 34.0 | | | 53.0 | 150.0 | |
| Total Maine Province | | | | | | 21(1,755) |
| Bradford | — | — | — | 1(45) | — | 1(45) |
| | | | | 45.0 | | |
| Haverhill | 1(50) | — | — | — | — | 1(50) |
| | 50.0 | | | | | |
| Salisbury | 1(40) | — | — | — | — | 1(40) |
| | 40.0 | | | | | |
| Newbury | 28(975) | — | 2(60) | 11(525) | 11(1,065) | 52(2,625) |
| | 34.8 | | 30.0 | 47.7 | 96.8 | |
| Total Merrimack River | | | | | | 55(2,760) |
| Rowley | 1(35) | — | — | — | — | 1(35) |
| | 35.0 | | | | | |
| Ipswich | 3(90) | — | — | 1(100) | — | 4(190) |
| | 30.0 | | | 100.0 | | |
| Gloucester | 17(506) | — | — | — | — | 17(506) |
| | 29.8 | | | | | |
| Salem | 13(440) | — | 1(65) | 4(300) | 7(860) | 25(1,665) |
| | 33.8 | | 65.0 | 75.0 | 122.9 | |
| Total Salem area | | | | | | 47(2,396) |
| Lynn | 3(110) | — | 1(30) | 2(110) | — | 6(250) |
| | 36.7 | | 30.0 | 55.0 | | |

Table 4 (*cont.*)

| Construction site | Sloop | Ketch | Bark | Brig | Ship | Total |
|---|---|---|---|---|---|---|
| Charlestown | 6(210) | — | — | 3(170) | 20(2,675) | 29(3,055) |
| | 35.0 | | | 56.7 | 133.8 | |
| Boston | 58(1,972) | — | 3(180) | 25(1,410) | 97(9,953) | 183(13,515) |
| | 34.0 | | 60.0 | 56.4 | 102.6 | |
| Dorchester | 1(50) | — | — | — | — | 1(50) |
| | 50.0 | | | | | |
| Milton | 1(40) | — | — | — | — | 1(40) |
| | 40.0 | | | | | |
| Weymouth | 1(30) | — | — | — | — | 1(30) |
| | 30.0 | | | | | |
| Total Boston area | | | | | | 221(16,940) |
| Hingham | 5(131) | — | 1(40) | — | — | 6(171) |
| | 26.2 | | 40.0 | | | |
| Cohasset | — | — | — | — | 1(60) | 1(60) |
| | | | | | 60.0 | |
| Scituate | 5(160) | — | — | 4(210) | 5(340) | 14(710) |
| | 32.0 | | | 52.5 | 68.0 | |
| Marshfield | 1(30) | — | — | — | 1(70) | 2(100) |
| | 30.0 | | | | 70.0 | |
| Duxbury | 8(225) | — | — | 1(45) | — | 9(270) |
| | 28.1 | | | 45.0 | | |
| Plymouth | 13(395) | — | — | — | — | 13(395) |
| | 30.4 | | | | | |
| Total Plymouth area | | | | | | 45(1,706) |
| Eastham | 1(20) | — | — | — | — | 1(20) |
| | 20.0 | | | | | |
| Total Cape Cod area | | | | | | 1(20) |

Table 4 *(cont.)*

| Construction site | Sloop | Ketch | Bark | Brig | Ship | Total |
|---|---|---|---|---|---|---|
| Tiverton | 1(14) | — | — | — | — | 1(14) |
| | 14.0 | | | | | |
| Taunton | 2(55) | — | — | 1(50) | 5(1,330) | 8(1,435) |
| | 27.5 | | | 50.0 | 266.0 | |
| Dighton | — | — | — | — | 2(150) | 2(150) |
| | | | | | 75.0 | |
| Swansea | 1(34) | — | — | 3(160) | 1(80) | 5(274) |
| | 34.0 | | | 53.3 | 80.0 | |
| Bristol | 1(50) | — | — | — | 2(150) | 3(200) |
| | 50.0 | | | | 75.0 | |
| Total Bristol County | | | | | | 19(2,073) |
| Massachusetts (location unspecified) | 1(40) | — | — | — | — | 1(40) |
| | 40.0 | | | | | |
| Total Massachusetts | 181(5,992) | — | 8(375) | 61(3,390) | 160(17,933) | 410(27,690) |
| | 33.1 | | 46.9 | 55.6 | 112.1 | |
| New Hampshire | 2(69) | — | — | 1(50) | 11(1,405) | 14(1,524) |
| | 34.5 | | | 50.0 | 127.7 | |
| Rhode Island | 5(117) | — | — | 1(55) | — | 6(172) |
| | 23.4 | | | 55.0 | | |
| Connecticut | 14(490) | — | — | — | 2(160) | 16(650) |
| | 35.0 | | | | 80.0 | |
| Pennsylvania | — | — | — | — | 1(80) | 1(80) |
| | | | | | 80.0 | |
| Total non-Massachusetts | 21(676) | — | — | 1(105) | 14(1,645) | 37(2,426) |
| | 32.2 | | | 52.5 | 117.5 | |

Table 4 *(cont.)*

| Vessels registered in Massachusetts | | % of tonnage |
|---|---|---|
| Massachusetts-built | 410(27,690) | 91.9 |
| New Hampshire–built | 14(1,524) | 5.1 |
| Other colonial-built | 23(902) | 3.0 |
| Total | 447(30,116) | 100.0 |
| Vessels built in Massachusetts | | |
| Kittery-built | 18(1,635) | 5.9 |
| Newbury-built | 52(2,625) | 9.5 |
| Salem-built | 25(1,665) | 6.0 |
| Charlestown-built | 29(3,055) | 11.0 |
| Boston-built | 183(13,515) | 48.8 |
| Other | 103(5,195) | 18.8 |
| Total | 410(27,690) | 100.0 |

Table 5. Boston port records, 1753

| Construction site | Sloop | Schooner | Brig | Snow | Ship | Total |
|---|---|---|---|---|---|---|
| Falmouth and Casco Bay | 16(720) | 12(565) | 4(220) | — | — | 32(1,505) |
| | 45.0 | 47.1 | 55.0 | | | |
| Scarborough | 1(25) | 2(115) | — | — | — | 3(140) |
| | 25.0 | 57.5 | | | | |
| Wells | 7(285) | — | — | — | — | 7(285) |
| | 40.7 | | | | | |
| York | 6(330) | 2(95) | — | — | — | 8(425) |
| | 55.0 | 47.5 | | | | |
| Elsewhere in Maine | 5(215) | — | 2(105) | 2(170) | — | 9(490) |
| | 43.0 | | 52.5 | 85.0 | | |
| Total Maine Province | | | | | | 59(2,845) |
| Andover | — | 1(55) | — | — | — | 1(55) |
| | | 55.0 | | | | |
| Bradford | — | 3(80) | — | — | — | 3(80) |
| | | 26.7 | | | | |
| Haverhill | 4(141) | 3(123) | — | 1(100) | 1(140) | 9(504) |
| | 35.3 | 41.0 | | 100.0 | 140.0 | |
| Amesbury | — | 1(30) | 1(70) | — | 1(120) | 3(200) |
| | | 30.0 | 70.0 | | 120.0 | |
| Salisbury | — | 2(90) | 3(150) | 1(105) | — | 6(345) |
| | | 45.0 | 50.0 | 105.0 | | |
| Newbury | 11(435) | 15(650) | 11(690) | 13(1,190) | 9(1,165) | 59(4,130) |
| | 39.5 | 43.3 | 62.7 | 91.5 | 129.4 | |
| Total Merrimack River | | | | | | 81(5,334) |

Table 5 (*cont.*)

| Construction site | Sloop | Schooner | Brig | Snow | Ship | Total |
|---|---|---|---|---|---|---|
| Rowley | 1(60) | 2(110) | — | 1(85) | — | 4(255) |
|  | 60.0 | 55.0 |  | 85.0 |  |  |
| Ipswich | — | 1(30) | — | — | — | 1(30) |
|  |  | 30.0 |  |  |  |  |
| Gloucester | 1(50) | 3(100) | — | — | — | 4(150) |
|  | 50.0 | 33.3 |  |  |  |  |
| Manchester | — | 1(50) | — | — | — | 1(50) |
|  |  | 50.0 |  |  |  |  |
| Salem | — | 3(105) | — | — | — | 3(105) |
|  |  | 35.0 |  |  |  |  |
| Total Salem area |  |  |  |  |  | 13(590) |
| Lynn | 1(67) | — | — | — | — | 1(67) |
|  | 67.0 |  |  |  |  |  |
| Medford | — | 2(70) | — | 1(75) | — | 3(145) |
|  |  | 35.0 |  | 75.0 |  |  |
| Charlestown | — | — | 1(50) | 1(140) | — | 3(190) |
|  |  |  | 50.0 | 70.0 |  |  |
| Boston | 6(390) | 9(470) | 12(751) | 22(1,940) | 22(3,092) | 71(6,643) |
|  | 65.0 | 52.2 | 62.6 | 82.2 | 140.5 |  |
| Braintree | 1(40) | 3(80) | — | — | — | 4(120) |
|  | 40.0 | 26.7 |  |  |  |  |
| Weymouth | 5(148) | 2(55) | 2(200) | — | — | 9(403) |
|  | 29.6 | 27.5 | 100.0 |  |  |  |
| Total Boston area |  |  |  |  |  | 91(7,568) |
| Hingham | 8(325) | 4(130) | 1(50) | — | — | 13(505) |
|  | 40.6 | 32.5 | 50.0 |  |  |  |

Table 5 (*cont.*)

| Construction site | Sloop | Schooner | Brig | Snow | Ship | Total |
|---|---|---|---|---|---|---|
| Hull | — | 1(50) | — | — | — | 1(50) |
| | | 50.0 | | | | |
| Scituate | 15(605) | 7(195) | 6(455) | 2(180) | — | 30(1,435) |
| | 40.3 | 27.9 | 75.8 | 90.0 | | |
| Hanover | 3(105) | 4(170) | 1(70) | — | — | 8(345) |
| | 35.0 | 42.5 | 70.0 | | | |
| Bridgewater | — | 2(80) | — | — | — | 2(80) |
| | | 40.0 | | | | |
| Pembroke | 5(221) | 4(203) | 1(70) | — | — | 10(494) |
| | 42.2 | 50.8 | 70.0 | | | |
| Marshfield | 5(245) | 4(195) | — | 3(255) | — | 12(695) |
| | 49.0 | 48.8 | | 85.0 | | |
| Duxbury | 4(160) | 1(25) | — | — | — | 5(185) |
| | 40.0 | 25.0 | | | | |
| Kingston | 4(205) | 10(330) | 1(30) | 1(60) | 1(115) | 17(740) |
| | 51.3 | 33.0 | 30.0 | 60.0 | 115.0 | |
| Plymouth | 1(20) | 17(525) | 2(110) | — | — | 20(655) |
| | 20.0 | 30.9 | 55.0 | | | |
| Total Plymouth area | | | | | | 118(5,184) |
| Sandwich | — | — | 1(65) | — | — | 1(65) |
| | | | 65.0 | | | |
| Barnstable | — | 3(105) | — | — | — | 3(105) |
| | | 35.0 | | | | |
| Harwich | 1(30) | — | — | — | — | 1(30) |
| | 30.0 | | | | | |
| Total Cape Cod area | | | | | | 5(200) |

Table 5 (*cont.*)

| Construction site | Sloop | Schooner | Brig | Snow | Ship | Total |
|---|---|---|---|---|---|---|
| Dartmouth | 1(40) | 2(70) | — | — | — | 3(110) |
| | 40.0 | 35.0 | | | | |
| Dighton | — | 1(40) | — | — | — | 1(40) |
| | | 40.0 | | | | |
| Freetown | 1(30) | — | — | — | — | 1(30) |
| | 30.0 | | | | | |
| Swansea | — | — | — | 1(120) | — | 1(120) |
| | | | | 120.0 | | |
| Total Bristol County | | | | | | 6(300) |
| Massachusetts (location unspecified) | 3(95) | 1(45) | — | 1(90) | — | 5(230) |
| | 31.7 | 45.0 | | 90.0 | | |
| Total Massachusetts | 116(4,987) | 128(5,036) | 49(3,086) | 51(4,510) | 34(4,632) | 378(22,251) |
| | 43.0 | 39.3 | 63.0 | 88.4 | 136.2 | |
| New Hampshire | 1(40) | 4(125) | 3(190) | 3(280) | 2(240) | 13(875) |
| | 40.0 | 31.3 | 63.3 | 93.3 | 120.0 | |
| Rhode Island | — | 1(65) | — | 2(130) | 1(65) | 4(260) |
| | | 65.0 | | 65.0 | 65.0 | |
| Connecticut | 8(249) | — | — | — | — | 8(249) |
| | 31.2 | | | | | |
| New York | 7(148) | — | — | — | — | 7(148) |
| | 21.1 | | | | | |
| Pennsylvania and Delaware | 3(80) | — | 1(50) | — | — | 4(130) |
| | 26.7 | | 50.0 | | | |

Table 5 (*cont.*)

| Construction site | Sloop | Schooner | Brig | Snow | Ship | Total |
|---|---|---|---|---|---|---|
| Maryland | 5(165) | 2(60) | — | 1(80) | — | 8(305) |
|  | 33.0 | 30.0 | | 80.0 | | |
| Virginia | 9(442) | 2(55) | — | 1(80) | — | 12(577) |
|  | 49.1 | 27.5 | | 80.0 | | |
| North Carolina | 1(40) | 1(40) | — | — | — | 2(80) |
|  | 40.0 | 40.0 | | | | |
| South Carolina | — | 8(265) | — | — | — | 8(265) |
|  | | 33.1 | | | | |
| Total non-Massachusetts | 34(1,164) | 18(610) | 4(240) | 7(570) | 3(305) | 66(2,889) |
|  | 34.2 | 33.9 | 60.0 | 81.4 | 101.7 | |

| Vessels in Boston port records, 1753 | | % of tonnage |
|---|---|---|
| Massachusetts-built | 378(22,251) | 88.5 |
| New Hampshire–built | 13(875) | 3.5 |
| Maryland- and Virginia-built | 12(882) | 3.5 |
| Other colonial-built | 41(1,132) | 4.5 |
| Total | 444(25,140) | 100.00 |

| Vessels built in Massachusetts* | | |
|---|---|---|
| Falmouth- and Casco Bay–built | 32(1,505) | 6.8 |
| Newbury-built | 59(4,130) | 18.6 |
| Boston-built | 71(6,643) | 29.9 |
| Plymouth area–built | 118(5,184) | 23.3 |
| Other | 98(4,789) | 21.5 |
| Total | 378(22,251) | 100.0 |

*Of the 378 Massachusetts-built vessels, all but 29 were registered in Massachusetts.

Table 6. New Hampshire port records, 1744–45

| Construction site | Sloop | Schooner | Brig | Snow | Ship | Total |
|---|---|---|---|---|---|---|
| New Hampshire | 9(380) | 20(881) | 12(725) | 5(410) | 20(3,238) | 66(5,634) |
|  | 42.2 | 44.1 | 60.4 | 82.0 | 161.5 |  |
| Massachusetts |  |  |  |  |  |  |
| Falmouth and Casco Bay | — | — | — | — | 1(250) | 1(250) |
|  |  |  |  |  | 250.0 |  |
| Haverhill | — | 1(50) | — | — | — | 1(50) |
|  |  | 50.0 |  |  |  |  |
| Newbury | — | 1(60) | 1(60) | — | 1(210) | 3(330) |
|  |  | 60.0 | 60.0 |  | 210.0 |  |
| Salem | — | 1(35) | — | 1(70) | — | 2(105) |
|  |  | 35.0 |  | 70.0 |  |  |
| Boston | — | 1(60) | — | — | 2(530) | 3(590) |
|  |  | 60.0 |  |  | 265.0 |  |
| Scituate | 3(160) | — | — | — | — | 3(160) |
|  | 53.3 |  |  |  |  |  |
| Plymouth | — | — | — | 2(160) | — | 2(160) |
|  |  |  |  | 80.0 |  |  |
| Total Massachusetts | 3(160) | 4(205) | 1(60 | 3(230) | 4(990) | 15(1,645) |
|  | 53.3 | 51.2 | 60.0 | 76.7 | 247.5 |  |

Table 6 (*cont.*)

| | | |
|---|---|---|
| Vessels entering and clearing New Hampshire ports | | % of tonnage |
| New Hampshire–built | 66(5,634) | 77·4 |
| Massachusetts-built | 15(1,645) | 22.6 |
| Total | 81(7,279) | 100.0 |
| Registration | | |
| New Hampshire–built vessels | | % of tonnage |
| New Hampshire | 63(5,514) | 97·9 |
| Antigua | 2(90) | 1.6 |
| Boston | 1(30) | 0.5 |
| Total | 66(5,634) | 100.0 |
| Massachusetts-built vessels | | |
| Massachusetts | 11(995) | 60.5 |
| New Hampshire | 4(650) | 39·5 |
| Total | 15(1,645) | 100.0 |
| Vessels registered in New Hampshire, 1744–45 | | % of tonnage |
| New Hampshire–built | 63(5,514) | 89·5 |
| Massachusetts-built | 4(650) | 10.5 |
| Total | 67(6,164) | 100.0 |

Table 7. New Hampshire port records, 1756–57

| Construction site | Sloop | Schooner | Brig | Snow | Ship | Total |
|---|---|---|---|---|---|---|
| New Hampshire | 21(376) | 20(685) | 15(925) | 12(860) | 18(2,320) | 86(5,666) |
|  | 41.7 | 34.3 | 61.7 | 71.7 | 128.9 | |
| Massachusetts | | | | | | |
| Brunswick | 1(60) | — | — | — | — | 1(60) |
|  | 60.0 | | | | | |
| Falmouth | — | 2(110) | — | — | — | 2(110) |
|  | | 55.0 | | | | |
| Scarborough | 1(25) | — | 1(70) | — | — | 2(95) |
|  | 25.0 | | 70.0 | | | |
| Yarmouth | — | — | 1(50) | — | — | 1(50) |
|  | | | 50.0 | | | |
| Total Penobscot to Cape Elizabeth area | | | | | | 6(315) |
| Biddeford | — | 1(45) | — | — | — | 1(45) |
|  | | 45.0 | | | | |
| Arundel | 2(85) | 2(80) | — | — | — | 4(165) |
|  | 42.5 | 40.0 | | | | |
| Wells | 5(235) | — | — | — | — | 5(235) |
|  | 47.0 | | | | | |
| York | 2(120) | 2(130) | — | — | — | 4(250) |
|  | 60.0 | 65.0 | | | | |
| Total Saco River to York area | | | | | | 14(695) |
| Berwick | 2(100) | 1(15) | 2(120) | — | — | 5(235) |
|  | 50.0 | 15.0 | 60.0 | | | |
| Kittery | 4(185) | 13(185) | 3(220) | 2(140) | 2(250) | 24(1,190) |
|  | 46.3 | 30.4 | 73.3 | 70.0 | 125.0 | |
| Total Maine side of Piscataqua River | | | | | | 29(1,425) |

Table 7 (*cont.*)

| Construction site | Sloop | Schooner | Brig | Snow | Ship | Total |
|---|---|---|---|---|---|---|
| Total Maine Province | 17(810) | 21(775) | 7(460) | 2(140) | 2(250) | 49(2,435) |
| | 47.6 | 36.9 | 65.7 | 70.0 | 125.0 | |
| Haverhill | — | 2(64) | — | — | — | 2(64) |
| | | 32.0 | | | | |
| Newbury | 8(360) | 10(439) | 4(255) | — | 2(230) | 24(1,284) |
| | 45.0 | 43.9 | 63.8 | | 115.0 | |
| Salisbury | 2(75) | 1(40) | — | 1(90) | — | 4(205) |
| | 37.5 | 40.0 | | 90.0 | | |
| Total Merrimack River area | | | | | | 30(1,553) |
| Elsewhere in Massachusetts | 2(85) | 1(35) | — | 2(115) | — | 5(235) |
| | 42.5 | 35.0 | | 57.5 | | |
| Total Massachusetts | 29(1,330) | 35(1,353) | 11(715) | 5(345) | 4(480) | 84(4,223) |
| | 45.9 | 38.7 | 65.0 | 69.0 | 120.0 | |
| Connecticut | 1(44) | — | — | — | — | 1(44) |
| | 44.0 | | | | | |
| Maryland | — | 1(15) | — | — | — | 1(15) |
| | | 15.0 | | | | |
| Virginia | — | 1(40) | — | — | — | 1(40) |
| | | 40.0 | | | | |
| North Carolina | 1(30) | — | — | — | — | 1(30) |
| | 30.0 | | | | | |
| South Carolina | — | 2(40) | — | — | — | 2(40) |
| | | 20.0 | | | | |
| Total other colonies | | | | | | 6(169) |

Table 7 (*cont.*)

| Vessels entering and clearing | | | |
|---|---|---|---|
| New Hampshire ports | | | % of tonnage |
| New Hampshire–built | 86(5,666) | | 56.3 |
| Massachusetts-built | 84(4,223) | | 42.0 |
| Maine-built | | 49(2,435) | 24.2 |
| Merrimack River–built | | 30(1,553) | 15.4 |
| Other colonial-built | 6(169) | | 1.7 |
| Total | 176(10,058) | | 100.0 |

| Registration | | % of tonnage |
|---|---|---|
| New Hampshire–built vessels | | |
| New Hampshire | 85(5,506) | 97.2 |
| Boston | 1(160) | 2.8 |
| Total | 86(5,666) | 100.0 |
| | | |
| Massachusetts-built vessels (not Maine) | | |
| New Hampshire | 32(1,618) | 90.5 |
| Massachusetts | 2(120) | 6.7 |
| England | (1(50) | 2.8 |
| Total | 35(1,788) | 100.0 |
| | | |
| Maine-built vessels | | |
| New Hampshire | 42(1,990) | 81.7 |
| Boston | 6(405) | 16.6 |
| Antigua | 1(40) | 1.6 |
| Total | 49(2,435) | 99.9 |
| | | |
| Other colonial-built vessels | | |
| South Carolina | 2(40) | 23.7 |
| St. Christopher | 2(84) | 49.7 |
| Rhode Island | 1(15) | 8.9 |
| North Carolina | 1(30) | 17.8 |
| Total | 6(169) | 100.1 |
| Vessels registered in New Hampshire, 1756–57 | | |
| New Hampshire–built | 85(5,506) | 60.4 |
| Massachusetts-built | 74(3,608) | 39.6 |
| Total | 159(9,114) | 100.0 |

Table 8. New Hampshire port records, 1768

| Construction site | Sloop | Schooner | Brig | Snow | Ship | Total |
|---|---|---|---|---|---|---|
| New Hampshire | 9(418) | 25(1,290) | 37(2,935) | 3(260) | 13(1,550) | 87(6,453) |
| | 35.4 | 51.6 | 79.4 | 86.7 | 119.2 | |
| Massachusetts | | | | | | |
| Penobscot to Cape Elizabeth | 1(30) | 2(85) | — | — | — | 3(115) |
| | 30.0 | 42.5 | | | | |
| Wells | 1(40) | 1(61) | — | — | — | 2(101) |
| | 40.0 | 61.0 | | | | |
| York | — | 3(120) | — | — | — | 3(120) |
| | | 40.0 | | | | |
| Total Saco River to York area | | | | | | 5(221) |
| Berwick | — | 1(60) | 1(80) | — | — | 2(140) |
| | | 60.0 | 80.0 | | | |
| Kittery | — | 3(100) | 1(85) | — | — | 4(185) |
| | | 33.3 | 85.0 | | | |
| Total Maine side of Piscataqua River | | | | | | 6(325) |
| Total Maine Province | 2(70) | 14(426) | 2(165) | — | — | 14(661) |
| | 35.0 | 42.6 | 82.5 | | | |
| Pepperellborough | — | — | — | — | 1(90) | 1(90) |
| | | | | | 90.0 | |
| Almsbury | — | 1(50) | 1(60) | — | 3(370) | 5(480) |
| | | 50.0 | 60.0 | | 123.3 | |
| Newbury | 1(50) | 6(290) | 8(550) | — | 5(550) | 20(1,440) |
| | 50.0 | 48.3 | 68.8 | | 110.0 | |
| Salisbury | — | 2(92) | 4(335) | — | 1(140) | 7(567) |
| | | 46.0 | 83.5 | | 140.0 | |

Table 8 (*cont.*)

| Construction site | Sloop | Schooner | Brig | Snow | Ship | Total |
|---|---|---|---|---|---|---|
| Total Merrimack River area | 1(50) | 9(432) | 13(945) | — | 10(1,150) | 33(2,577) |
| | 50.0 | 48.0 | 72.7 | | 115.0 | |
| Elsewhere in Massachusetts | — | 3(73) | — | — | — | 3(73) |
| | | 24.3 | | | | |
| Total Massachusetts | 3(120) | 22(931) | 15(1,110) | — | 10(1,150) | 50(3,311) |
| | 40.0 | 43.3 | 74.0 | | 115.0 | |
| Other colonies | 2(55) | — | — | — | — | 2(55) |
| | 27.5 | | | | | |

| | | | % of tonnage |
|---|---|---|---|
| Vessels entering and clearing New Hampshire ports | | | |
| New Hampshire–built | 87(6,453) | | 65.7 |
| Massachusetts-built | 50(3,311) | | 33.7 |
| Maine-built* | | 14(611) | 6.7 |
| Merrimack-built | | 33(2,577) | 26.2 |
| Other colonial-built | | 2(55) | 0.6 |
| Total | | 139(9,819) | 100.0 |

| | | % of tonnage |
|---|---|---|
| Registration | | |
| New Hampshire–built vessels | | |
| New Hampshire | 85(6,298) | 97.6 |
| Salem | 1(70) | 1.1 |
| England | 1(85) | 1.3 |
| Total | 87(6,453) | 100.0 |
| | | |
| Massachusetts-built vessels (not Maine) | | |
| New Hampshire | 33(2,520) | 95.1 |
| Boston | 1(25) | 1.0 |
| Rhode Island | 1(15) | 0.6 |
| England | 1(90) | 3.4 |
| Total | 36(2,650) | 100.1 |

*Although covering only a one-year period instead of two, this table shows an increase in both New Hampshire and Merrimack River tonnage and a sharp decline in Maine shipbuilding.

Table 8 (*cont.*)

| Registration | | % of tonnage |
|---|---|---|
| Maine-built vessels | | |
| New Hampshire | 12(591) | 89.4 |
| Boston | 2(70) | 10.6 |
| Total | 16(661) | 100.0 |
| | | |
| Other colonial-built vessels | | |
| Philadelphia | 1(40) | |
| New Jersey | 1(15) | |
| Total | 2(55) | |
| Vessels registered in New Hampshire, 1768 | | |
| New Hampshire–built | 85(6,298) | 67.0 |
| Massachusetts-built | 45(3,111) | 33.1 |
| Total | 90(9,409) | 100.1 |

Table 9. Rhode Island shipping register, 1776–78: Vessels built 1764–75

| Construction site | Sloop | Schooner | Brig | Snow | Ship | Total |
|---|---|---|---|---|---|---|
| Rhode Island | 26(730) | 1(40) | 5(250) | — | — | 32(1,020) |
| | 28.1 | 40.0 | 50.0 | | | |
| Massachusetts | 18(409) | 4(210) | 4(230) | | 2(280) | 28(1,129) |
| | 22.7 | 52.5 | 57.5 | | 140.0 | |
| Connecticut | 1(18) | — | — | — | — | 1(18) |
| | 18.0 | | | | | |
| Virginia | — | 1(15) | — | — | — | 1(15) |
| | | 15.0 | | | | |
| North Carolina | — | — | 1(140) | — | — | 1(140) |
| | | | 140.0 | | | |
| Georgia | — | — | 1(40) | — | — | 1(40) |
| | | | 40.0 | | | |

| Vessels registered in Rhode Island | | % of tonnage |
|---|---|---|
| Rhode Island–built | 32(1,020) | 43.2 |
| Massachusetts-built | 28(1,129) | 47.8 |
| Other colonial-built | 4(213) | 9.0 |
| Total | 64(2,362) | 100.0 |

Table 10. Philadelphia shipping register, 1726–36

| Construction site | Shallop | Sloop | Schooner | Brig | Snow | Ship | Total |
|---|---|---|---|---|---|---|---|
| Philadelphia | 4(20) 5.0 | 29(657) 22.7 | 4(44) 11.0 | 19(875) 46.1 | 11(570) 51.8 | 24(1,810) 75.4 | 91(3,976) |
| Chester | 1(10) 10.0 | 2(27) 13.5 | — | 1(35) 35.0 | 1(70) 70.0 | 1(100) 100.0 | 6(242) |
| Bristol | 1(4) 4.0 | 1(25) 25.0 | — | 2(80) 40.0 | — | 2(160) 80.0 | 6(269) |
| Marcus Hook | — | — | — | — | — | 1(130) 130.0 | 1(130) |
| Pennsylvania (location unspecified) | 3(30) 10.0 | 1(10) 10.0 | 1(10) 10.0 | — | 2(90) 45.0 | 2(200) 100.0 | 9(340) |
| Total Pennsylvania | 9(64) 7.1 | 33(719) 21.8 | 5(54) 10.8 | 22(990) 45.0 | 14(730) 52.1 | 30(2,400) 80.0 | 113(4,957) |
| Delaware | 12(113) 9.4 | 15(287) 19.1 | 5(71) 14.2 | 3(110) 36.7 | 1(50) 50.0 | — | 36(631) |

Table 10 (*cont.*)

| Construction site | Shallop | Sloop | Schooner | Brig | Snow | Ship | Total |
|---|---|---|---|---|---|---|---|
| New Jersey | 11(85) 7.7 | 9(141) 15.7 | 1(15) 15.0 | — | 1(70) 70.0 | 2(340) 170.0 | 24(651) |
| New England (colony unspecified) | — | — | — | 1(60) 60.0 | — | 1(60) 60.0 | 2(120) |
| New Hampshire | — | 1(10) 10.0 | — | — | — | — | 1(10) |
| Boston | — | — | — | — | — | 1(80) 80.0 | 1(80) |
| Rhode Island | — | — | 1(10) 10.0 | — | — | — | 1(10) |
| Connecticut | 2(11) 5.5 | 2(37) 18.5 | — | 1(60) 60.0 | — | — | 5(108) |
| Maryland | 1(6) 6.0 | — | — | — | — | — | 1(6) |

Table 10 (*cont.*)

| Construction site | Shallop | Sloop | Schooner | Brig | Snow | Ship | Total |
|---|---|---|---|---|---|---|---|
| Virginia | 1(7) | 2(65) | — | — | — | — | 3(72) |
| | 7.0 | 32.5 | | | | | |
| Total non-Pennsylvania | 27(222) | 29(540) | 7(96) | 5(230) | 2(120) | 4(480) | 74(1,688) |
| | 8.2 | 18.6 | 13.7 | 46.0 | 60.0 | 120.0 | |

| Vessels registered in Philadelphia | % of tonnage |
|---|---|
| Pennsylvania-built | 113(4,957) | 74.6 |
| Philadelphia-built | 91(3,976) | 59.8 |
| Other | 22(981) | 14.8 |
| Delaware-built | 36(631) | 9.5 |
| New Jersey-built | 24(651) | 9.8 |
| New England-built | 10(328) | 4.9 |
| Virginia- and Maryland-built | 4(78) | 1.2 |
| Total | 187(6,645) | 100.0 |

Table 11. Philadelphia shipping register, 1734–41

| Construction site | Shallop | Sloop | Schooner | Brig | Snow | Ship | Total |
|---|---|---|---|---|---|---|---|
| Philadelphia | 2(22) 11.0 | 9(252) 28.0 | 2(47) 23.5 | 12(648) 54.0 | 13(681) 52.4 | 27(2,471) 91.5 | 65(4,121) |
| Chester | 3(32) 10.7 | 2(40) 20.0 | — | 4(165) 41.3 | — | — | 9(237) |
| Bristol | 1(9) 9.0 | — | — | 1(50) 50.0 | — | 2(200) 100.0 | 4(259) |
| Marcus Hook | — | — | — | 1(50) 50.0 | 1(80) 80.0 | — | 2(130) |
| Pennsylvania (location unspecified) | — | — | — | — | — | 1(80) 80.0 | 1(80) |
| Total Pennsylvania | 6(63) 10.5 | 11(292) 26.5 | 2(47) 23.5 | 18(913) 50.7 | 14(761) 54.4 | 30(2,751) 91.7 | 81(4,827) |
| Delaware | 8(96) 12.0 | 17(278) 16.4 | 1(20) 20.0 | 3(168) 56.0 | 2(90) 45.0 | 4(340) 85.0 | 35(992) |

Table 11 (*cont.*)

| Construction site | Shallop | Sloop | Schooner | Brig | Snow | Ship | Total |
|---|---|---|---|---|---|---|---|
| New Jersey | 5(63) 12.6 | 7(94) 13.4 | 1(24) 24.0 | 1(25) 25.0 | 3(205) 68.3 | 3(260) 86.7 | 20(671) |
| Maine | — | — | 1(30) 30.0 | — | — | — | 1(30) |
| Boston | — | — | — | — | — | 1(100) 100.0 | 1(100) |
| Maryland | — | — | 1(35) 35.0 | — | — | — | 1(35) |
| Virginia | — | 2(52) 26.0 | — | — | — | — | 2(52) |
| Total non-Pennsylvania | 13(159) 12.2 | 26(424) 16.3 | 4(109) 27.3 | 4(193) 48.3 | 5(295) 59.0 | 8(700) 87.5 | 60(1,880) |

Table 11 (*cont.*)

| Vessels registered in Philadelphia | | % of tonnage |
|---|---|---|
| Pennsylvania-built | 81(4,827) | 71.9 |
| Philadelphia-built | 65(4,121) | 61.4 |
| Other | 16(706) | 10.5 |
| Delaware-built | 35(992) | 14.8 |
| New Jersey-built | 20(671) | 10.0 |
| Massachusetts-built | 2(130) | 1.9 |
| Virginia- and Maryland-built | 3(87) | 1.3 |
| Total | 141(6,707) | 99.9 |

Table 12. Philadelphia shipping register, 1742–47

| Construction site | Shallop | Sloop | Schooner | Brig | Snow | Ship | Total |
|---|---|---|---|---|---|---|---|
| Philadelphia | 3(34) 11.3 | 13(312) 24.0 | 11(249) 22.6 | 26(1,500) 57.7 | 8(530) 66.3 | 33(3,510) 106.4 | 94(6,135) |
| Chester | 2(16) 8.0 | 1(10) 10.0 | 1(20) 20.0 | 5(235) 47.0 | 1(70) 70.0 | — | 10(351) |
| Marcus Hook | — | 1(25) 25.0 | 1(14) 14.0 | 5(280) 56.0 | — | 2(180) 90.0 | 9(499) |
| Kensington | — | — | 1(60) 60.0 | 1(60) 60.0 | — | — | 2(120) |
| Bristol | — | 1(25) 25.0 | — | — | — | — | 1(25) |
| Pennsylvania (location unspecified) | — | 1(30) 30.0 | — | — | — | 1(100) 100.0 | 2(130) |
| Total Pennsylvania | 5(50) 10.0 | 17(402) 23.6 | 14(343) 24.5 | 37(2,075) 56.1 | 9(600) 66.7 | 36(3,790) 105.3 | 118(7,260) |

Table 12 (*cont.*)

| Construction site | Shallop | Sloop | Schooner | Brig | Snow | Ship | Total |
|---|---|---|---|---|---|---|---|
| Delaware | 4(58) 14.5 | 19(357) 18.8 | 9(114) 12.7 | 8(422) 52.8 | — | 2(210) 105.0 | 42(1,161) |
| New Jersey | 2(24) 12.0 | 6(80) 13.3 | 2(41) 20.5 | 1(60) 60.0 | 2(150) 75.0 | 2(267) 133.5 | 15(622) |
| New England (colony unspecified) | — | 2(22) 11.0 | 2(97) 48.5 | — | — | — | 4(119) |
| New Hampshire | — | — | 1(40) 40.0 | 2(130) 65.0 | — | — | 3(170) |
| Massachusetts | — | 2(70) 35.0 | 1(20) 20.0 | 1(50) 50.0 | 3(305) 101.7 | — | 7(445) |
| Rhode Island | — | 3(72) 24.0 | — | — | — | — | 3(72) |
| Connecticut | — | 1(30) 30.0 | 1(35) 35.0 | — | 1(90) 90.0 | — | 3(155) |

Table 12 (*cont.*)

| Construction site | Shallop | Sloop | Schooner | Brig | Snow | Ship | Total |
|---|---|---|---|---|---|---|---|
| New York | — | 1(15) | — | 2(70) | — | — | 3(85) |
|  |  | 15.0 |  | 35.0 |  |  |  |
| Maryland | 1(11) | — |  |  | — | — | 1(11) |
|  | 11.0 |  |  |  |  |  |  |
| South Carolina | — | 1(15) |  |  | — | — | 1(15) |
|  |  | 15.0 |  |  |  |  |  |
| Total non-Pennsylvania | 7(93) | 35(661) | 16(347) | 14(732) | 6(545) | 4(477) | 82(2,855) |
|  | 13.3 | 18.9 | 21.7 | 52.3 | 90.8 | 119.3 |  |

| Vessels registered in Philadelphia | | % of tonnage |
|---|---|---|
| Pennsylvania-built | 118(7,260) | 71.8 |
| Philadelphia-built | 94(6,135) | 60.7 |
| Other | 24(1,125) | 11.1 |
| Delaware-built | 42(1,161) | 11.5 |
| New Jersey-built | 15(622) | 6.1 |
| New England-built | 20(961) | 9.5 |
| Other colonial-built | 5(111) | 1.1 |
| Total | 200(10,115) | 100.0 |

Table 13. Philadelphia shipping register, 1748–52

| Construction site | Shallop | Sloop | Schooner | Brig | Snow | Ship | Total |
|---|---|---|---|---|---|---|---|
| Philadelphia | 1(8) 8.0 | 17(293) 17.2 | 11(210) 19.1 | 39(2,049) 52.5 | 34(2,568) 75.5 | 64(6,150) 96.1 | 166(11,278) |
| Marcus Hook | — | 7(118) 16.9 | 1(15) 15.0 | 4(180) 45.0 | 3(195) 65.0 | 5(420) 84.0 | 20(928) |
| Kensington | | — | 1(25) 25.0 | — | — | — | 1(25) |
| Chester | | — | 1(20) 20.0 | — | — | — | 1(20) |
| Pennsylvania (location unspecified) | — | 2(42) 21.0 | — | 1(60) 60.0 | 3(160) 53.3 | — | 6(262) |
| Total Pennsylvania | 1(8) 8.0 | 26(453) 17.4 | 14(270) 19.3 | 44(2,289) 52.0 | 40(2,923) 73.1 | 69(6,570) 95.2 | 194(12,513) |
| Delaware | 2(20) 10.0 | 21(407) 19.4 | 12(117) 9.8 | 8(355) 44.4 | 4(260) 65.0 | 2(145) 72.5 | 49(1,304) |

Table 13 *(cont.)*

| Construction site | Shallop | Sloop | Schooner | Brig | Snow | Ship | Total |
|---|---|---|---|---|---|---|---|
| New Jersey | 1(15) <br> 15.0 | 23(398) <br> 17.3 | 1(5) <br> 5.0 | 2(95) <br> 47.5 | — | 1(200) <br> 200.0 | 28(713) |
| New England (colony unspecified) | — | 5(123) <br> 24.6 | 1(20) <br> 20.0 | — | 1(60) <br> 60.0 | — | 7(203) |
| Massachusetts | — | 3(90) <br> 30.0 | 2(70) <br> 35.0 | 2(100) <br> 50.0 | 1(120) <br> 120.0 | 1(180) <br> 180.0 | 9(560) |
| Rhode Island | — | 1(30) <br> 30.0 | — | — | — | — | 1(30) |
| Connecticut | — | 1(25) <br> 25.0 | — | 1(45) <br> 45.0 | — | — | 2(70) |
| New York | — | 2(45) <br> 22.5 | — | — | 1(100) <br> 100.0 | 1(100) <br> 100.0 | 4(245) |
| Maryland | — | 3(32) <br> 10.7 | 2(50) <br> 25.0 | — | 2(130) <br> 65.0 | 3(230) <br> 76.7 | 10(442) |

Table 13 (cont.)

| Construction site | Shallop | Sloop | Schooner | Brig | Snow | Ship | Total |
|---|---|---|---|---|---|---|---|
| Virginia | — | 3(65) | — | — | — | — | 3(65) |
|  |  | 21.7 |  |  |  |  |  |
| North Carolina | — | 1(20) | — | — | — | — | 1(20) |
|  |  | 20.0 |  |  |  |  |  |
| South Carolina | — | — | 1(15) | — | — | — | 1(15) |
|  |  |  | 15.0 |  |  |  |  |
| Total non-Pennsylvania | 3(35) | 63(1,235) | 19(277) | 13(595) | 9(670) | 8(855) | 115(3,667) |
|  | 11.7 | 19.6 | 14.6 | 45.8 | 74.4 | 106.9 |  |

Vessels registered in Philadelphia

| | | % of tonnage |
|---|---|---|
| Pennsylvania-built | 194(12,513) | 77.3 |
| Philadelphia-built | 166(11,278) | 69.7 |
| Other | 28(1,235) | 7.6 |
| Delaware-built | 49(1,304) | 8.1 |
| New Jersey-built | 28(713) | 4.4 |
| New England-built | 19(863) | 5.3 |
| Other colonial-built | 19(787) | 4.9 |
| Total | 309(16,180) | 100.0 |

Table 14. Philadelphia shipping register, 1753–57

| Construction site | Shallop | Sloop | Schooner | Brig | Snow | Ship | Total |
|---|---|---|---|---|---|---|---|
| Philadelphia | — | 18(370) 20.6 | 6(95) 15.8 | 33(1,867) 56.6 | 17(1,133) 66.6 | 46(4,605) 100.1 | 120(8,070) |
| Marcus Hook | — | 7(71) 10.1 | 2(50) 25.0 | 6(285) 47.5 | 1(100) 100.0 | 5(340) 68.0 | 21(846) |
| Pennsylvania (location unspecified) | — | 2(55) 52.5 | — | — | — | 1(100) 100.0 | 3(155) |
| Total Pennsylvania | — | 27(496) 18.4 | 8(145) 18.1 | 39(2,152) 55.2 | 18(1,233) 68.5 | 52(5,045) 97.0 | 144(9,071) |
| Delaware | — | 17(270) 15.9 | 8(81) 10.1 | 2(80) 40.0 | 1(60) 60.0 | 1(80) 80.0 | 29(571) |
| New Jersey | — | 17(273) 16.1 | 1(10) 10.0 | 5(260) 52.0 | — | — | 23(543) |
| New England (colony unspecified) | — | — | 1(8) 8.0 | — | — | 1(70) 70.0 | 2(78) |

Table 14 (*cont.*)

| Construction site | Shallop | Sloop | Schooner | Brig | Snow | Ship | Total |
|---|---|---|---|---|---|---|---|
| New Hampshire | — | — | 1(20) 20.0 | 2(120) 60.0 | — | — | 3(140) |
| Massachusetts | — | 8(235) 29.4 | 9(325) 36.1 | 2(65) 32.5 | — | — | 19(625) |
| Rhode Island | — | 2(40) 20.0 | 1(20) 20.0 | — | — | — | 3(60) |
| Connecticut | — | 4(125) 31.3 | — | — | — | 1(60) 60.0 | 5(185) |
| New York | — | 4(110) 27.5 | — | — | — | — | 4(110) |
| Maryland | — | 1(50) 50.0 | 2(67) 33.5 | — | — | — | 3(117) |
| Virginia | — | 2(35) 17.5 | 2(35) 17.5 | — | — | — | 4(70) |

Table 14 (*cont.*)

| Construction site | Shallop | Sloop | Schooner | Brig | Snow | Ship | Total |
|---|---|---|---|---|---|---|---|
| South Carolina | — | — | 1(15) | — | — | — | 1(15) |
|  |  |  | 15.0 |  |  |  |  |
| Total non-Pennsylvania | — | 55(1,138) | 26(581) | 11(525) | 1(60) | 3(210) | 96(2,514) |
|  |  | 20.7 | 22.3 | 47.7 | 60.0 | 70.0 |  |

| Vessels registered in Philadelphia | | % of tonnage |
|---|---|---|
| Pennsylvania-built | 144(9,017) | 78.3 |
| Philadelphia-built | 120(8,070) | 69.7 |
| Other | 24(1,001) | 8.6 |
| Delaware-built | 29(571) | 4.9 |
| New Jersey-built | 23(543) | 4.7 |
| New England-built | 32(1,088) | 8.4 |
| Other colonial-built | 12(312) | 2.7 |
| Total | 240(11,585) | 100.0 |

Table 15. Philadelphia shipping register, 1758–65

| Construction site | Shallop | Sloop | Schooner | Brig | Snow | Ship | Total |
|---|---|---|---|---|---|---|---|
| Philadelphia | 1(5) | 19(498) | 13(278) | 47(2,970) | 9(630) | 66(6,735) | 155(11,116) |
|  | 5.0 | 26.2 | 21.4 | 63.2 | 70.0 | 102.0 |  |
| Marcus Hook | — | 2(19) | 1(25) | 3(120) | — | 3(200) | 9(364) |
|  |  | 9.5 | 25.0 | 40.0 |  | 66.7 |  |
| Kensington | — | — | — | — | — | 1(80) | 1(80) |
|  |  |  |  |  |  | 80.0 |  |
| Pennsylvania (location unspecified) | — | — | 1(7) | — | 1(60) | 2(250) | 4(317) |
|  |  |  | 7.0 |  | 60.0 | 125.0 |  |
| Total Pennsylvania | 1(5) | 21(517) | 15(310) | 50(3,090) | 10(690) | 72(7,265) | 169(11,877) |
|  | 5.0 | 24.6 | 20.7 | 61.8 | 69.0 | 100.9 |  |
| Delaware | — | 20(283) | 23(352) | 4(190) | — | 5(415) | 52(1,240) |
|  |  | 14.2 | 15.3 | 47.5 |  | 83.0 |  |
| New Jersey | — | 11(185) | 4(55) | 6(280) | — | — | 21(520) |
|  |  | 16.8 | 13.8 | 46.7 |  |  |  |

Table 15 (*cont.*)

| Construction site | Shallop | Sloop | Schooner | Brig | Snow | Ship | Total |
|---|---|---|---|---|---|---|---|
| New England (colony unspecified) | — | 4(145) 36.3 | — | 5(235) 47.0 | — | — | 9(380) |
| New Hampshire | — | — | — | 3(240) 80.0 | — | 1(80) 80.0 | 4(320) |
| Massachusetts | — | 16(580) 36.3 | 13(478) 36.8 | 9(485) 53.9 | 3(185) 61.7 | 2(220) 110.0 | 43(1,948) |
| Rhode Island | — | 3(75) 25.0 | 1(25) 25.0 | 1(25) 25.0 | 2(120) 60.0 | — | 7(245) |
| Connecticut | — | 3(42) 14.0 | — | 2(65) 32.5 | 1(70) 70.0 | — | 6(177) |
| Total New England | — | 26(842) 32.4 | 14(503) 35.9 | 20(1,050) 52.5 | 6(375) 62.5 | 3(300) 100.0 | 69(3,070) |
| New York | — | 2(45) 22.5 | — | 1(50) 50.0 | 3(275) 91.7 | 2(120) 60.0 | 8(490) |

Table 15 (*cont.*)

| Construction site | Shallop | Sloop | Schooner | Brig | Snow | Ship | Total |
|---|---|---|---|---|---|---|---|
| Maryland | — | 1(30) 30.0 | 2(90) 45.0 | 4(190) 47.5 | 3(220) 73.3 | 1(120) 120.0 | 11(650) |
| Virginia | — | 4(85) 21.3 | 4(105) 26.3 | 5(260) 52.0 | — | — | 13(450) |
| North Carolina | — | 1(25) 25.0 | — | 2(80) 40.0 | — | — | 3(105) |
| Total non-Pennsylvania | — | 65(1,495) 23.0 | 47(1,105) 23.5 | 42(2,100) 50.0 | 12(870) 72.5 | 11(995) 90.5 | 177(6,525) |

| Vessels registered in Philadelphia | | % of tonnage |
|---|---|---|
| Pennsylvania-built | 169(11,877) | 64.5 |
|   Philadelphia-built | 155(11,116) | 60.4 |
|   Other | 14(761) | 4.1 |
| Delaware-built | 52(1,240) | 6.7 |
| New Jersey-built | 21(520) | 2.8 |
| Massachusetts-built | 43(1,948) | 10.6 |
| Other New England-built | 26(1,122) | 6.1 |
| Other colonial-built | 35(1,695) | 9.2 |
| Total | 346(18,402) | 99.9 |

Table 16. Philadelphia shipping register, 1766–70

| Construction site | Shallop | Sloop | Schooner | Brig | Snow | Ship | Total |
|---|---|---|---|---|---|---|---|
| Philadelphia | — | 15(325) 21.7 | 15(409) 27.3 | 51(3,390) 66.5 | 14(1,205) 86.1 | 51(5,890) 115.5 | 146(11,219) |
| Kensington | — | 1(15) 15.0 | 2(22) 11.0 | 4(258) 64.5 | 3(250) 83.3 | 1(90) 90.0 | 11(635) |
| Marcus Hook | — | — | 2(45) 22.5 | 2(60) 30.0 | — | — | 4(105) |
| Pennsylvania (location unspecified) | — | 3(45) 15.0 | 3(50) 16.7 | 2(105) 52.5 | — | 1(90) 90.0 | 9(290) |
| Total Pennsylvania | — | 19(385) 20.3 | 22(526) 23.9 | 59(3,813) 64.6 | 17(1,455) 85.6 | 53(6,070) 114.5 | 170(12,249) |
| Delaware | — | 14(297) 21.2 | 20(374) 18.7 | 8(385) 48.1 | — | 3(310) 103.3 | 45(1,366) |
| New Jersey | — | 24(415) 17.3 | 3(23) 7.7 | 6(280) 46.7 | — | 1(100) 100.0 | 34(818) |

Table 16 *(cont.)*

| Construction site | Shallop | Sloop | Schooner | Brig | Snow | Ship | Total |
|---|---|---|---|---|---|---|---|
| New England (colony unspecified) | — | 3(100) 100.0 | 4(150) 37.5 | 7(315) 45.0 | — | 3(340) 113.3 | 17(905) |
| New Hampshire | — | — | 1(30) 30.0 | — | — | 1(180) 180.0 | 2(210) |
| Massachusetts | — | 14(550) 39.3 | 11(364) 33.1 | 14(780) 55.7 | 2(180) 90.0 | 5(540) 108.0 | 46(2,414) |
| Rhode Island | — | — | — | — | 1(60) 60.0 | 2(210) 105.0 | 3(270) |
| Connecticut | — | 5(112) 56.0 | 2(39) 19.5 | 2(80) 40.0 | 1(80) 80.0 | — | 10(311) |
| Total New England | — | 22(762) 34.6 | 18(583) 32.4 | 23(1,175) 51.1 | 4(320) 80.0 | 11(1,270) 115.5 | 78(4,110) |
| New York | — | 5(90) 18.0 | — | — | — | — | 5(90) |

Table 16 (*cont.*)

| Construction site | Shallop | Sloop | Schooner | Brig | Snow | Ship | Total |
|---|---|---|---|---|---|---|---|
| Maryland | — | 8(230) | 5(144) | 5(275) | 2(300) | 4(564) | 24(7,513) |
| | | 28.8 | 28.8 | 55.0 | 150.0 | 141.0 | |
| Virginia | — | 3(95) | 8(275) | 1(30) | — | — | 12(400) |
| | | 31.7 | 34.4 | 30.0 | | | |
| North Carolina | — | — | 7(192) | 6(350) | — | 3(384) | 16(926) |
| | | | 27.4 | 58.3 | | 128.0 | |
| Total non-Pennsylvania | — | 76(1,889) | 61(1,591) | 49(2,495) | 6(620) | 22(2,628) | 214(9,223) |
| | | 24.9 | 26.1 | 50.9 | 103.3 | 119.5 | |

Vessels registered in Philadelphia

| | | % of tonnage |
|---|---|---|
| Pennsylvania-built | 170(12,249) | 57.0 |
| Philadelphia-built | 146(11,219) | 52.2 |
| Other | 24(1,030) | 4.8 |
| Delaware-built | 45(1,366) | 6.4 |
| New Jersey-built | 34(818) | 3.8 |
| Massachusetts-built | 46(2,414) | 11.2 |
| Other New England-built | 32(1,696) | 7.9 |
| Other colonial-built | 57(2,929) | 13.6 |
| Total | 384(21,472) | 99.9 |

Table 17. Philadelphia shipping register, 1771–75

| Construction site | Shallop | Sloop | Schooner | Brig | Snow | Ship | Total |
|---|---|---|---|---|---|---|---|
| Philadelphia | 1(15) | 12(255) | 18(538) | 35(2,245) | 6(500) | 104(15,180) | 176(18,733) |
|  | 15.0 | 21.3 | 29.9 | 64.1 | 83.3 | 146.0 |  |
| Kensington | — | — | 2(50) | 4(325) | — | 1(200) | 7(575) |
|  |  |  | 25.0 | 81.3 |  | 200.0 |  |
| Pennsylvania (location unspecified) | — | 5(115) | 1(15) | 6(230) | — | 1(90) | 13(450) |
|  |  | 23.0 | 15.0 | 38.3 |  | 90.0 |  |
| Total Pennsylvania | 1(15) | 17(370) | 21(603) | 45(2,800) | 6(500) | 106(15,470) | 196(19,758) |
|  | 15.0 | 21.8 | 28.7 | 62.2 | 83.3 | 145.9 |  |
| Delaware | 1(10) | 6(72) | 18(434) | 7(345) | — | 2(260) | 34(1,121) |
|  | 10.0 | 12.0 | 24.1 | 49.3 |  | 130.0 |  |
| New Jersey | — | 20(330) | 7(200) | 7(470) | 1(80) | 2(310) | 37(1,390) |
|  |  | 16.5 | 28.6 | 67.1 | 80.0 | 155.0 |  |
| New England (colony unspecified) | — | 5(187) | 10(425) | 16(965) | — | 2(105) | 33(1,682) |
|  |  | 37.4 | 42.5 | 60.3 |  | 52.5 |  |

Table 17 (*cont.*)

| Construction site | Shallop | Sloop | Schooner | Brig | Snow | Ship | Total |
|---|---|---|---|---|---|---|---|
| New Hampshire | — | — | — | 1(90) 90.0 | — | 1(80) 80.0 | 1(170) |
| Massachusetts | — | 18(640) 35.6 | 21(861) 41.0 | 16(945) 59.1 | 1(90) 90.0 | 2(270) 135.0 | 58(2,806) |
| Rhode Island | — | 4(130) 32.5 | 1(34) 34.0 | 6(330) 55.0 | — | 1(80) 80.0 | 12(574) |
| Connecticut | — | 9(281) 31.2 | 4(142) 35.5 | 5(235) 47.0 | — | 1(95) 95.0 | 19(753) |
| Total New England | — | 36(1,238) 34.4 | 36(1,462) 40.6 | 44(2,565) 58.3 | 1(90) 90.0 | 7(630) 90.0 | 124(5,985) |
| New York | — | 4(65) 16.3 | 4(60) 15.0 | 4(205) 51.3 | — | — | 12(330) |
| Maryland | — | 2(50) 25.0 | 3(150) 50.0 | 5(350) 70.0 | — | — | 10(550) |

Table 17 (*cont.*)

| Construction site | Shallop | Sloop | Schooner | Brig | Snow | Ship | Total |
|---|---|---|---|---|---|---|---|
| Virginia | — | 7(173) | 6(152) | 3(342) | — | — | 16(667) |
|  |  | 24.7 | 25.3 | 114.0 |  |  |  |
| North Carolina | — | — | 2(66) | 8(475) | 1(60) | 2(175) | 13(776) |
|  |  |  | 33.0 | 59.4 | 60.0 | 87.5 |  |
| South Carolina | — | — | — | 3(130) | — | — | 3(130) |
|  |  |  |  | 43.3 |  |  |  |
| Total non-Pennsylvania | 1(10) | 75(1,928) | 76(2,524) | 81(4,882) | 3(230) | 13(1,375) | 249(10,949) |
|  | 10.0 | 25.7 | 33.2 | 60.3 | 76.7 | 105.8 |  |

| Vessels registered in Philadelphia | | % of tonnage |
|---|---|---|
| Pennsylvania-built | 196(19,758) | 64.3 |
| Philadelphia-built | 176(18,733) | 61.0 |
| Other | 20(1,025) | 3.3 |
| Delaware-built | 34(1,121) | 3.7 |
| New Jersey–built | 37(1,390) | 4.5 |
| Massachusetts-built | 58(2,806) | 9.1 |
| Other New England–built | 66(3,179) | 10.4 |
| Other colonial-built | 54(2,453) | 8.0 |
| Total | 445(30,707) | 100.0 |

Table 18. Annapolis port records to 1747

| Construction site | Sloop | Schooner | Brig | Snow | Ship | Total |
|---|---|---|---|---|---|---|
| New England | 18(680) | 15(510) | 8(470) | 7(605) | 30(4,540) | 78(6,805) |
| | 37.8 | 34.0 | 58.8 | 86.4 | 151.3 | |
| Maryland | 11(290) | 8(138) | 1(35) | 2(180) | 2(200) | 24(843) |
| | 26.4 | 17.3 | 35.0 | 90.0 | 100.0 | |
| Virginia | 5(94) | 3(32) | 1(60) | 1(100) | 1(100) | 11(386) |
| | 18.8 | 10.7 | 60.0 | 100.0 | 100.0 | |
| Pennsylvania | — | — | — | — | 3(310) | 3(310) |
| | | | | | 103.3 | |
| New Jersey | 1(40) | — | — | — | — | 1(40) |
| | 40.0 | | | | | |
| New York | 2(45) | — | — | — | 1(120) | 3(165) |
| | 22.5 | | | | 120.0 | |
| North Carolina | — | 2(18) | — | — | — | 2(18) |
| | | 9.0 | | | | |
| South Carolina | — | 1(15) | — | — | — | 1(15) |
| | | 15.0 | | | | |
| Total | 37(1,149) | 29(713) | 10(565) | 10(885) | 37(5,270) | 123(8,582) |
| | 31.1 | 24.6 | 56.5 | 88.5 | 142.4 | |

| Vessels entering and clearing Annapolis | | % of tonnage |
|---|---|---|
| New England–built | 78(6,805) | 79.3 |
| Maryland-built | 24(843) | 9.8 |
| Virginia-built | 11(386) | 4.5 |
| Middle colonies–built | 7(515) | 6.0 |
| Carolina-built | 3(33) | 0.4 |
| Total | 123(8,582) | 100.0 |

Table 19. Annapolis port records to 1747

| Registration | Sloop | Schooner | Brig | Snow | Ship | Total |
|---|---|---|---|---|---|---|
| New England–built vessels | | | | | | |
| Boston | 15(580) | 8(275) | 4(220) | 1(100) | 6(900) | 34(2,075) |
| | 38.7 | 34.4 | 105.0 | 100.0 | 150.0 | |
| Other Massachusetts ports | 3(95) | — | — | — | 1(180) | 4(275) |
| | 37.7 | | | | 180.0 | |
| Total Massachusetts | | | | | | 38(2,350) |
| New Hampshire | 1(40) | 1(20) | — | — | 1(160) | 3(220) |
| | 40.0 | 20.0 | | | 160.0 | |
| Rhode Island | 2(60) | — | 1(60) | — | — | 2(120) |
| | 30.0 | | 60.0 | | | |
| Total New England | | | | | | 44(2,690) |
| London | — | — | 2(120) | 1(100) | 14(2,130) | 17(2,350) |
| | | | 60.0 | 100.0 | 152.1 | |
| Bideford | — | — | — | 4(305) | 3(300) | 7(605) |
| | | | | 76.3 | 100.0 | |
| Other British ports | — | — | 1(70) | 1(100) | 4(490) | 6(660) |
| | | | 70.0 | 100.0 | 122.5 | |
| Total Great Britain | | | | | | 30(3,615) |
| Maryland | — | 2(80) | — | — | 1(380) | 4(460) |
| | | 40.0 | | | 380.0 | |
| West Indies | — | 1(40) | — | — | — | 1(40) |
| | | 40.0 | | | | |

Table 19 (*cont.*)

| Registration | Sloop | Schooner | Brig | Snow | Ship | Total |
|---|---|---|---|---|---|---|
| **Maryland-built vessels** | | | | | | |
| Maryland | 10(280) | 8(138) | 1(35) | — | 2(200) | 21(653) |
| | 28.0 | 17.3 | 35.0 | | 100.0 | |
| North Carolina | 1(10) | — | — | — | — | 1(10) |
| | 10.0 | | | | | |
| Great Britain | — | — | — | 2(180) | — | 2(180) |
| | | | | 90.0 | | |
| **Virginia-built vessels** | | | | | | |
| Virginia | 3(65) | 3(32) | 1(60) | — | — | 7(157) |
| | 21.7 | 10.7 | 60.0 | | | |
| Maryland | 1(14) | — | — | — | — | 1(14) |
| | 14.0 | | | | | |
| Rhode Island | 1(15) | — | — | — | — | 1(15) |
| | 15.0 | | | | | |
| Great Britain | — | — | — | 1(100) | 1(100) | 2(200) |
| | | | | 100.0 | 100.0 | |
| **Other colonial-built vessels** | | | | | | |
| Rhode Island | 2(45) | — | — | — | — | 2(45) |
| | 22.5 | | | | | |
| Pennsylvania | 1(40) | — | — | — | 1(90) | 2(130) |
| | 40.0 | | | | 90.0 | |
| North Carolina | — | 3(33) | — | — | — | 3(33) |
| | | 11.0 | | | | |
| Great Britain | — | — | — | — | 3(340) | 3(340) |
| | | | | | 113.3 | |

Table 19 (*cont.*)

| Vessels entering and clearing Annapolis | | % of tonnage |
|---|---|---|
| Maryland-registered | 25(1,127) | 13.1 |
| Great Britain–registered | 37(4,335) | 50.5 |
| London-registered | 20(2,690) | 31.3 |
| Other | 20(1,645) | 19.2 |
| New England-registered | 47(2,750) | 32.1 |
| Boston-registered | 34(2,075) | 24.2 |
| Other | 13(675) | 7.9 |
| Other | 14(370) | 4.3 |
| Total | 123(8,582) | 100.0 |
| Maryland-registered vessels | | |
| New England–built | 3(460) | 40.8 |
| Maryland-built | 21(653) | 57.9 |
| Virginia-built | 1(14) | 1.2 |
| Total | 25(1,127) | 99.9 |

Table 20. Annapolis port records, 1748–51

| Construction site | Sloop | Schooner | Brig | Snow | Ship | Total |
|---|---|---|---|---|---|---|
| Maryland | 23(703) | 11(394) | 8(660) | 6(580) | 13(1,915) | 61(4,252) |
| | 30.6 | 35.8 | 82.5 | 96.7 | 147.3 | |
| New England | 17(695) | 9(355) | 6(380) | 8(825) | 6(940) | 46(3,195) |
| | 40.9 | 39.4 | 63.3 | 103.1 | 156.7 | |
| Virginia | 14(472) | 10(293) | 1(80) | 3(320) | 2(420) | 30(1,585) |
| | 33.7 | 29.3 | 80.0 | 106.7 | 210.0 | |
| Pennsylvania | 5(108) | 1(20) | 2(200) | 7(475) | 4(355) | 20(1,158) |
| | 21.6 | 20.0 | 66.7 | 67.9 | 88.8 | |
| New York | 4(95) | — | — | 2(180) | 1(90) | 7(365) |
| | 23.8 | | | 90.0 | 90.0 | |
| New Jersey | 2(35) | — | — | — | — | 2(35) |
| | 17.5 | | | | | |
| Total | 65(2,108) | 31(1,062) | 18(1,320) | 26(2,380) | 26(3,720) | 166(10,590) |
| | 32.4 | 34.3 | 73.3 | 91.5 | 143.1 | |

| Vessels entering and clearing Annapolis | | % of tonnage |
|---|---|---|
| Maryland-built | 61(4,252) | 40.2 |
| New England–built | 46(3,195) | 30.2 |
| Virginia-built | 30(1,585) | 15.0 |
| Pennsylvania-built | 20(1,158) | 10.9 |
| Other colonial-built | 9(400) | 3.8 |
| Total | 166(10,590) | 100.1 |

Table 21. Annapolis port records, 1748–51

| Registration | Sloop | Schooner | Brig | Snow | Ship | Total |
|---|---|---|---|---|---|---|
| **Maryland-built vessels** | | | | | | |
| Maryland | 20(597) | 11(394) | 8(660) | 5(480) | 8(1,250) | 52(3,381) |
| | 29.9 | 35.8 | 82.5 | 96.0 | 156.3 | |
| Virginia | 1(60) | — | — | — | — | 1(60) |
| | 60.0 | | | | | |
| Pennsylvania | — | — | — | — | 1(75) | 1(75) |
| | | | | | 75.0 | |
| North Carolina | 1(16) | — | — | — | — | 1(16) |
| | 16.0 | | | | | |
| West Indies | 1(30) | — | — | — | — | 1(30) |
| | 30.0 | | | | | |
| London | — | — | — | 1(100) | 2(280) | 3(380) |
| | | | | 100.0 | 140.0 | |
| Other British ports | — | — | — | — | 2(310) | 2(310) |
| | | | | | 155.0 | |
| **New England–built vessels** | | | | | | |
| Boston | 8(345) | 6(225) | 3(230) | 1(150) | 3(430) | 21(1,380) |
| | 43.1 | 37.5 | 76.7 | 150.0 | 143.3 | |
| Other Massachusetts ports | — | 2(80) | — | — | — | 2(80) |
| | | 40.0 | | | | |
| Total Massachusetts | | | | | | 23(1,460) |
| New Hampshire | 1(70) | — | — | — | 1(190) | 2(260) |
| | 70.0 | | | | | |
| Rhode Island | 4(90) | — | — | — | — | 4(90) |
| | 22.5 | | | | | |

Table 21 (*cont.*)

| Registration | Sloop | Schooner | Brig | Snow | Ship | Total |
|---|---|---|---|---|---|---|
| Connecticut | 1(45) | — | — | 1(50) | — | 2(95) |
| | 45.0 | | | 50.0 | | |
| Total New England | | | | | | 31(1,905) |
| Pennsylvania | — | — | 1(40) | — | — | 1(40) |
| | | | 40.0 | | | |
| Maryland | 3(145) | — | — | 1(75) | — | 4(220) |
| | 48.3 | | | 75.0 | | |
| West Indes | — | 1(50) | 1(60) | 1(80) | — | 3(190) |
| | | 50.0 | 60.0 | 80.0 | | |
| London | — | — | 1(50) | 3(370) | 2(320) | 7(740) |
| | | | 50.0 | 123.3 | 160.0 | |
| Other British ports | — | — | — | 1(100) | — | 1(100) |
| | | | | 100.0 | | |
| Total Great Britain | | | | | | 8(840) |
| Virginia-built vessels | | | | | | |
| Virginia | 14(472) | 10(293) | 1(80) | 1(100) | — | 26(945) |
| | 33.7 | 29.3 | 80.0 | 100.0 | | |
| London | — | — | — | 2(220) | 2(420) | 4(640) |
| | | | | 110.0 | 210.0 | |
| Other colonial-built vessels | | | | | | |
| Pennsylvania | 4(95) | — | 2(150) | 6(415) | 2(125) | 14(785) |
| | 23.8 | | 75.0 | 69.2 | 62.5 | |
| New York | 2(45) | — | — | 2(180) | — | 4(225) |
| | 22.5 | | | 90.0 | | |
| Maryland | 2(33) | — | — | 1(60) | — | 3(93) |
| | 16.5 | | | 60.0 | | |

Table 21 (*cont.*)

| Registration | Sloop | Schooner | Brig | Snow | Ship | Total |
|---|---|---|---|---|---|---|
| Other colonies | 3(65) | 1(20) | — | — | — | 4(85) |
| | 21.7 | 20.0 | | | | |
| West Indies | — | — | 1(50) | — | — | 1(50) |
| | | | 50.0 | | | |
| Great Britain | — | — | — | — | 3(320) | 3(320) |
| | | | | | 106.7 | |

| Vessels entering and clearing Annapolis | | % of tonnage | |
|---|---|---|---|
| Maryland-registered | 59(3,694) | 34.9 | |
| Great Britain–registered | 19(2,490) | 23.5 | |
| London-registered | 15(1,930) | | 18.2 |
| Other | 4(560) | | 5.3 |
| New England–registered | 31(1,905) | 18.0 | |
| Boston-registered | 21(1,380) | | 13.0 |
| Other | 10(525) | | 5.0 |
| Virginia-registered | 27(1,005) | 9.5 | |
| Pennsylvania-registered | 16(900) | 8.5 | |
| Other colonial-registered | 14(596) | 5.6 | |
| Total | 166(10,590) | 100.0 | |

| Maryland-registered vessels | | |
|---|---|---|
| Maryland-built | 52(3,381) | 91.5 |
| New England–built | 4(220) | 6.0 |
| Pennsylvania-built | 3(93) | 2.5 |
| Total | 59(3,694) | 100.0 |

Table 22. Annapolis port records, 1752–55

| Construction site | Sloop | Schooner | Brig | Snow | Ship | Total |
|---|---|---|---|---|---|---|
| Maryland | 17(482) | 12(451) | 8(540) | 6(555) | 10(1,625) | 53(3,653) |
| | 28.4 | 37.6 | 67.5 | 92.5 | 162.5 | |
| New England | 13(448) | 25(845) | 4(370) | 5(380) | 6(891) | 53(2,934) |
| | 34.5 | 33.8 | 92.5 | 76.0 | 148.5 | |
| Virginia | 6(160) | 8(220) | 3(400) | — | — | 17(780) |
| | 26.7 | 27.5 | 133.3 | | | |
| Pennsylvania | — | 2(40) | 1(180) | — | 7(720) | 11(940) |
| | | 20.0 | 90.0 | | 102.9 | |
| New York | 3(85) | — | — | — | 2(200) | 5(285) |
| | 28.3 | | | | 100.0 | |
| New Jersey | — | — | 2(110) | 1(110) | — | 3(220) |
| | | | 55.0 | 110.0 | | |
| North Carolina | — | — | 1(90) | — | 1(132) | 2(222) |
| | | | 90.0 | | 132.0 | |
| Total | 39(1,175) | 47(1,556) | 20(1,690) | 12(1,045) | 26(3,568) | 144(9,034) |
| | 30.1 | 33.1 | 84.5 | 87.1 | 137.2 | |

| Vessels entering and clearing Annapolis | | % of tonnage |
|---|---|---|
| Maryland-built | 53(3,653) | 40.4 |
| New England–built | 53(2,934) | 32.5 |
| Virginia-built | 17(780) | 8.6 |
| Pennsylvania-built | 11(940) | 10.4 |
| Other colonial-built | 10(727) | 8.0 |
| Total | 144(9,034) | 99.9 |

Table 23. Annapolis port records, 1752–55

| Registration | Sloop | Schooner | Brig | Snow | Ship | Total |
|---|---|---|---|---|---|---|
| **Maryland-built vessels** | | | | | | |
| Maryland | 16(462) | 10(366) | 7(460) | 6(555) | 8(1,300) | 47(3,143) |
| | 28.9 | 36.6 | 65.7 | 92.5 | 162.5 | |
| New York | 1(20) | — | — | — | — | 1(20) |
| | 20.0 | | | | | |
| Massachusetts | — | 1(40) | — | — | — | 1(40) |
| | | 40.0 | | | | |
| West Indies | — | 1(45) | — | — | — | 1(45) |
| | | 45.0 | | | | |
| London | — | — | 1(80) | — | 2(325) | 3(405) |
| | | | 80.0 | | 162.5 | |
| **New England–built vessels** | | | | | | |
| Boston | 3(130) | 6(213) | 1(50) | — | — | 10(393) |
| | 43.3 | 35.5 | 50.0 | | | |
| Other Massachusetts ports | — | 8(315) | — | — | — | 8(315) |
| | | 39.4 | | | | |
| Total Massachusetts | | | | | | 18(708) |
| New Hampshire | 2(90) | 2(45) | — | — | 1(140) | 5(275) |
| | 45.0 | 22.5 | | | 140.0 | |
| Rhode Island | 3(83) | 4(82) | — | — | — | 7(165) |
| | 27.7 | 20.5 | | | | |
| Connecticut | 1(20) | — | — | — | — | 1(20) |
| | 20.0 | | | | | |
| Total New England | | | | | | 31(1,168) |
| Maryland | 1(15) | 2(65) | 2(220) | — | — | 5(300) |
| | 15.0 | 32.5 | 110.0 | | | |

Table 23 (*cont.*)

| Registration | Sloop | Schooner | Brig | Snow | Ship | Total |
|---|---|---|---|---|---|---|
| New York | 1(20) | — | — | — | — | 1(20) |
|  | 20.0 |  |  |  |  |  |
| Halifax | — | 1(35) | — | — | — | 1(35) |
|  |  | 35.0 |  |  |  |  |
| West Indies | 2(90) | 2(90) | — | 1(65) | — | 5(245) |
|  | 45.0 | 45.0 |  | 65.0 |  |  |
| London | — | — | — | 2(170) | 4(631) | 6(801) |
|  |  |  |  | 85.0 | 157.8 |  |
| Other British ports | — | — | 1(100) | 2(145) | 1(120) | 4(365) |
|  |  |  | 100.0 | 72.5 | 120.0 |  |
| **Virginia-built vessels** |  |  |  |  |  |  |
| Virginia | 2(80) | 4(140) | — | 2(250) | — | 8(470) |
|  | 40.0 | 35.0 |  | 125.0 |  |  |
| Maryland | 2(50) | 3(50) | — | — | — | 5(100) |
|  | 25.0 | 16.7 |  |  |  |  |
| Other colonies | 2(30) | — | — | — | — | 2(30) |
|  | 15.0 |  |  |  |  |  |
| West Indies | — | 1(30) | — | — | — | 1(30) |
|  |  | 30.0 |  |  |  |  |
| Guernsey | — | — | — | 1(150) | — | 1(150) |
|  |  |  |  | 150.0 |  |  |
| **Pennsylvania-built vessels** |  |  |  |  |  |  |
| Pennsylvania | — | 2(40) | — | — | 4(400) | 6(440) |
|  |  | 20.0 |  |  | 100.0 |  |
| Maryland | — | — | 1(90) | — | — | 1(90) |
|  |  |  | 90.0 |  |  |  |

Table 23 *(cont.)*

| Registration | Sloop | Schooner | Brig | Snow | Ship | Total |
|---|---|---|---|---|---|---|
| West Indies | — | — | 1(90) | — | — | 1(90) |
| | | | 90.0 | | | |
| London | — | — | — | — | 3(320) | 3(320) |
| | | | | | 106.7 | |
| **New York–built vessels** | | | | | | |
| New York | 3(85) | — | — | — | 1(100) | 4(185) |
| | 28.3 | | | | 100.0 | |
| Great Britain | — | — | — | — | 1(100) | 1(100) |
| | | | | | 100.0 | |
| **Other colonial-built vessels** | | | | | | |
| Maryland | — | — | 2(110) | — | 1(132) | 3(242) |
| | | | 55.0 | | 132.0 | |
| Great Britain | — | — | 1(90) | 1(110) | — | 2(200) |
| | | | 90.0 | 110.0 | | |

| Vessels entering and clearing Annapolis | | % of tonnage | |
|---|---|---|---|
| Maryland-registered | 61(3,875) | 42.9 | |
| Great Britain–registered | 20(2,341) | 25.9 | |
| London-registered | 12(1,526) | | 16.9 |
| Other | 8(815) | | 9.0 |
| New England–registered | 32(1,208) | 13.4 | |
| Boston-Registered | 10(393) | | 4.4 |
| Other | 22(815) | | 9.0 |
| Virginia-registered | 8(470) | 5.2 | |
| Pennsylvania-registered | 6(440) | 4.9 | |
| West Indies–registered | 8(410) | 4.5 | |
| Other colonial-registered | 9(290) | 3.2 | |
| Total | 144(9,034) | 100.0 | |

| Maryland-registered vessels | | | |
|---|---|---|---|
| Maryland-built | 47(3,143) | 81.1 | |
| New England–built | 5(300) | 7.7 | |
| Virginia-built | 5(100) | 2.6 | |
| Other | 4(332) | 8.6 | |
| Total | 61(3,875) | 100.0 | |

Table 24. Annapolis port records, 1756–59

| Construction site | Sloop | Schooner | Brig | Snow | Ship | Total |
|---|---|---|---|---|---|---|
| Maryland | 10(309) | 12(495) | 4(270) | 5(440) | 10(1,980) | 41(3,494) |
|  | 30.9 | 41.3 | 67.5 | 88.0 | 198.0 |  |
| New England | 10(376) | 8(202) | 4(310) | 4(390) | 6(850) | 32(2,128) |
|  | 37.6 | 25.3 | 77.5 | 97.5 | 141.7 |  |
| Pennsylvania | 1(10) | — | 4(300) | — | 7(810) | 12(1,120) |
|  | 10.0 |  | 75.0 |  | 115.7 |  |
| Virginia | 2(45) | 2(40) | 1(40) | 1(100) | 1(140) | 7(365) |
|  | 22.5 | 20.0 | 40.0 | 100.0 | 140.0 |  |
| Other colonies | 3(42) | 1(8) | — | — | — | 4(50) |
|  | 14.0 | 8.0 |  |  |  |  |
| Total | 26(782) | 23(745) | 13(920) | 10(930) | 24(3,780) | 96(7,157) |
|  | 30.1 | 32.4 | 70.8 | 93.0 | 157.5 |  |

| Vessels entering and clearing Annapolis |  | % of tonnage |
|---|---|---|
| Maryland-built | 41(3,494) | 48.8 |
| New England–built | 32(2,128) | 29.7 |
| Pennsylvania-built | 12(1,120) | 15.6 |
| Virginia-built | 7(365) | 5.1 |
| Other colonial-built | 4(50) | 0.7 |
| Total | 96(7,157) | 99.9 |

Table 25. Annapolis port records, 1756–59

| Registration | Sloop | Schooner | Brig | Snow | Ship | Total |
|---|---|---|---|---|---|---|
| Maryland-built vessels | | | | | | |
| Maryland | 9(289) | 12(495) | 4(270) | 4(370) | 8(1,630) | 37(3,054) |
|  | 32.1 | 41.3 | 67.5 | 92.5 | 203.8 | |
| Virginia | 1(20) | — | — | — | — | 1(20) |
|  | 20.0 | | | | | |
| Pennsylvania | — | — | — | 1(70) | — | 1(70) |
|  | | | | 70.0 | | |
| London | — | — | — | — | 1(200) | 1(200) |
|  | | | | | 200.0 | |
| Other British ports | — | — | — | — | 1(150) | 1(150) |
|  | | | | | 150.0 | |
| New England–built vessels | | | | | | |
| Boston | 2(110) | — | — | 2(210) | — | 4(320) |
|  | 55.0 | | | 105.0 | | |
| Other Massachusetts ports | 2(70) | 2(70) | — | — | 1(110) | 5(250) |
|  | 35.0 | 35.0 | | | 110.0 | |
| Total Massachusetts | | | | | | 9(570) |
| New Hampshire | 1(50) | — | — | — | 1(230) | 2(280) |
|  | 50.0 | | | | 230.0 | |
| Rhode Island | 3(86) | 3(52) | 1(50) | 1(50) | — | 8(238) |
|  | 28.7 | 17.3 | 50.0 | 50.0 | | |
| Connecticut | — | 1(30) | — | — | — | 1(30) |
|  | | 30.0 | | | | |
| Total New England | | | | | | 20(1,118) |

Table 25 (*cont.*)

| Registration | Sloop | Schooner | Brig | Snow | Ship | Total |
|---|---|---|---|---|---|---|
| New York | 1(30) | 1(20) | 1(60) | — | — | 3(110) |
| | 30.0 | 20.0 | 60.0 | | | |
| Maryland | — | — | 2(200) | — | — | 2(200) |
| | | | 100.0 | | | |
| West Indies | 1(30) | 1(30) | — | — | — | 2(60) |
| | 30.0 | 30.0 | | | | |
| London | — | — | — | — | 3(410) | 3(410) |
| | | | | | 136.7 | |
| Other British ports | — | — | — | 1(130) | 1(100) | 2(230) |
| | | | | 130.0 | 100.0 | |
| **Pennsylvania-built vessels** | | | | | | |
| Pennsylvania | — | — | — | — | 2(200) | 2(200) |
| | | | | | 100.0 | |
| New York | 1(10) | — | — | — | — | 1(10) |
| | 10.0 | | | | | |
| Maryland | — | — | — | — | 2(280) | 2(280) |
| | | | | | 140.0 | |
| London | — | — | 1(50) | — | 2(230) | 3(280) |
| | | | 50.0 | | 115.0 | |
| Other British ports | — | — | 3(250) | — | 1(100) | 4(350) |
| | | | 83.3 | | 100.0 | |
| **Other colonial-built vessels** | | | | | | |
| Virginia | 1(15) | 2(40) | — | — | — | 3(55) |
| | 15.0 | 20.0 | | | | |

Table 25 (*cont.*)

| Registration | Sloop | Schooner | Brig | Snow | Ship | Total |
|---|---|---|---|---|---|---|
| Other colonies | 3(42) | 1(8) | — | — | — | 4(50) |
|  | 14.0 | 8.0 | | | | |
| West Indies | 1(30) | — | 1(40) | — | — | 2(70) |
|  | 30.0 | | 40.0 | | | |
| London | — | — | — | — | 1(140) | 1(140) |
|  | | | | | 140.0 | |
| Other British ports | — | — | — | 1(100) | — | 1(100) |
|  | | | | 100.0 | | |

| Vessels entering and clearing Annapolis | | % of tonnage |
|---|---|---|
| Maryland-registered | 41(3,534) | 49.4 |
| Great Britain–registered | 16(1,860) | 26.0 |
| London-registered | 8(1,030) | 14.4 |
| Other | 8(830) | 11.6 |
| New England–registered | 20(1,118) | 15.6 |
| Boston-registered | 4(320) | 4.5 |
| Other | 16(798) | 11.1 |
| Other colonial-registered | 19(645) | 9.0 |
| Total | 96(7,157) | 100.0 |

| Maryland-registered vessels | | |
|---|---|---|
| Maryland-built | 37(3,054) | 86.4 |
| Pennsylvania-built | 2(280) | 7.9 |
| New England–built | 2(200) | 5.7 |
| Total | 41(3,534) | 100.0 |

Table 26. Annapolis port records, 1760–63

| Construction site | Sloop | Schooner | Brig | Snow | Ship | Total |
|---|---|---|---|---|---|---|
| Maryland | 23(800) | 28(1,047) | 5(455) | 12(1,223) | 14(2,415) | 82(5,940) |
| | 34.8 | 37.4 | 91.0 | 101.9 | 172.5 | |
| New England | 41(1,572) | 18(776) | 13(920) | 8(770) | 12(1,670) | 92(5,708) |
| | 38.3 | 43.1 | 70.8 | 96.3 | 139.2 | |
| Delaware and Pennsylvania | 5(83) | 3(70) | 6(360) | 3(260) | 7(615) | 24(1,388) |
| | 16.6 | 23.3 | 60.0 | 86.7 | 87.9 | |
| Virginia | 9(247) | 4(155) | 2(170) | 1(80) | 3(570) | 19(1,222) |
| | 27.4 | 38.8 | 85.0 | 80.0 | 190.0 | |
| North Carolina | — | 3(55) | 1(150) | — | — | 4(205) |
| | | 18.3 | 150.0 | | | |
| New York | 2(35) | — | 1(20) | — | 1(70) | 4(125) |
| | 17.5 | | 20.0 | | 70.0 | |
| Other colonies | — | 2(55) | — | — | — | 2(55) |
| | | 27.5 | | | | |
| Total | 80(2,737) | 58(2,158) | 28(2,075) | 24(2,333) | 37(5,340) | 227(14,643) |
| | 34.2 | 37.2 | 74.1 | 97.2 | 144.3 | |

| Vessels entering and clearing Annapolis | | % of tonnage |
|---|---|---|
| Maryland-built | 82(5,940) | 40.6 |
| New England–built | 92(5,708) | 39.0 |
| Pennsylvania-built | 24(1,388) | 9.5 |
| Virginia-built | 19(1,222) | 8.3 |
| Other colonial-built | 10(385) | 2.6 |
| Total | 227(14,643) | 100.0 |

Table 27. Annapolis port records, 1760–63

| Registration | Sloop | Schooner | Brig | Snow | Ship | Total |
|---|---|---|---|---|---|---|
| **Maryland-built vessels** | | | | | | |
| Maryland | 19(690) | 26(950) | 5(445) | 11(1,143) | 12(2,070) | 73(5,308) |
| | 36.3 | 36.5 | 91.0 | 103.9 | 172.5 | |
| Virginia | 1(30) | 1(50) | — | — | — | 2(80) |
| | 30.0 | 50.0 | | | | |
| Pennsylvania | 1(35) | 1(47) | — | — | — | 2(82) |
| | 35.0 | 47.0 | | | | |
| New England | 2(45) | — | — | — | — | 2(45) |
| | 22.5 | | | | | |
| London | — | — | — | — | 1(200) | 1(200) |
| | | | | | 200.0 | |
| Other British ports | — | — | — | 1(80) | 1(145) | 2(225) |
| | | | | 80.0 | 145.0 | |
| **New England–built vessels** | | | | | | |
| Boston | 10(435) | 9(400) | 3(275) | 1(100) | 1(130) | 24(1,340) |
| | 43.5 | 44.4 | 91.7 | 100.0 | 130.0 | |
| Other Massachusetts ports | 5(210) | 2(90) | 1(50) | — | — | 8(350) |
| | 42.0 | 45.0 | 50.0 | | | |
| Total Massachusetts | | | | | | 32(1,690) |
| New Hampshire | 1(30) | — | 1(60) | — | — | 2(90) |
| | 30.0 | | 60.0 | | | |
| Rhode Island | 15(502) | 1(16) | — | 1(70) | — | 17(588) |
| | 33.5 | 16.0 | | 70.0 | | |
| Connecticut | — | — | — | 1(100) | 1(130) | 2(230) |
| | | | | 100.0 | 130.0 | |
| Total New England | | | | | | 53(2,598) |

Table 27 (*cont.*)

| Registration | Sloop | Schooner | Brig | Snow | Ship | Total |
|---|---|---|---|---|---|---|
| New Jersey | 1(25) | — | — | — | — | 1(25) |
|  | 25.0 |  |  |  |  |  |
| Pennsylvania | — | 1(45) | 3(145) | 2(180) | — | 6(370) |
|  |  | 45.0 | 48.3 | 90.0 |  |  |
| Maryland | 7(295) | 3(175) | — | — | — | 10(470) |
|  | 42.1 | 58.3 |  |  |  |  |
| Virginia | — | — | — | — | 1(130) | 1(130) |
|  |  |  |  |  | 130.0 |  |
| West Indies | 2(75) | 2(50) | 1(70) | — | — | 5(195) |
|  | 37.5 | 25.0 | 70.0 |  |  |  |
| London | — | — | 1(50) | 1(150) | 5(770) | 7(970) |
|  |  |  | 50.0 | 150.0 | 154.0 |  |
| Other British ports | — | — | 3(270) | 2(170) | 4(510) | 9(950) |
|  |  |  | 90.0 | 85.0 | 127.5 |  |

Delaware- and Pennsylvania-built vessels

| Registration | Sloop | Schooner | Brig | Snow | Ship | Total |
|---|---|---|---|---|---|---|
| Delaware and Pennsylvania | 5(83) | 2(50) | 5(250) | 2(120) | 4(385) | 18(888) |
|  | 27.7 | 25.0 | 50.0 | 60.0 | 96.3 |  |
| Virginia | — | 1(20) | — | — | — | 1(20) |
|  |  | 20.0 |  |  |  |  |
| Connecticut | — | — | — | — | 1(70) | 1(70) |
|  |  |  |  |  | 70.0 |  |
| British ports (not London) | — | — | 1(110) | 1(140) | 2(160) | 4(410) |
|  |  |  | 110.0 | 140.0 | 80.0 |  |

Virginia-built vessels

| Registration | Sloop | Schooner | Brig | Snow | Ship | Total |
|---|---|---|---|---|---|---|
| Virginia | 2(42) | 2(45) | 1(60) | — | — | 5(147) |
|  | 21.0 | 22.5 | 60.0 |  |  |  |

Table 27 (cont.)

| Registration | Sloop | Schooner | Brig | Snow | Ship | Total |
|---|---|---|---|---|---|---|
| Maryland | 2(75) | 1(50) | — | — | — | 3(125) |
|  | 37.5 | 50.0 |  |  |  |  |
| Other colonies | 4(100) | — | — | 1(80) | — | 5(180) |
|  | 25.0 |  |  | 80.0 |  |  |
| West Indies | 1(30) | 1(60) | — | — | — | 2(90) |
|  | 30.0 | 60.0 |  |  |  |  |
| London | — | — | — | — | 2(310) | 2(310) |
|  |  |  |  |  | 155.0 |  |
| Other British ports | — | — | 1(110) | — | 1(260) | 2(370) |
|  |  |  | 110.0 |  | 260.0 |  |
| **Other colonial-built vessels** |  |  |  |  |  |  |
| Colonies | 2(35) | 5(110) | 1(20) | — | — | 8(165) |
|  | 17.5 | 21.0 | 20.0 |  |  |  |
| London | — | — | — | — | 1(70) | 1(70) |
|  |  |  |  |  | 70.0 |  |
| Other British ports | — | — | 1(150) | — | — | 1(150) |
|  |  |  | 150.0 |  |  |  |

| Vessels entering and clearing Annapolis |  | % of tonnage |
|---|---|---|
| Maryland-registered | 86(5,903) | 40.3 |
| Great Britain–registered | 29(3,655) | 25.0 |
| London-registered | 11(1,550) | 10.6 |
| Other | 18(2,105) | 14.4 |
| New England–registered | 56(2,713) | 18.5 |
| Boston-registered | 24(1,340) | 9.2 |
| Other | 32(1,373) | 9.4 |
| Pennsylvania-registered | 26(1,340) | 9.2 |
| Other colonial-registered | 30(1,032) | 7.0 |
| Total | 227(14,643) | 100.0 |

| Maryland-registered vessels |  |  |
|---|---|---|
| Maryland-built | 73(5,308) | 89.9 |
| New England–built | 10(470) | 8.0 |
| Virginia-built | 3(125) | 2.1 |
| Total | 86(5,903) | 100.0 |

Table 28. Annapolis port records, 1764–67

| Construction site | Sloop | Schooner | Brig | Snow | Ship | Total |
|---|---|---|---|---|---|---|
| Maryland | 10(284) | 18(683) | 21(1,721) | 8(868) | 16(2,303) | 73(5,859) |
| | 28.4 | 37.9 | 82.0 | 108.5 | 143.9 | |
| New England | 27(947) | 23(905) | 23(1,705) | 4(325) | 13(1,481) | 90(5,363) |
| | 35.1 | 39.3 | 74.1 | 81.3 | 113.9 | |
| Delaware and Pennsylvania | — | 2(23) | 12(921) | 4(410) | 9(970) | 27(2,324) |
| | | 11.5 | 76.8 | 102.5 | 107.8 | |
| Virginia | 5(165) | 9(245) | 4(390) | 2(250) | 3(601) | 23(1,651) |
| | 33.0 | 27.2 | 97.5 | 125.0 | 200.3 | |
| New York | 2(40) | 1(10) | 1(80) | — | 4(530) | 8(660) |
| | 20.0 | 10.0 | 80.0 | | 132.5 | |
| New Jersey | 2(23) | — | — | — | 1(80) | 3(103) |
| | 11.5 | | | | 80.0 | |
| North Carolina | 1(30) | 2(40) | — | 1(60) | 2(285) | 6(415) |
| | 30.0 | 20.0 | | 60.0 | 142.5 | |
| South Carolina | — | 2(75) | 2(95) | — | 1(240) | 5(410) |
| | | 37.5 | 47.5 | | 240.0 | |
| Total | 47(1,489) | 57(1,981) | 63(4,912) | 19(1,913) | 49(6,490) | 235(16,785) |
| | 31.7 | 34.8 | 78.0 | 100.7 | 132.4 | |

| Vessels entering and clearing Annapolis | | % of tonnage |
|---|---|---|
| Maryland-built | 73(5,859) | 34.9 |
| New England–built | 90(5,363) | 32.0 |
| Pennsylvania-built | 27(2,324) | 13.8 |
| Virginia-built | 23(1,651) | 9.8 |
| Other colonial-built | 22(1,588) | 9.5 |
| Total | 235(16,785) | 100.0 |

Table 29. Annapolis port records, 1764–67

| Registration | Sloop | Schooner | Brig | Snow | Ship | Total |
|---|---|---|---|---|---|---|
| **Maryland-built vessels** | | | | | | |
| Maryland | 10(284) | 16(635) | 17(1,428) | 8(868) | 12(1,753) | 63(4,968) |
|  | 28.4 | 39.7 | 84.0 | 108.5 | 146.1 | |
| Philadelphia | — | — | 2(120) | — | — | 2(120) |
|  | | | 60.0 | | | |
| North Carolina | — | 2(48) | — | — | — | 2(48) |
|  | | 24.0 | | | | |
| London | — | — | — | — | 3(430) | 3(430) |
|  | | | | | 143.3 | |
| Other British ports | — | — | 2(173) | — | 1(120) | 3(293) |
|  | | | 86.5 | | 120.0 | |
| **New England–built vessels** | | | | | | |
| Boston | 11(505) | 4(175) | 6(490) | — | — | 21(1,170) |
|  | 45.9 | 43.8 | 81.7 | | | |
| Other Massachusetts ports | 3(120) | 10(445) | 2(175) | — | — | 15(740) |
|  | 40.0 | 44.5 | 87.5 | | | |
| New Hampshire | 2(75) | 1(30) | — | — | 1(100) | 4(205) |
|  | 37.5 | 30.0 | | | | |
| Rhode Island | 7(137) | 2(40) | 1(40) | — | — | 10(217) |
|  | 19.6 | 20.0 | 40.0 | | | |
| Connecticut | 1(20) | — | — | — | — | 1(20) |
|  | 20.0 | | | | | |
| New York | — | — | 3(200) | — | 3(235) | 6(435) |
|  | | | 66.7 | | 78.3 | |
| Pennsylvania | 1(20) | — | — | — | 1(160) | 2(180) |
|  | 20.0 | | | | 160.0 | |

Table 29 (*cont.*)

| Registration | Sloop | Schooner | Brig | Snow | Ship | Total |
|---|---|---|---|---|---|---|
| Maryland | 2(70) | 5(180) | 4(205) | 1(60) | — | 12(515) |
| | 35.0 | 36.0 | 51.3 | 60.0 | | |
| Virginia | — | 1(35) | — | — | — | 1(35) |
| | | 35.0 | | | | |
| West Indies | — | — | 3(185) | — | — | 3(185) |
| | | | 61.7 | | | |
| London | — | — | 1(70) | 1(60) | 4(470) | 6(600) |
| | | | 70.0 | 60.0 | 117.5 | |
| Other British ports | — | — | 3(340) | 2(205) | 4(516) | 9(1,061) |
| | | | 113.3 | 102.5 | 129.0 | |

Delaware- and Pennsylvania-built vessels

| | | | | | | |
|---|---|---|---|---|---|---|
| Pennsylvania | — | 1(8) | 8(596) | 3(270) | 7(760) | 19(1,634) |
| | | 8.0 | 74.5 | 90.0 | 108.6 | |
| North Carolina | — | 1(15) | — | — | — | 1(15) |
| | | 15.0 | | | | |
| West Indies | — | — | 1(65) | — | 1(100) | 2(165) |
| | | | 65.0 | | 100.0 | |
| London | — | — | 1(60) | — | — | 1(60) |
| | | | 60.0 | | | |
| Other British ports | — | — | 2(200) | 1(140) | 1(110) | 4(450) |
| | | | 100.0 | 140.0 | 110.0 | |

Virginia-built vessels

| | | | | | | |
|---|---|---|---|---|---|---|
| Virginia | 5(165) | 5(122) | 1(75) | — | 1(165) | 12(527) |
| | 33.0 | 24.4 | 75.0 | | 165.0 | |
| Maryland | — | 2(90) | — | — | — | 2(90) |
| | | 45.0 | | | | |

Table 29 (*cont.*)

| Registration | Sloop | Schooner | Brig | Snow | Ship | Total |
|---|---|---|---|---|---|---|
| Pennsylvania | — | 1(20) | — | — | — | 1(20) |
| | | 20.0 | | | | |
| West Indies | — | 1(13) | — | — | — | 1(13) |
| | | 13.0 | | | | |
| London | — | — | — | — | 1(236) | 1(236) |
| | | | | | 236.0 | |
| Other British ports | — | — | 3(315) | 2(250) | 1(200) | 6(765) |
| | | | 105.0 | 125.0 | 200.0 | |
| **Other colonial-built vessels** | | | | | | |
| New York | 3(48) | — | — | — | 1(70) | 4(118) |
| | 16.0 | | | | 70.0 | |
| Maryland | — | — | 1(65) | — | — | 1(65) |
| | | | 65.0 | | | |
| North Carolina | 1(30) | 2(40) | — | 1(60) | 1(200) | 5(330) |
| | 30.0 | 20.0 | | 60.0 | 200.0 | |
| Other colonies | 1(15) | 2(40) | 1(30) | — | 1(85) | 5(170) |
| | 15.0 | 20.0 | 30.0 | | 85.0 | |
| West Indies | — | 1(45) | — | — | — | 1(45) |
| | | 45.0 | | | | |
| London | — | — | — | — | 4(700) | 4(700) |
| | | | | | 175.0 | |
| Other British ports | — | — | 1(80) | — | 1(80) | 2(160) |
| | | | 80.0 | | 80.0 | |

Table 29 *(cont.)*

| Vessels entering and clearing Annapolis | | % of tonnage | |
| --- | --- | --- | --- |
| Maryland-registered | 78(5,638) | 33.6 | |
| Great Britain–registered | 39(4,755) | 28.3 | |
| London-registered | 15(2,026) | | 12.1 |
| Other | 24(2,729) | | 16.2 |
| New England–registered | 51(2,352) | 14.0 | |
| Boston-registered | 21(1,170) | | 7.0 |
| Other | 30(2,182) | | 7.0 |
| Pennsylvania-registered | 24(1,954) | 11.6 | |
| Other colonial-registered | 43(2,086) | 12.4 | |
| Total | 235(16,785) | 99.9 | |
| Maryland-registered vessels | | | |
| Maryland-built | 63(4,968) | 88.1 | |
| New England–built | 12(515) | 9.1 | |
| Virginia-built | 2(90) | 1.6 | |
| Other | 1(65) | 1.2 | |
| Total | 78(5,638) | 100.0 | |

Table 30. Annapolis port records, 1768–71

| Construction site | Sloop | Schooner | Brig | Snow | Ship | Total |
|---|---|---|---|---|---|---|
| Maryland | 7(229) | 21(614) | 17(1,380) | 4(465) | 16(2,665) | 65(5,353) |
| | 32.7 | 29.2 | 81.2 | 116.3 | 166.6 | |
| New England | 12(435) | 12(535) | 7(670) | — | 6(750) | 37(2,390) |
| | 36.3 | 44.6 | 95.7 | | 125.0 | |
| Virginia | 7(220) | 6(200) | 6(500) | 1(120) | 1(90) | 21(1,130) |
| | 31.4 | 33.3 | 83.3 | 120.0 | 90.0 | |
| Delaware and Pennsylvania | 2(35) | — | 5(310) | 1(100) | 4(440) | 12(885) |
| | 17.5 | | 62.0 | 100.0 | 110.0 | |
| North Carolina | 1(20) | 5(99) | 1(50) | — | — | 7(169) |
| | 20.0 | 19.8 | 50.0 | | | |
| South Carolina | 1(15) | — | — | — | — | 1(15) |
| | 15.0 | | | | | |
| New York | 1(25) | — | — | — | — | 1(25) |
| | 25.0 | | | | | |
| Total | 31(979) | 44(1,448) | 36(2,910) | 6(685) | 27(3,945) | 144(9,967) |
| | 31.6 | 32.9 | 80.8 | 114.2 | 146.1 | |

| Vessels entering and clearing Annapolis | | % of tonnage |
|---|---|---|
| Maryland-built | 65(5,353) | 53.7 |
| New England–built | 37(2,390) | 24.0 |
| Virginia-built | 21(1,130) | 11.3 |
| Pennsylvania-built | 12(885) | 8.9 |
| Other colonial-built | 9(209) | 2.1 |
| Total | 144(9,967) | 100.0 |

Table 31. Annapolis port records, 1768–71

| Registration | Sloop | Schooner | Brig | Snow | Ship | Total |
|---|---|---|---|---|---|---|
| Maryland-built vessels | | | | | | |
| Maryland | 7(229) | 21(614) | 16(1,300) | 4(465) | 13(2,070) | 61(4,678) |
| | 32.7 | 29.2 | 81.3 | 116.3 | 159.2 | |
| London | — | — | 1(80) | — | 3(595) | 4(675) |
| | | | 80.0 | | 198.3 | |
| New England–built vessels | | | | | | |
| Boston | 3(120) | 4(160) | — | — | — | 7(280) |
| | 40.0 | 40.0 | | | | |
| Other Massachusetts ports | 4(155) | 5(265) | 3(245) | — | — | 12(665) |
| | 38.8 | 53.0 | 81.7 | | | |
| New Hampshire | 2(75) | — | — | — | — | 2(75) |
| | 37.5 | | | | | |
| Rhode Island | 1(40) | 1(20) | — | — | — | 2(60) |
| | 40.0 | 20.0 | | | | |
| Maryland | 2(45) | 1(60) | — | — | — | 3(105) |
| | 22.5 | 60.0 | | | | |
| West Indies | — | 1(30) | — | — | — | 1(30) |
| | | 30.0 | | | | |
| London | — | — | 1(115) | — | 2(200) | 3(315) |
| | | | 115.0 | | 100.0 | |
| Other British ports | — | — | 3(310) | — | 4(550) | 7(860) |
| | | | 103.3 | | 137.5 | |
| Virginia-built vessels | | | | | | |
| Virginia | 7(220) | 4(130) | 1(100) | 1(120) | — | 13(570) |
| | 31.4 | 32.5 | 100.0 | 120.0 | | |

Table 31 (*cont.*)

| Registration | Sloop | Schooner | Brig | Snow | Ship | Total |
|---|---|---|---|---|---|---|
| Maryland | — | 2(70) | 3(245) | — | — | 5(315) |
| | | 35.0 | 81.7 | | | |
| West Indies | — | — | 1(85) | — | — | 1(85) |
| | | | 85.0 | | | |
| London | — | — | 1(70) | — | — | 1(70) |
| | | | 70.0 | | | |
| Other British ports | — | — | — | — | 1(90) | 1(90) |
| | | | | | 90.0 | |

**Delaware- and Pennsylvania-built vessels**

| | | | | | | |
|---|---|---|---|---|---|---|
| Pennsylvania | 20(35) | — | 2(160) | 1(100) | 4(440) | 9(735) |
| | 17.5 | | 80.0 | 100.0 | 110.0 | |
| Maryland | — | — | 2(100) | — | — | 2(100) |
| | | | 50.0 | | | |
| London | — | — | 1(50) | — | — | 1(50) |
| | | | 50.0 | | | |

**Other colonial-built vessels**

| | | | | | | |
|---|---|---|---|---|---|---|
| North Carolina | 2(35) | 3(74) | 1(50) | — | — | 6(159) |
| | 17.5 | 24.7 | 50.0 | | | |
| Maryland | — | 1(15) | — | — | — | 1(15) |
| | | 15.0 | | | | |
| Pensacola | — | 1(10) | — | — | — | 1(10) |
| | | 10.0 | | | | |
| West Indies | 1(25) | — | — | — | — | 1(25) |
| | 25.0 | | | | | |

Table 31 *(cont.)*

| Vessels entering and clearing Annapolis | | % of tonnage |
|---|---|---|
| Maryland-registered | 72(5,213) | 52.3 |
| Great Britain–registered | 17(2,060) | 20.7 |
|   London-registered | 9(1,110) | 11.1 |
|   Other | 8(950) | 9.5 |
| New England–registered | 23(1,080) | 10.8 |
|   Boston-registered | 7(280) | 2.8 |
|   Other | 16(800) | 8.0 |
| Pennsylvania-registered | 9(735) | 7.4 |
| Virginia-registered | 13(570) | 5.7 |
| Other colonial-registered | 10(309) | 3.1 |
| Total | 144(9,967) | 100.0 |
| Maryland-registered vessels | | |
| Maryland-built | 61(4,678) | 89.7 |
| Virginia-built | 5(315) | 6.0 |
| New England–built | 3(105) | 2.0 |
| Other | 3(115) | 2.2 |
| Total | 72(5,213) | 99.9 |

Table 32. Annapolis port records, 1772–75

| Construction site | Sloop | Schooner | Brig | Snow | Ship | Total |
|---|---|---|---|---|---|---|
| Maryland | 3(75) | 11(349) | 9(604) | — | 23(4,368) | 46(5,396) |
| | 25.0 | 31.7 | 67.1 | | 189.9 | |
| New England | 7(165) | 19(868) | 13(1,082) | 1(100) | 6(705) | 46(2,920) |
| | 23.6 | 45.7 | 83.2 | 100.0 | 117.6 | |
| Pennsylvania | — | — | 1(80) | — | 5(710) | 6(790) |
| | | | 80.0 | | 142.0 | |
| Virginia | 6(180) | 9(274) | — | — | — | 15(454) |
| | 30.0 | 30.4 | | | | |
| North Carolina | 1(16) | 2(50) | — | — | — | 3(66) |
| | 16.0 | 25.0 | | | | |
| New Jersey | 1(15) | — | — | — | — | 1(15) |
| | 15.0 | | | | | |
| Total | 18(451) | 41(1,541) | 23(1,766) | 1(100) | 34(5,783) | 117(9,641) |
| | 25.1 | 37.6 | 76.8 | 100.0 | 170.1 | |

| Vessels entering and clearing Annapolis | | % of tonnage |
|---|---|---|
| Maryland-built | 46(5,396) | 56.0 |
| New England–built | 46(2,920) | 30.3 |
| Pennsylvania-built | 6(790) | 8.2 |
| Virginia-built | 15(454) | 4.7 |
| Other colonial-built | 4(81) | 0.8 |
| Total | 117(9,641) | 100.0 |

Table 33. Annapolis port records, 1772–75

| Registration | Sloop | Schooner | Brig | Snow | Ship | Total |
|---|---|---|---|---|---|---|
| Maryland-built vessels | | | | | | |
| Maryland | 3(75) | 11(349) | 9(604) | — | 22(4,168) | 45(5,196) |
| | 25.0 | 31.7 | 67.1 | | 189.5 | |
| London | — | — | — | — | 1(200) | 1(200) |
| | | | | | 200.0 | |
| New England–built vessels | | | | | | |
| Boston | 1(35) | 7(368) | — | — | — | 8(403) |
| | 35.0 | 52.6 | | | | |
| Other Massachusetts ports | 2(60) | 4(195) | 4(303) | 1(100) | 1(105) | 12(763) |
| | 30.0 | 48.8 | 75.8 | 100.0 | 105.0 | |
| New Hampshire | 1(20) | — | 4(360) | — | — | 5(380) |
| | 20.0 | | 90.0 | | | |
| Rhode Island | 2(35) | — | — | — | 1(90) | 3(125) |
| | 17.5 | | | | 90.0 | |
| Connecticut | 1(15) | — | 1(49) | — | — | 2(64) |
| | 15.0 | | 49.0 | | | |
| Maryland | — | 5(197) | 2(180) | — | — | 7(377) |
| | | 39.4 | 90.0 | | | |
| North Carolina | — | 2(70) | — | — | — | 2(70) |
| | | 35.0 | | | | |
| South Carolina | — | 1(38) | — | — | — | 1(38) |
| | | 38.0 | | | | |
| West Indies | — | — | 1(90) | — | — | 1(90) |
| | | | 90.0 | | | |
| London | — | — | — | — | 1(140) | 1(140) |
| | | | | | 140.0 | |

Table 33 (*cont.*)

| Registration | Sloop | Schooner | Brig | Snow | Ship | Total |
|---|---|---|---|---|---|---|
| Other British ports | — | — | 1(100) | — | 3(370) | 4(470) |
| | | | 100.0 | | 123.3 | |
| **Pennsylvania-built vessels** | | | | | | |
| Pennsylvania | — | — | 1(80) | — | 4(510) | 5(590) |
| | | | 80.0 | | 127.5 | |
| London | — | — | — | — | 1(200) | 1(200) |
| | | | | | 200.0 | |
| **Virginia-built vessels** | | | | | | |
| Virginia | 5(140) | 6(179) | — | — | — | 11(319) |
| | 28.0 | 29.8 | | | | |
| Maryland | 1(40) | 3(95) | — | — | — | 4(135) |
| | 40.0 | 31.7 | | | | |
| **Other colonial-built vessels** | | | | | | |
| North Carolina | 1(16) | 2(50) | — | — | — | 3(66) |
| | 16.0 | 25.0 | | | | |
| Pennsylvania | 1(15) | — | — | — | — | 1(15) |
| | 15.0 | | | | | |

| Vessels entering and clearing Annapolis | | % of tonnage | |
|---|---|---|---|
| Maryland-registered | 56(5,708) | 59.2 | |
| New England–registered | 30(1,735) | 18.0 | |
|   Boston-registered | 8(403) | | 4.2 |
|   Other | 22(1,332) | | 13.8 |
| Great Britain–registered | 7(1,010) | 10.5 | |
|   London-registered | 3(540) | | 5.6 |
|   Other | 4(470) | | 4.9 |
| Pennsylvania-registered | 6(605) | 6.3 | |
| Other colonial-registered | 18(583) | 6.0 | |
| Total | 117(9,641) | 100.0 | |
| **Maryland-registered vessels** | | | |
| Maryland-built | 45(5,196) | 91.0 | |
| New England–built | 7(377) | 6.6 | |
| Virginia-built | 4(135) | 2.4 | |
| Total | 56(5,708) | 100.0 | |

Table 34. Register of vessels trading with North Carolina, 1725–51: Vessels built 1710–39

| Construction site | Sloop | Schooner | Brig | Snow | Ship | Total |
|---|---|---|---|---|---|---|
| New Hampshire | 4(120) | 9(215) | — | — | 1(60) | 14(395) |
| | 30.0 | 23.9 | | | 60.0 | |
| Massachusetts | 65(2,161) | 29(813) | 5(225) | 1(70) | — | 100(3,269) |
| | 33.2 | 28.0 | 45.0 | 70.0 | | |
| Rhode Island | 6(103) | 3(55) | — | — | — | 9(158) |
| | 17.2 | 18.3 | | | | |
| Connecticut | 15(344) | 1(30) | — | — | — | 16(374) |
| | 22.9 | 30.0 | | | | |
| New York | 16(245) | — | — | — | — | 16(245) |
| | 15.3 | | | | | |
| New Jersey | 14(188) | — | — | — | — | 14(188) |
| | 13.4 | | | | | |
| Pennsylvania and Delaware | 3(43) | 1(5) | — | — | — | 4(48) |
| | 14.3 | 5.0 | | | | |
| Maryland | 5(40) | 1(20) | — | — | — | 6(60) |
| | 8.0 | 20.0 | | | | |
| Virginia | 10(90) | — | — | — | — | 10(90) |
| | 9.0 | | | | | |
| North Carolina | 24(561) | 9(86) | 3(205) | — | 2(290) | 38(1,142) |
| | 23.4 | 9.6 | 68.3 | | 145.0 | |
| South Carolina | — | 2(24) | — | — | — | 2(24) |
| | | 12.0 | | | | |
| Total | 162(3,895) | 55(1,248) | 8(430) | 1(70) | 3(350) | 229(5,993) |
| | 24.0 | 22.7 | 53.8 | 70.0 | 116.7 | |

Table 34 (*cont.*)

| Vessels trading with North Carolina | | % of tonnage |
|---|---|---|
| New England–built | 139(4,196) | 70.0 |
| Massachusetts-built | 100(3,269) | 54.5 |
| New York-, New Jersey-, Pennsylvania-, and Delaware-built | 34(481) | 8.0 |
| Maryland- and Virginia-built | 16(150) | 2.5 |
| North Carolina–built | 38(1,142) | 19.1 |
| South Carolina–built | 2(24) | 0.4 |
| Total | 229(5,993) | 100.0 |

Table 35. Register of vessels trading with North Carolina, 1725–51: Origin of vessels built in Massachusetts, 1710–39

| Construction site | Sloop* | Schooner | Brig | Snow | Ship | Total |
|---|---|---|---|---|---|---|
| Maine Province | 5(190) | 3(90) | — | — | — | 8(280) |
| | 38.0 | 30.0 | | | | |
| Haverhill | 1(40) | 1(50) | — | — | — | 2(90) |
| | 40.0 | 50.0 | | | | |
| Newbury | 9(355) | 3(60) | 2(95) | 1(70) | — | 15(580) |
| | 39.4 | 20.0 | 47.5 | 70.0 | | |
| Salisbury | — | 2(85) | — | — | — | 2(85) |
| | | 42.5 | | | | |
| Total Merrimack River | | | | | | 19(755) |
| Salem | 2(50) | 2(65) | — | — | — | 4(115) |
| | 25.0 | 32.5 | | | | |
| Gloucester | — | 4(95) | — | — | — | 4(95) |
| | | 23.8 | | | | |
| Rowly | — | 2(70) | — | — | — | 2(70) |
| | | 35.0 | | | | |
| Total Salem area | | | | | | 10(280) |
| Boston | 3(85) | 1(8) | 1(50) | — | — | 5(143) |
| | 28.3 | 8.0 | 50.0 | | | |
| Lynn | — | 2(65) | — | — | — | 2(65) |
| | | 32.5 | | | | |
| Total Boston area | | | | | | 7(208) |
| Bridgewater | 1(15) | — | — | — | — | 1(15) |
| | 15.0 | | | | | |
| Cohasset | 1(30) | — | — | — | — | 1(30) |
| | 30.0 | | | | | |
| Duxbury | 3(125) | 1(50) | — | — | — | 4(175) |
| | 41.7 | 50.0 | | | | |

*Figures do not include one 20-ton sloop for which no construction site is given.

Table 35 (cont.)

| Construction site | Sloop | Schooner | Brig | Snow | Ship | Total |
|---|---|---|---|---|---|---|
| Kingston | 2(62) | — | — | — | — | 2(62) |
|  | 31.0 | | | | | |
| Marshfield | 3(110) | 1(20) | — | — | — | 4(130) |
|  | 36.7 | 20.0 | | | | |
| Middleboro | 1(35) | — | — | — | — | 1(35) |
|  | 35.0 | | | | | |
| Plymouth | 7(173) | 7(155) | — | — | — | 14(328) |
|  | 24.7 | 22.1 | | | | |
| Scituate | 12(585) | — | 1(50) | — | — | 13(635) |
|  | 48.8 | | 50.0 | | | |
| Total Plymouth County | | | | | | 40(1,410) |
| Bristol | 1(20) | — | — | — | — | 1(20) |
|  | 20.0 | | | | | |
| Dighton | 4(73) | — | — | — | — | 4(73) |
|  | 18.3 | | | | | |
| Freetown | 1(23) | — | — | — | — | 1(23) |
|  | 23.0 | | | | | |
| Swansea | 8(170) | — | 1(30) | — | — | 9(200) |
|  | 21.3 | | 30.0 | | | |
| Total Bristol County | | | | | | 15(316) |

| Vessels trading with North Carolina | | % of tonnage |
|---|---|---|
| Merrimack River–built | 19(755) | 23.2 |
| Plymouth County–built | 40(1,410) | 43.4 |
| Bristol County–built | 15(316) | 9.7 |
| Salem area–built | 10(280) | 8.6 |
| Maine Province–built | 8(280) | 8.6 |
| Boston area–built | 7(208) | 6.4 |
| Total | 99(3,249) | 99.9 |

Table 36. Register of vessels trading with North Carolina, 1725–51: Registration of vessels built in Massachusetts, 1710–39

| Registration | Sloop | Schooner | Brig | Snow | Ship | Total |
|---|---|---|---|---|---|---|
| New Hampshire | 4(155) | 3(80) | — | — | — | 7(235) |
| | 38.8 | 26.7 | | | | |
| Massachusetts | 42(1,572) | 22(665) | 5(195) | — | — | 68(2,422) |
| | 37.4 | 30.2 | 48.8 | | | |
| Rhode Island | 12(226) | — | — | — | — | 12(226) |
| | 18.8 | | | | | |
| North Carolina | 7(208) | 4(78) | 1(30) | 1(70) | — | 13(386) |
| | 29.7 | 19.5 | 30.0 | 70.0 | | |

| Vessels trading with North Carolina | | % of tonnage |
|---|---|---|
| Massachusetts-registered | | |
|   Massachusetts-built | 68(2,422) | 74.1 |
| New Hampshire–registered | | |
|   Maine Province–built | 5(170) | 5.2 |
|   Newbury (Massachusetts)–built | 2(65) | 2.0 |
| Rhode Island–registered | | |
|   Bristol County–built | 12(226) | 6.9 |
| North Carolina–registered | | |
|   Massachusetts-built | 13(386) | 11.8 |
| Total | 100(3,269) | 100.0 |

Table 37. Register of vessels trading with North Carolina, 1725–51: Origin of North Carolina–registered vessels built 1710–39

| Construction site | Sloop | Schooner | Brig | Snow | Ship | Total |
|---|---|---|---|---|---|---|
| New Hampshire | — | 2(40) | — | — | — | 2(40) |
| | | 20.0 | | | | |
| Massachusetts | 7(208) | 4(78) | 1(30) | 1(70) | — | 13(386) |
| | 29.7 | 19.5 | 30.0 | 70.0 | | |
| Rhode Island | — | 1(10) | — | — | — | 1(10) |
| | | 10.0 | | | | |
| Connecticut | 7(149) | 1(30) | — | — | — | 8(179) |
| | 21.3 | 30.0 | | | | |
| New York | 7(115) | — | — | — | — | 7(115) |
| | 16.4 | | | | | |
| New Jersey | 3(36) | — | — | — | — | 3(36) |
| | 12.0 | | | | | |
| Pennsylvania and Delaware | 2(27) | 1(5) | — | — | — | 3(32) |
| | 13.5 | 5.0 | | | | |
| Maryland | 3(27) | — | — | — | — | 3(27) |
| | 9.0 | | | | | |
| Virginia | 5(37) | — | — | — | — | 5(37) |
| | 7.4 | | | | | |
| North Carolina | 22(486) | 9(86) | 3(205) | — | 2(290) | 36(1,067) |
| | 22.1 | 9.6 | 68.3 | | 145.0 | |
| South Carolina | — | 1(5) | — | — | — | 1(5) |
| | | 5.0 | | | | |

| Vessels registered in North Carolina | | % of tonnage |
|---|---|---|
| North Carolina–built | 36(1,067) | 55.2 |
| New England–built | 24(615) | 31.8 |
| Massachusetts-built | 13(386) | 20.0 |
| Other | 11(229) | 11.8 |
| Other colonial-built | 22(252) | 13.0 |
| Total | 82(1,934) | 100.0 |

Table 38. North Carolina port records, 1767–75

| Construction site | Sloop | Schooner | Brig | Snow | Ship | Total |
|---|---|---|---|---|---|---|
| Plantation | 8(190) | 10(265) | 12(820) | 2(200) | 8(1,050) | 40(2,525) |
| | 23.8 | 26.5 | 68.3 | 100.0 | 131.3 | |
| New England | 17(558) | 10(391) | 7(430) | — | 2(225) | 36(1,604) |
| | 32.8 | 39.1 | 61.4 | | 112.5 | |
| Massachusetts | 102(3,578) | 115(3,968) | 31(2,245) | 6(640) | 6(724) | 260(11,155) |
| | 35.1 | 34.6 | 72.4 | 106.7 | 120.7 | |
| Rhode Island | 16(365) | 3(120) | 11(600) | — | 1(147) | 31(1,232) |
| | 22.8 | 40.0 | 54.5 | | 147.0 | |
| Connecticut | 21(581) | 5(155) | 3(127) | — | — | 29(863) |
| | 28.2 | 31.0 | 42.3 | | | |
| New Hampshire | 6(285) | 3(85) | 3(170) | — | 5(770) | 17(1,310) |
| | 47.5 | 28.3 | 56.7 | | 154.0 | |
| New York | 10(145) | 1(10) | 2(90) | — | — | 13(245) |
| | 14.5 | 10.0 | 45.0 | | | |
| New Jersey | 3(38) | 1(25) | — | — | — | 4(63) |
| | 12.7 | 25.0 | | | | |
| Pennsylvania and Delaware | 4(91) | 7(170) | 4(170) | — | 1(160) | 16(591) |
| | 22.8 | 24.3 | 42.5 | | 160.0 | |
| Maryland | 3(67) | 10(366) | 1(103) | — | 2(240) | 16(776) |
| | 25.7 | 36.6 | 103.0 | | 120.0 | |
| Virginia | 15(400) | 8(238) | 9(751) | 2(200) | — | 34(1,589) |
| | 26.7 | 29.8 | 83.4 | 100.0 | | |
| North Carolina | 13(324) | 19(465) | 27(2,009) | 2(180) | 5(695) | 66(3,673) |
| | 24.9 | 24.5 | 74.4 | 90.0 | 139.0 | |
| South Carolina | — | 3(49) | — | — | — | 3(49) |
| | | 16.3 | | | | |

Table 38 (*cont.*)

| Construction site | Sloop | Schooner | Brig | Snow | Ship | Total |
|---|---|---|---|---|---|---|
| Georgia | — | 1(35) | — | — | — | 1(35) |
| | | 35.0 | | | | |
| Total | 218(6,622) | 196(6,342) | 110(7,515) | 12(1,220) | 30(4,011) | 566(25,710) |
| | 30.4 | 32.4 | 68.3 | 101.8 | 133.7 | |

| Vessels trading with North Carolina* | | % of tonnage |
|---|---|---|
| New England–built | 373(16,164) | 69.7 |
| Middle colonies–built | 33(899) | 3.9 |
| Southern colonies–built | 120(6,122) | 26.4 |
| Total | 526(23,185) | 100.0 |

*Figures for plantation-built vessels not included.

Table 39. North Carolina port records, 1767–75: Origin of Massachusetts-built vessels

| Construction site | Sloop | Schooner | Brig | Snow | Ship | Total |
|---|---|---|---|---|---|---|
| Falmouth | 4(165) | 4(98) | 3(141) | — | — | 11(404) |
| | 41.3 | 24.5 | 47.0 | | | |
| Other | 3(130) | 2(38) | 3(220) | — | — | 8(388) |
| | 32.5 | 19.0 | 73.3 | | | |
| Total Maine Province | | | | | | 19(792) |
| Salisbury | 2(60) | 4(175) | — | 1(120) | — | 7(355) |
| | 30.0 | 43.8 | | 120.0 | | |
| Newbury | 7(285) | 11(483) | 5(422) | — | 1(104) | 24(1,294) |
| | 46.7 | 43.9 | 84.4 | | 104.0 | |
| Other | — | 3(135) | — | — | — | 1(135) |
| | | 45.0 | | | | |
| Total Merrimack River | | | | | | 34(1,784) |
| Salem, Ipswich, and Danvers | 1(25) | 7(245) | — | — | — | 8(270) |
| | 25.0 | 35.0 | | | | |
| Total Salem area | | | | | | 8(270) |
| Boston | 2(65) | 1(30) | 8(701) | 5(520) | 5(620) | 21(1,936) |
| | 32.5 | 30.0 | 87.6 | 104.0 | 124.0 | |
| Other | — | 2(70) | — | — | — | 2(70) |
| | | 35.0 | | | | |
| Total Boston area | | | | | | 23(2,006) |
| Hingham | 1(40) | 7(285) | 1(50) | — | — | 9(375) |
| | 40.0 | 40.7 | 50.0 | | | |
| Scituate | 2(110) | 6(204) | — | — | — | 8(314) |
| | 55.0 | 34.0 | | | | |

Table 39 (*cont.*)

| Construction site | Sloop | Schooner | Brig | Snow | Ship | Total |
|---|---|---|---|---|---|---|
| Hanover | 5(220) | 8(260) | — | — | — | 13(480) |
| | 44.0 | 32.5 | | | | |
| Duxbury | 5(205) | 7(230) | 1(80) | — | — | 13(515) |
| | 41.0 | 32.8 | 80.0 | | | |
| Kingston | 5(235) | 9(296) | — | — | — | 14(531) |
| | 47.0 | 32.9 | | | | |
| Plymouth | 3(100) | 10(301) | — | — | — | 13(401) |
| | 33.3 | 30.1 | | | | |
| Other | 7(291) | 4(105) | 1(45) | — | — | 12(441) |
| | 41.6 | 26.3 | 45.0 | | | |
| Total Plymouth County | | | | | | 82(3,057) |
| Swansea | 12(258) | 2(55) | 1(30) | — | — | 15(343) |
| | 21.5 | 27.5 | 30.0 | | | |
| Other | 8(204) | 6(180) | 1(50) | — | — | 15(434) |
| | 25.5 | 30.0 | 50.0 | | | |
| Total Bristol County | | | | | | 30(777) |
| Massachusetts (location unspecified) | 35(1,185) | 22(778) | 7(506) | — | — | 64(2,469) |
| | 33.9 | 35.4 | 72.3 | | | |

| Vessels built in Massachusetts | | % of tonnage |
|---|---|---|
| Maine Province–built | 19(792) | 9.1 |
| Merrimack River–built | 34(1,784) | 20.5 |
| Newbury-built | 24(1,294) | 14.9 |
| Other | 10(490) | 5.6 |
| Salem area–built | 8(270) | 3.1 |
| Boston area–built | 23(2,006) | 23.1 |
| Boston-built | 21(1,936) | 22.3 |
| Other | 2(70) | 0.8 |
| Plymouth County–built | 82(3,057) | 35.2 |
| Bristol County–built | 30(777) | 8.9 |
| Total | 196(8,686) | 99.9 |

Table 40. North Carolina port records, 1767–75: Registration of Massachusetts-built vessels

| Registration | Sloop | Schooner | Brig | Snow | Ship | Total |
|---|---|---|---|---|---|---|
| Massachusetts | 41(1,755) | 93(3,256) | 13(897) | 1(120) | 3(370) | 151(6,398) |
|  | 42.8 | 35.0 | 69.0 | 120.0 | 123.3 |  |
| New Hampshire | — | 6(222) | 2(120) | — | — | 8(342) |
|  |  | 37.0 | 60.0 |  |  |  |
| Rhode Island | 37(951) | 7(195) | 2(90) | — | — | 46(1,236) |
|  | 25.7 | 27.9 | 45.0 |  |  |  |
| Connecticut | 2(90) | 1(40) | — | — | — | 3(130) |
|  | 45.0 | 40.0 |  |  |  |  |
| New York | 2(40) | — | — | — | 1(104) | 3(144) |
|  | 20.0 |  |  |  | 104.0 |  |
| Pennsylvania | — | — | 1(70) | — | — | 1(70) |
|  |  |  | 70.0 |  |  |  |
| Maryland | — | 1(25) | — | — | — | 1(25) |
|  |  | 25.0 |  |  |  |  |
| North Carolina | 20(742) | 7(230) | 2(130) | — | — | 29(1,102) |
|  | 37.1 | 32.9 | 65.0 |  |  |  |
| Jamaica | — | — | 2(151) | — | — | 2(151) |
|  |  |  | 75.5 |  |  |  |
| Scotland | — | — | 8(737) | 3(280) | 2(250) | 13(1,267) |
|  |  |  | 92.1 | 93.3 | 125.0 |  |
| England | — | — | 1(50) | 2(240) | — | 3(290) |
|  |  |  | 50.0 | 120.0 |  |  |

| Vessels built in Massachusetts |  | % of tonnage |
|---|---|---|
| Massachusetts-registered | 151(6,398) | 57.4 |
| New England–registered (not Mass.) | 57(1,708) | 15.3 |
| Other colonial-registered | 36(1,492) | 13.4 |
| Great Britain–registered | 16(1,557) | 14.0 |
| Total | 260(11,155) | 100.1 |

Table 41. North Carolina port records, 1767-75: Origin of North Carolina-registered vessels

| Construction site | Sloop | Schooner | Brig | Snow | Ship | Total |
|---|---|---|---|---|---|---|
| Plantation | 3(75) | 3(85) | 1(70) | — | 1(100) | 8(330) |
| | 25.0 | 28.3 | 70.0 | | 100.0 | |
| New England | 5(200) | 2(90) | 3(150) | — | — | 10(440) |
| | 40.0 | 45.0 | 50.0 | | | |
| Massachusetts | 20(742) | 7(230) | 2(130) | — | — | 29(1,102) |
| | 37.1 | 32.9 | 65.0 | | | |
| Rhode Island | — | — | 1(70) | — | — | 1(70) |
| | | | 70.0 | | | |
| Connecticut | 2(37) | — | — | — | — | 2(37) |
| | 18.5 | | | | | |
| New Hampshire | 2(120) | — | 2(120) | — | — | 4(240) |
| | 60.0 | | 60.0 | | | |
| New York | 2(30) | 1(10) | 1(40) | — | — | 4(80) |
| | 15.0 | 10.0 | 40.0 | | | |
| New Jersey | 1(15) | — | — | — | — | 1(15) |
| | 15.0 | | | | | |
| Pennsylvania and Delaware | 2(31) | 1(20) | 1(70) | — | — | 4(121) |
| | 15.5 | 20.0 | 70.0 | | | |
| Maryland | 1(8) | 1(5) | — | — | — | 2(13) |
| | 8.0 | 5.0 | | | | |
| Virginia | 8(225) | — | — | — | — | 8(225) |
| | 28.1 | | | | | |
| North Carolina | 11(269) | 18(470) | 23(1,682) | 1(80) | 3(445) | 56(2,946) |
| | 24.5 | 26.1 | 73.1 | 80.0 | 148.8 | |

| Vessels registered in North Carolina* | | % of tonnage |
|---|---|---|
| New England–built | 46(1,889) | 35.7 |
| Middle colonies–built | 9(216) | 4.1 |
| Southern colonies–built | 66(3,184) | 60.2 |
| Total | 121(5,289) | 100.0 |

*Figures for plantation-built vessels not included.

Table 42. North Carolina port records, 1767–75: Registration of vessels built in colonies (except Massachusetts) producing more than 1,000 tons

| Registration | Sloop | Schooner | Brig | Snow | Ship | Total |
|---|---|---|---|---|---|---|
| **New Hampshire–built vessels** | | | | | | |
| New Hampshire | 3(105) | 1(30) | 1(50) | — | 1(100) | 6(285) |
| | 35.0 | 30.0 | 50.0 | | 100.0 | |
| Massachusetts | 1(60) | 1(25) | — | — | — | 2(85) |
| | 60.0 | 25.0 | | | | |
| North Carolina | 2(120) | — | 2(120) | — | — | 4(240) |
| | 60.0 | | 60.0 | | | |
| England | — | — | — | — | 4(670) | 4(670) |
| | | | | | 167.5 | |
| Bermuda | — | 1(30) | — | — | — | 1(30) |
| | | 30.0 | | | | |
| Total | | | | | | 17(1,310) |
| **Rhode Island–built vessels** | | | | | | |
| Rhode Island | 16(365) | 3(120) | 9(415) | — | 1(147) | 29(1,047) |
| | 22.8 | 40.0 | 46.1 | | 147.0 | |
| North Carolina | — | — | 1(70) | — | — | 1(70) |
| | | | 70.0 | | | |
| England | — | — | 1(115) | — | — | 1(115) |
| | | | 115.0 | | | |
| Total | | | | | | 31(1,232) |
| **Virginia-built vessels** | | | | | | |
| Virginia | 4(75) | 6(183) | 3(210) | — | — | 13(468) |
| | 18.8 | 30.5 | 70.0 | | | |
| North Carolina | 8(225) | — | — | — | — | 8(225) |
| | 28.1 | | | | | |

Table 42 (*cont.*)

| Registration | Sloop | Schooner | Brig | Snow | Ship | Total |
|---|---|---|---|---|---|---|
| New York | 1(30) | 1(20) | — | — | — | 2(50) |
|  | 30.0 | 20.0 |  |  |  |  |
| Rhode Island | — | — | 1(60) | — | — | 1(60) |
|  |  |  | 60.0 |  |  |  |
| Massachusetts | 1(45) | — | — | — | — | 1(45) |
|  | 45.0 |  |  |  |  |  |
| British West Indies | 1(25) | 1(35) | 2(110) | — | — | 4(170) |
|  | 25.0 | 35.0 | 55.0 |  |  |  |
| Great Britain | — | — | 3(371) | 2(200) | — | 5(571) |
|  |  |  | 123.7 | 100.0 |  |  |
| Total |  |  |  |  |  | 34(1,589) |

North Carolina–built vessels

| Registration | Sloop | Schooner | Brig | Snow | Ship | Total |
|---|---|---|---|---|---|---|
| North Carolina | 11(269) | 18(470) | 23(1,682) | 1(80) | 3(445) | 56(2,946) |
|  | 24.5 | 26.1 | 73.1 | 80.0 | 148.3 |  |
| Pennsylvania | — | — | 1(90) | — | — | 1(90) |
|  |  |  | 90.0 |  |  |  |
| New York | 1(10) | — | — | — | — | 1(10) |
|  | 10.0 |  |  |  |  |  |
| British West Indies | — | 2(40) | — | — | — | 2(40) |
|  |  | 20.0 |  |  |  |  |
| Great Britain | — | — | 3(237) | 1(100) | 2(250) | 6(587) |
|  |  |  | 79.0 | 100.0 | 125.0 |  |
| Total |  |  |  |  |  | 66(3,673) |

Table 42 *(cont.)*

| | | % of tonnage |
|---|---|---|
| Vessels built in New Hampshire | | |
| New Hampshire–registered | 6(285) | 21.8 |
| Other colonial-registered | 6(325) | 24.8 |
| Bermuda-registered | 1(30) | 2.3 |
| Great Britain–registered | 4(670) | 51.1 |
| Total | 17(1,310) | 100.0 |
| Vessels built in Rhode Island | | |
| Rhode Island–registered | 29(1,047) | 85.0 |
| Other colonial-registered | 1(70) | 5.7 |
| Great Britain–registered | 1(115) | 9.3 |
| Total | 31(1,232) | 100.0 |
| Vessels built in Virginia | | |
| Virginia-registered | 13(468) | 29.5 |
| Other colonial-registered | 12(380) | 23.9 |
| West Indies–registered | 4(170) | 10.7 |
| Great Britain–registered | 5(571) | 35.9 |
| Total | 34(1,589) | 100.0 |
| Vessels built in North Carolina | | |
| North Carolina–registered | 56(2,946) | 80.2 |
| Other colonial-registered | 2(100) | 2.7 |
| West Indies–registered | 2(40) | 1.1 |
| Great Britain–registered | 6(587) | 16.0 |
| Total | 66(3,673) | 100.0 |

Table 43. South Carolina shipping register, 1735–39

| Construction site | Sloop | Schooner | Brig | Snow | Ship | Total |
|---|---|---|---|---|---|---|
| Charleston | — | 1(15) | 2(90) | — | — | 3(105) |
| | | 15.0 | 45.0 | | | |
| Georgetown | 1(5) | — | — | — | — | 1(5) |
| | 5.0 | | | | | |
| South Carolina | — | 6(110) | — | — | — | 6(110) |
| | | 18.3 | | | | |
| Total | | | | | | |
| South Carolina | 1(5) | 7(125) | 2(90) | — | — | 10(220) |
| | 5.0 | 17.8 | 45.0 | | | |
| New England | 8(230) | 2(90) | 1(80) | 1(75) | 1(80) | 13(555) |
| | 27.8 | 45.0 | 80.0 | 75.0 | 80.0 | |
| New York | 4(84) | — | — | — | — | 4(84) |
| | 21.0 | | | | | |
| Philadelphia | 1(15) | 1(20) | 1(30) | — | — | 3(65) |
| | 15.0 | 20.0 | 30.0 | | | |

| Vessels registered in South Carolina | | % of tonnage |
|---|---|---|
| South Carolina–built | 10(220) | 23.8 |
| New England–built | 13(555) | 60.1 |
| Other | 7(149) | 16.1 |
| Total | 30(924) | 100.0 |

Table 44. South Carolina shipping register, 1740–44

| Construction site | Sloop | Schooner | Brig | Snow | Ship | Total |
|---|---|---|---|---|---|---|
| Santee River | — | 1(12) | — | — | — | 1(12) |
| | | 12.0 | | | | |
| Total Georgetown area | | | | | | 1(12) |
| Ashley River | — | 1(20) | — | — | — | 1(20) |
| | | 20.0 | | | | |
| Charleston | 1(40) | 4(85) | — | — | 1(100) | 6(225) |
| | 40.0 | 21.3 | | | 100.0 | |
| James Island | — | 6(120) | — | — | — | 6(120) |
| | | 20.0 | | | | |
| Total Charleston area | | | | | | 13(365) |
| Beaufort | — | 1(12) | — | — | — | 1(12) |
| | | 12.0 | | | | |
| Combaltee | — | 1(12) | — | — | — | 1(12) |
| | | 12.0 | | | | |
| Port Royal | — | 4(73) | — | — | — | 4(73) |
| | | 18.3 | | | | |
| Total Port Royal area | | | | | | 6(97) |
| South Carolina (location unspecified) | — | 20(287) | — | — | — | 20(287) |
| | | 14.4 | | | | |
| Total South Carolina | 1(40) | 38(621) | — | — | 1(100) | 40(761) |
| | 40.0 | 16.3 | | | 100.0 | |
| New England | 1(25) | 1(40) | — | — | — | 2(65) |
| | 25.0 | 40.0 | | | | |
| Pennsylvania | — | — | 1(50) | — | — | 1(50) |
| | | | 50.0 | | | |
| North Carolina | — | — | 1(70) | — | — | 1(70) |
| | | | 70.0 | | | |

Table 44 (*cont.*)

| Vessels registered in South Carolina | | % of tonnage |
|---|---|---|
| South Carolina–built | 40(761) | 80.4 |
| New England–built | 2(65) | 6.9 |
| Other | 2(120) | 12.7 |
| Total | 44(946) | 100.0 |

Table 45. South Carolina shipping register, 1745–49

| Construction site | Sloop | Schooner | Brig | Snow | Ship | Total |
|---|---|---|---|---|---|---|
| Winyaw | — | 2(55) | 1(90) | — | — | 3(145) |
| | | 27.5 | 90.0 | | | |
| Georgetown | — | 1(25) | 2(90) | 2(210) | — | 5(325) |
| | | 25.0 | 45.0 | 105.0 | | |
| Santee River | — | 1(20) | — | — | — | 1(20) |
| | | 20.0 | | | | |
| Wacomaw River | — | — | — | 1(120) | — | 1(120) |
| | | | | 120.0 | | |
| Total Georgetown area | | | | | | 10(610) |
| Charleston | — | 4(81) | 1(80) | — | 1(130) | 6(291) |
| | | 20.3 | 80.0 | | 130.0 | |
| Dorchester | — | 2(36) | — | — | — | 2(36) |
| | | 18.0 | | | | |
| James Island | 1(35) | 2(40) | 3(170) | — | 1(125) | 7(370) |
| | 35.0 | 20.0 | 56.7 | | 125.0 | |
| Hobcaw | — | 2(40) | — | — | — | 2(40) |
| | | 20.0 | | | | |
| Total Charleston area | | | | | | 17(737) |
| Port Royal | — | 2(35) | — | — | — | 2(35) |
| | | 17.5 | | | | |
| Beaufort | 1(15) | — | — | — | — | 1(15) |
| | 15.0 | | | | | |
| Total Port Royal area | | | | | | 3(50) |

Table 45 *(cont.)*

| Construction site | Sloop | Schooner | Brig | Snow | Ship | Total |
|---|---|---|---|---|---|---|
| South Carolina (location unspecified) | 1(10) | 29(638) | 2(100) | 1(60) | — | 33(808) |
| | 10.0 | 22.0 | 50.0 | 60.0 | | |
| Total South Carolina | 3(60) | 45(970) | 9(530) | 4(390) | 2(255) | 63(2,205) |
| | 20.0 | 21.6 | 58.9 | 97.5 | 127.5 | |
| New England | 7(247) | 5(200) | 4(310) | 4(330) | — | 20(1,087) |
| | 35.3 | 40.0 | 77.5 | 82.5 | | |
| New York | 1(40) | — | — | — | — | 1(40) |
| | 40.0 | | | | | |
| New Jersey | 2(26) | 1(24) | — | — | — | 3(50) |
| | 13.0 | 24.0 | | | | |
| Pennsylvania | 2(26) | — | 1(50) | — | — | 3(76) |
| | 13.0 | | 50.0 | | | |

| Vessels registered in South Carolina | | % of tonnage |
|---|---|---|
| South Carolina–built | 63(2,205) | 63.8 |
| New England–built | 20(1,087) | 31.4 |
| Other | 7(166) | 4.8 |
| Total | 90(3,458) | 100.0 |

Table 46. South Carolina shipping register, 1750–54

| Construction site | Sloop | Schooner | Brig | Snow | Ship | Total |
|---|---|---|---|---|---|---|
| Winyaw | — | 1(15) | — | 1(90) | 1(180) | 3(285) |
| | | 15.0 | | 90.0 | 180.0 | |
| Georgetown | — | 7(147) | 1(50) | 1(75) | — | 9(272) |
| | | 21.0 | 50.0 | 75.0 | | |
| Total Georgetown area | | | | | | 12(557) |
| Charleston | 2(44) | 5(89) | — | 1(80) | — | 8(213) |
| | 22.0 | 17.8 | | 80.0 | | |
| Cooper River | 1(20) | — | — | — | — | 1(20) |
| | 20.0 | | | | | |
| James Island | — | 7(175) | 2(130) | 1(90) | 1(130) | 11(525) |
| | | 25.0 | 65.0 | 90.0 | 130.0 | |
| Total Charleston area | | | | | | 20(758) |
| Port Royal | — | 1(14) | — | — | — | 1(14) |
| | | 14.0 | | | | |
| Little River | — | 1(20) | — | — | — | 1(20) |
| | | 20.0 | | | | |
| Total Port Royal area | | | | | | 2(34) |
| South Carolina (location unspecified) | 1(35) | 14(266) | 1(45) | — | — | 16(346) |
| | 35.0 | 19.0 | 45.0 | | | |
| Total South Carolina | 4(99) | 36(726) | 4(225) | 4(335) | 2(310) | 50(1,695) |
| | 24.8 | 20.2 | 56.3 | 83.8 | 155.0 | |
| New England | 4(110) | 1(25) | 1(60) | 2(110) | 2(270) | 10(575) |
| | 27.5 | 25.0 | 60.0 | 55.0 | 135.0 | |
| New York | — | — | — | 1(90) | — | 1(90) |
| | | | | 90.0 | | |

Table 46 (*cont.*)

| Construction site | Sloop | Schooner | Brig | Snow | Ship | Total |
|---|---|---|---|---|---|---|
| Pennsylvania | 1(15) | — | — | — | — | 2(115) |
| | 15.0 | | | | | |
| Virginia | 1(15) | — | 1(100) | — | — | 2(115) |
| | 15.0 | | 100.0 | | | |
| Georgia | 1(40) | — | — | — | — | 1(40) |
| | 40.0 | | | | | |

| Vessels registered in South Carolina | | % of tonnage |
|---|---|---|
| South Carolina–built | 50(1,695) | 64.4 |
| New England–built | 10(575) | 21.9 |
| Other | 6(360) | 13.7 |
| Total | 65(2,630) | 100.0 |

Table 47. South Carolina shipping register, 1755–59

| Construction site | Sloop | Schooner | Brig | Snow | Ship | Total |
|---|---|---|---|---|---|---|
| Winyaw | 1(29) | 1(20) | — | — | — | 2(49) |
| | 29.0 | 20.0 | | | | |
| Georgetown | 1(25) | — | 1(40) | — | — | 2(65) |
| | 25.0 | | 40.0 | | | |
| Total Georgetown area | | | | | | 4(114) |
| Charleston | — | 1(15) | — | — | — | 1(15) |
| | | 15.0 | | | | |
| James Island | — | 5(98) | — | — | — | 5(98) |
| | | 19.6 | | | | |
| Wadmalaw | — | 1(14) | — | — | — | 1(14) |
| | | 14.0 | | | | |
| Total Charleston area | | | | | | 7(127) |
| Beaufort | 1(10) | — | — | — | — | 1(10) |
| | 10.0 | | | | | |
| Bulls Island | — | 1(40) | — | — | — | 1(40) |
| | | 40.0 | | | | |
| Total Port Royal area | | | | | | 2(50) |
| South Carolina (location unspecified) | — | 5(84) | 1(50) | — | 1(180) | 7(314) |
| | | 16.8 | 50.0 | | 180.0 | |
| Total South Carolina | 3(64) | 14(271) | 2(90) | — | 1(180) | 20(605) |
| | 21.3 | 19.4 | 45.0 | | 180.0 | |
| New England | 1(40) | 3(85) | 1(40) | — | — | 5(165) |
| | 40.0 | 28.3 | 40.0 | | | |
| Maryland | — | 1(45) | — | — | — | 1(45) |
| | | 45.0 | | | | |

Table 47 (*cont.*)

| Construction site | Sloop | Schooner | Brig | Snow | Ship | Total |
|---|---|---|---|---|---|---|
| North Carolina | — | 1(5) | — | — | — | 1(5) |
| | | 5.0 | | | | |
| Georgia | 1(10) | — | — | — | — | 1(10) |
| | 10.0 | | | | | |

| Vessels registered in South Carolina | | % of tonnage |
|---|---|---|
| South Carolina–built | 20(605) | 72.9 |
| New England–built | 5(165) | 19.9 |
| Other | 3(60) | 7.2 |
| Total | 28(830) | 100.0 |

Table 48. South Carolina shipping register, 1760–64

| Construction site | Sloop | Schooner | Brig | Snow | Ship | Total |
|---|---|---|---|---|---|---|
| South Carolina | — | 32(607) | 1(60) | — | 5(870) | 38(1,537) |
| | | 19.0 | 60.0 | | 174.0 | |
| New England | 8(235) | 2(50) | 2(175) | 1(110) | — | 13(570) |
| | 29.4 | 25.0 | 87.5 | 110.0 | | |
| Pennsylvania | 1(15) | — | 1(60) | — | — | 2(75) |
| | 15.0 | | 60.0 | | | |
| Maryland | 1(20) | — | — | — | — | 1(20) |
| | 20.0 | | | | | |
| Virginia | — | — | — | — | 1(120) | 1(120) |
| | | | | | 120.0 | |
| Georgia | — | 3(52) | — | — | — | 3(52) |
| | | 17.3 | | | | |

| Vessels registered in South Carolina | | % of tonnage |
|---|---|---|
| South Carolina–built | 38(1,537) | 64.7 |
| New England–built | 13(570) | 24.0 |
| Other | 7(267) | 11.2 |
| Total | 58(2,374) | 99.9 |

Table 49. South Carolina shipping register, 1765–69

| Construction site | Sloop | Schooner | Brig | Snow | Ship | Total |
|---|---|---|---|---|---|---|
| James Island | — | 1(16) | — | — | — | 1(16) |
| | | 16.0 | | | | |
| Total Charleston area | | | | | | 1(16) |
| Port Royal | 1(30) | 2(45) | — | 1(100) | — | 4(175) |
| | 30.0 | 22.5 | | 100.0 | | |
| Beaufort | — | 4(87) | — | — | 2(410) | 6(497) |
| | | 21.8 | | | 205.0 | |
| Lady's Island | — | 1(30) | — | — | — | 1(30) |
| | | 30.0 | | | | |
| Pocotaligo | — | 1(20) | — | — | — | 1(20) |
| | | 20.0 | | | | |
| Total Port Royal area | | | | | | 12(722) |
| South Carolina (location unspecified) | — | 38(770) | 4(275) | — | 3(530) | 45(1,585) |
| | | 20.1 | 68.8 | | 176.7 | |
| Total South Carolina | 1(30) | 47(968) | 4(275) | 1(100) | 5(940) | 58(2,313) |
| | 30.0 | 20.6 | 68.8 | 100.0 | 188.0 | |
| New England | 8(215) | 4(90) | 4(260) | 1(70) | 1(120) | 18(755) |
| | 26.9 | 22.5 | 65.0 | 70.0 | 120.0 | |
| New York | 2(28) | — | — | — | — | 2(28) |
| | 14.0 | | | | | |
| Pennsylvania | — | — | 1(100) | — | — | 1(100) |
| | | | 100.0 | | | |
| Virginia | 1(20) | — | 1(45) | — | — | 2(65) |
| | 20.0 | | 45.0 | | | |
| North Carolina | — | — | 1(50) | — | — | 1(50) |
| | | | 50.0 | | | |
| Georgia | — | 1(30) | — | — | — | 1(30) |
| | | 30.0 | | | | |

Table 49 (*cont.*)

| Vessels registered in South Carolina | | % of tonnage |
|---|---|---|
| South Carolina–built | 58(2,313) | 69.2 |
| New England–built | 18(755) | 22.6 |
| Other | 7(273) | 8.2 |
| Total | 83(3,341) | 100.0 |

Table 50. South Carolina shipping register, 1770–74

| Construction site | Sloop | Schooner | Brig | Snow | Ship | Total |
|---|---|---|---|---|---|---|
| Georgetown | — | 1(20) | — | — | — | 1(20) |
| | | 20.0 | | | | |
| Santee River | — | 1(16) | — | — | — | 1(16) |
| | | 16.0 | | | | |
| Total Georgetown area | | | | | | 2(36) |
| Charleston | — | 1(20) | — | — | — | 1(20) |
| | | 20.0 | | | | |
| Dewee's Island | — | — | 1(65) | — | — | 1(65) |
| | | | 65.0 | | | |
| Hobcaw | — | 1(12) | — | — | 1(200) | 2(212) |
| | | 12.0 | | | 200.0 | |
| James Island | — | 1(16) | — | — | — | 1(16) |
| | | 16.0 | | | | |
| Total Charleston area | | | | | | 5(313) |
| Port Royal | — | — | — | — | 2(460) | 2(460) |
| | | | | | 230.0 | |
| Beaufort | — | 4(112) | 2(180) | — | 2(320) | 8(612) |
| | | 28.0 | 90.0 | | 160.0 | |
| Total Port Royal area | | | | | | 10(1,072) |
| South Carolina (location unspecified) | — | 12(227) | 4(180) | — | 2(400) | 18(807) |
| | | 18.9 | 45.0 | | 200.0 | |
| Total South Carolina | — | 21(423) | 7(425) | — | 7(1,380) | 35(2,228) |
| | | 20.2 | 60.7 | | 197.2 | |
| New England | 7(200) | 7(190) | 5(270) | — | 2(140) | 21(800) |
| | 28.6 | 27.1 | 54.0 | | 70.0 | |

Table 50 *(cont.)*

| Construction site | Sloop | Schooner | Brig | Snow | Ship | Total |
|---|---|---|---|---|---|---|
| New Jersey, Pennsylvania, and Delaware | 1(20) | — | 2(145) | 2(110) | 1(100) | 6(375) |
|  | 20.0 |  | 72.5 | 55.0 | 100.0 |  |
| Maryland | — | 1(25) | — | — | 2(335) | 3(360) |
|  |  | 25.0 |  |  | 167.5 |  |
| Virginia | 1(15) | 1(25) | 1(40) | — | 1(200) | 4(280) |
|  | 15.0 | 25.0 | 40.0 |  | 200.0 |  |
| North Carolina | — | 1(5) | — | — | — | 1(5) |
|  |  | 5.0 |  |  |  |  |
| Georgia | — | 1(20) | — | — | — | 1(20) |
|  |  | 20.0 |  |  |  |  |

| Vessels registered in South Carolina |  | % of tonnage |
|---|---|---|
| South Carolina–built | 35(2,228) | 54.8 |
| New England–built | 21(800) | 19.7 |
| Other | 15(1,040) | 25.5 |
| Total | 71(4,068) | 100.0 |

Table 51. *Lloyd's Register of Shipping, 1776*

| Construction site | Sloop | Schooner | Brig | Snow | Ship | Total |
|---|---|---|---|---|---|---|
| America (location unspecified) | 13(975) | 26(1,780) | 218(28,995) | 29(4,120) | 96(20,130) | 382(56,00( |
| | 75.0 | 68.5 | 133.0 | 142.1 | 209.7 | |
| New England (location unspecified) | 11(915) | 27(1,870) | 154(19,000) | 12(1,840) | 59(12,070) | 263(35,69! |
| | 83.2 | 69.3 | 123.4 | 153.3 | 204.6 | |
| Massachusetts | 5(340) | 21(1,510) | 226(27,805) | 33(4,740) | 152(30,405) | 437(64,80( |
| | 68.0 | 71.9 | 123.0 | 143.6 | 200.0 | |
| New Hampshire | — | 6(390) | 45(6,060) | 5(720) | 126(27,495) | 182(34,66! |
| | | 65.0 | 134.7 | 144.0 | 218.2 | |
| Rhode Island | 6(485) | 2(120) | 56(6,680) | 6(850) | 21(4,310) | 91(12,44! |
| | 80.8 | 60.0 | 119.3 | 141.7 | 205.2 | |
| Connecticut | 3(170) | 1(120) | 17(2,280) | 3(500) | 16(4,102) | 40(7,17! |
| | 56.7 | 120.0 | 134.1 | 166.7 | 256.4 | |
| New York | 9(740) | 4(330) | 41(5,640) | 7(1,040) | 50(11,775) | 111(19,52! |
| | 82.2 | 82.5 | 137.6 | 148.6 | 235.5 | |
| New Jersey | — | — | 2(340) | — | — | 2(34( |
| | | | 170.0 | | | |
| Pennsylvania | 2(110) | 1(60) | 48(6,740) | 21(3,290) | 132(31,125) | 204(41,32! |
| | 55.0 | 60.0 | 140.4 | 156.7 | 235.8 | |
| Maryland | — | 7(540) | 33(4,390) | 7(1,260) | 75(18,668) | 122(24,85! |
| | | 77.1 | 133.0 | 180.0 | 248.9 | |
| Virginia | 3(210) | 7(570) | 59(8,400) | 22(3,220) | 59(14,205) | 150(26,60! |
| | 70.0 | 80.0 | 142.4 | 146.4 | 240.8 | |
| "Carolina" (not listed as North or South) | — | — | 6(880) | 1(160) | 8(1,630) | 15(2,67( |
| | | | 146.7 | 160.0 | 203.8 | |

Table 51 (*cont.*)

| Construction site | Sloop | Schooner | Brig | Snow | Ship | Total |
|---|---|---|---|---|---|---|
| North Carolina | — | 2(140) | 21(2,780) | 1(130) | 10(2,160) | 34(5,210) |
| | | 70.0 | 132.4 | 130.0 | 216.0 | |
| South Carolina | — | — | 4(440) | 3(360) | 14(4,235) | 21(5,035) |
| | | | 110.0 | 120.0 | 302.5 | |
| Georgia | — | — | 2(270) | — | 6(1,760) | 8(2,030) |
| | | | 135.0 | | 293.3 | |
| Total | 53(3,945) | 104(7,430) | 932(120,700) | 150(22,230) | 824(184,070) | 2,062(338,375) |
| | 74.4 | 71.4 | 129.5 | 148.2 | 223.4 | |
| Total without American-built | 39(2,770) | 78(5,650) | 714(91,705) | 121(18,110) | 728(163,940) | 1,680(282,375) |
| | 71.0 | 72.4 | 128.4 | 149.7 | 225.2 | |

| Vessels listed in *Lloyd's Register of Shipping*, 1776* | | % of tonnage |
|---|---|---|
| New England–built | 1,013(154,777) | 54.8 |
| New York–built | 111(19,525) | 6.9 |
| New Jersey–built | 2(340) | 0.1 |
| Pennsylvania-built | 204(41,325) | 14.6 |
| Maryland-built | 122(24,858) | 8.8 |
| Virginia-built | 150(26,605) | 9.4 |
| North and South Carolina–built | 70(12,915) | 4.6 |
| Georgia-built | 8(2,030) | 0.7 |
| Total | 1,680(282,375) | 99.9 |

*Figures do not include vessels listed under the category of American-built.

Table 52. *Lloyd's Register of Shipping,* 1776: Origin of Massachusetts vessels

| Construction site | Sloop | Schooner | Brig | Snow | Ship | Total |
|---|---|---|---|---|---|---|
| Casco Bay and Falmouth | — | 1(40) | 6(920) | — | 9(2,315) | 16(3,275) |
| | | 40.0 | 153.3 | | 257.2 | |
| Kittery | — | 1(80) | 2(160) | — | 1(300) | 4(540) |
| | | 80.0 | 80.0 | | 300.0 | |
| Wells | — | — | 1(100) | — | — | 1(100) |
| | | | 100.0 | | | |
| Total Maine Province | | | | | | 21(3,915) |
| Haverhill | — | — | 2(180) | — | — | 2(180) |
| | | | 90.0 | | | |
| Almsbury | — | 1(60) | 3(270) | — | 3(570) | 7(900) |
| | | 60.0 | 90.0 | | 190.0 | |
| Salisbury | — | — | 1(250) | — | 1(140) | 2(390) |
| | | | 250.0 | | 140.0 | |
| Newbury | — | 11(830) | 64(7,675) | 8(1,320) | 40(8,120) | 123(17,945) |
| | | 75.4 | 119.9 | 165.0 | 203.0 | |
| Total Merrimack River | | | | | | 134(19,415) |
| Salem area | — | — | 6(520) | 1(140) | — | 7(660) |
| | | | 86.7 | 140.0 | | |
| Boston | 5(340) | 7(500) | 136(17,120) | 24(3,280) | 97(18,830) | 269(40,070) |
| | 68.0 | 71.4 | 125.9 | 136.7 | 194.1 | |
| Plymouth area | — | — | 3(260) | — | — | 3(260) |
| | | | 86.7 | | | |
| Dartmouth | — | — | 2(350) | — | — | 2(350) |
| | | | 175.0 | | | |
| Swansea | — | — | — | — | 1(130) | 1(130) |
| | | | | | 130.0 | |
| Total Plymouth and Bristol counties | | | | | | 6(740) |

Table 52 (*cont.*)

| Vessels built in Massachusetts | | % of tonnage | |
|---|---|---|---|
| Maine Province–built | 21(3,915) | 6.0 | |
| Merrimack River–built | 134(19,415) | 30.0 | |
| Newbury-built | 123(17,945) | | 27.7 |
| Other | 11(1,470) | | 2.3 |
| Salem area–built | 7(660) | 1.0 | |
| Boston-built | 269(40,070) | 61.8 | |
| Plymouth and Bristol County–built | 6(740) | 1.1 | |
| Total | 437(64,800) | 99.9 | |

Table 53. Rating of American-built* vessels in *Lloyd's Register of Shipping*, 1776

|        |   | Sloop | Schooner | Brig | Snow | Ship | Total |
|--------|---|-------|----------|------|------|------|-------|
| 1740s  | A | — | — | — | — | — | — |
|        | E | — | — | — | — | — | — |
|        | I | — | — | 1 | — | 1 | 2 |
|        | O | — | — | 1 | — | — | 1 |
| 1750s  | A | — | — | — | — | — | — |
|        | E | — | — | 4 | 1 | 1 | 6 |
|        | I | — | — | 5 | — | 2 | 7 |
|        | O | — | — | 1 | — | — | 1 |
|        | U | — | — | 1 | — | — | 1 |
| 1760s  | A | — | — | 1 | — | — | 1 |
|        | E | — | 3 | 43 | 2 | 19 | 67 |
|        | I | 2 | 1 | 20 | — | 3 | 26 |
|        | O | 2 | — | — | — | — | 2 |
|        | U | — | — | — | — | — | — |
| 1770s  | A | 1 | 3 | 14 | — | 6 | 24 |
|        | E | — | — | 6 | — | 2 | 8 |
| Total  |   |   |   |   |   |   | 146 |

* Specific location of construction unspecified.

Table 54. Rating of New England–built* vessels in *Lloyd's Register of Shipping*, 1776

|  |  | Sloop | Schooner | Brig | Snow | Ship | Total |
|---|---|---|---|---|---|---|---|
| 1750s | A | — | — | — | — | — | — |
|  | E | — | — | 1 | — | — | 1 |
|  | I | — | — | — | — | 1 | 1 |
|  | O | — | — | — | 1 | — | 1 |
|  | U | — | — | — | — | — | — |
| 1760s | A | — | — | 1 | — | — | 1 |
|  | E | 2 | 6 | 31 | 2 | 14 | 55 |
|  | I | 1 | — | 3 | 1 | 2 | 7 |
|  | O | — | — | — | — | 1 | 2 |
|  | U | — | — | — | — | 1 | 2 |
| 1770s | A | 1 | 2 | 17 | 2 | 11 | 33 |
|  | E | 3 | 1 | — | — | — | 4 |
|  | I | — | — | — | — | — | — |
|  | O | — | — | — | — | — | — |
|  | U | — | — | — | — | — | — |
| Total |  |  |  |  |  |  | 107 |

*Specific location of construction unspecified.

Table 55. Rating of American-built vessels, by colony, in *Lloyd's Register of Shipping*, 1776

|  |  | Sloop | Schooner | Brig | Snow | Ship | Total |
|---|---|---|---|---|---|---|---|
| | | New Hampshire–built vessels | | | | | |
| | A | — | — | — | — | — | — |
| 1760s | E | — | 3 | 15 | — | 13 | 31 |
| | I | — | — | 1 | 1 | — | 2 |
| 1770s | A | — | — | 3 | — | 36 | 39 |
| | E | — | — | 1 | — | 7 | 8 |
| Total | | | | | | | 80 |
| | | Rhode Island–built vessels | | | | | |
| | A | — | — | — | — | 1 | 1 |
| 1760s | E | — | — | 10 | 1 | 3 | 14 |
| | I | — | — | 1 | — | 1 | 2 |
| 1760s | A | 2 | 1 | 4 | 2 | 4 | 13 |
| | E | — | — | 4 | 1 | — | 5 |
| Total | | | | | | | 35 |
| | | Connecticut-built vessels | | | | | |
| 1740s | E | — | — | — | — | 1 | 1 |
| | A | — | — | — | — | — | — |
| 1750s | E | 1 | — | 1 | — | 2 | 4 |
| | I | — | — | — | — | 2 | 2 |
| | A | — | — | 2 | — | — | 2 |
| 1760s | E | 2 | — | 7 | 1 | 4 | 14 |
| | I | — | — | 1 | — | — | 1 |
| 1770s | A | — | 1 | 1 | 1 | 3 | 6 |
| | E | — | — | 1 | — | — | 1 |
| Total | | | | | | | 31 |
| | | Newbury (Massachusetts)-built vessels | | | | | |
| | A | — | — | — | — | — | — |
| 1750s | E | — | — | 3 | 1 | — | 4 |
| | I | — | — | — | — | 2 | 2 |
| | O | — | — | 1 | — | — | 1 |

Table 55 (*cont.*)

|  |  | Sloop | Schooner | Brig | Snow | Ship | Total |
|---|---|---|---|---|---|---|---|
| 1760s | A | — | — | — | — | — | — |
|  | E | — | 6 | 30 | 3 | 8 | 47 |
|  | I | — | 2 | 7 | 2 | 5 | 16 |
| 1770s | A | — | 2 | 19 | 2 | 24 | 47 |
|  | E | — | 1 | 3 | — | — | 4 |
| Total |  |  |  |  |  |  | 121 |

### Boston-built vessels

|  |  | Sloop | Schooner | Brig | Snow | Ship | Total |
|---|---|---|---|---|---|---|---|
| 1740s | O | — | — | 1 | — | — | 1 |
|  | U | — | — | 1 | — | — | 1 |
| 1750s | A | — | — | — | — | 1 | 1 |
|  | E | — | — | 1 | — | 1 | 2 |
|  | I | — | — | 2 | 2 | 1 | 5 |
|  | O | — | — | — | 2 | 1 | 3 |
| 1760s | A | — | — | 1 | — | 1 | 2 |
|  | E | — | 2 | 32 | 5 | 10 | 49 |
|  | I | — | — | 1 | — | 7 | 8 |
|  | O | — | — | — | — | 1 | 1 |
| 1770s | A | 3 | 1 | 22 | — | 16 | 42 |
|  | E | 1 | — | 6 | — | 3 | 10 |
| Total |  |  |  |  |  |  | 125 |

### New York–built vessels

|  |  | Sloop | Schooner | Brig | Snow | Ship | Total |
|---|---|---|---|---|---|---|---|
| 1770s | E | — | — | — | — | 2 | 2 |
|  | I | — | — | — | — | 1 | 1 |
| 1760s | A | 1 | — | — | — | 1 | 2 |
|  | E | 1 | 2 | 8 | — | 8 | 19 |
|  | I | — | — | 4 | 1 | 1 | 6 |
| 1750s | A | 3 | — | 8 | — | 10 | 21 |
|  | E | — | — | — | — | 2 | 2 |
| Total |  |  |  |  |  |  | 53 |

Table 55 (*cont.*)

|  |  | Sloop | Schooner | Brig | Snow | Ship | Total |
|---|---|---|---|---|---|---|---|
|  |  | Pennsylvania-built vessels | | | | | |
|  | E | — | — | — | 1 | 1 | 2 |
| 1750s | I | — | — | 1 | — | 2 | 3 |
|  | O | — | — | — | — | 1 | 1 |
|  | A | — | — | 2 | 1 | — | 3 |
|  | E | 1 | 1 | 9 | 3 | 18 | 32 |
| 1760s | I | — | — | 3 | 2 | 4 | 9 |
|  | O | — | — | — | — | — | — |
|  | U | — | — | 1 | — | — | 1 |
| 1770s | A | — | — | 7 | 1 | 36 | 44 |
|  | E | — | — | — | 1 | 3 | 4 |
| Total |  |  |  |  |  |  | 99 |
|  |  | Maryland-built vessels | | | | | |
| 1750s | E | — | — | — | — | 1 | 1 |
|  | I | — | — | 1 | — | 1 | 2 |
|  | A | — | — | 1 | — | — | 1 |
| 1760s | E | — | — | 4 | — | 13 | 17 |
|  | I | — | — | 5 | 1 | — | 6 |
| 1770s | A | — | — | 2 | 1 | 26 | 29 |
|  | E | — | 3 | — | — | 1 | 4 |
| Total |  |  |  |  |  |  | 60 |
|  |  | Virginia-built vessels | | | | | |
| 1750s | E | — | — | 1 | 1 | — | 2 |
|  | I | — | — | — | 1 | — | 1 |
| 1760s | E | — | 1 | 5 | 1 | 12 | 19 |
|  | I | — | 1 | 3 | 2 | 4 | 10 |
| 1770s | A | — | 2 | 16 | — | 7 | 25 |
|  | E | — | 1 | 4 | 1 | 2 | 8 |
| Total |  |  |  |  |  |  | 65 |

Table 55 (*cont.*)

|  |  | Sloop | Schooner | Brig | Snow | Ship | Total |
|---|---|---|---|---|---|---|---|
|  |  | North and South Carolina–built vessels | | | | | |
| 1760s | A | — | — | — | — | 1 | 1 |
|  | E | — | — | 5 | — | 3 | 8 |
|  | I | — | — | 2 | — | 3 | 5 |
|  | O | — | — | — | — | 1 | 1 |
| 1770s | A | — | 1 | 8 | 1 | 7 | 17 |
|  | E | — | — | 2 | — | 1 | 3 |
| Total |  |  |  |  |  |  | 35 |

| Vessels rated |  | % of vessels |
|---|---|---|
| Built in 1740s | 6 | 0.6 |
| Built in 1750s | 57 | 6.0 |
| Built in 1760s | 493 | 51.5 |
| Built in 1770s | 401 | 41.9 |
| Total | 957 | 100.0 |

*Notes*

*Bibliography*

# Notes

*Complete facts of publication for the sources are given in the Bibliography.*

PREFACE

1. Vernon Briggs, *History of Shipbuilding on North River, Plymouth County, Massachusetts, 1640–1872*; Robert Cheney, *Maritime History of the Merrimac and Shipbuilding.*
2. Arthur Pierce Middleton, *Tobacco Coast: A Maritime History of Chesapeake Bay in the Colonial Era*; William G. Saltonstall, *Ports of Piscataqua.*

CHAPTER I  Ships and Shipbuilding in the First Colonial Settlements

1. Hobart H. Holly, "Sparrow-Hawk: A Seventeenth-Century Vessel in Twentieth-Century America," p. 58.
2. William Salisbury, "Early Tonnage Measurement in England," p. 43; Ralph Davis, *The Rise of the English Shipping Industry in the Seventeenth and Eighteenth Centuries*, p. 7n; William A. Baker, *Colonial Vessels: Some Seventeenth-Century Sailing Craft*, pp. 25–26.
3. Salisbury, pp. 47–48.
4. *English Shipping*, p. 7n.
5. William Bradford, *Of Plymouth Plantation, 1620–1647*, ed. Samuel Eliot Morison, p. 64.
6. Davis, *English Shipping*, pp. 10–11; Hugh Talmage Lefler and Albert Ray Newsome, *The History of a Southern State: North Carolina*, p. 4.
7. R. H. Major, ed., *The Historie of Travaile into Virginia Britania*, p. 179; Henry Wilson Owen, *The Edward Clarence Plummer History of Bath, Maine*, pp. 19–20; Baker, p. 62; William Hutchinson Rowe, *The Maritime History of Maine, Three Centuries of Shipbuilding and Seafaring*, pp. 46–47.
8. Henry Wilkinson, *The Adventurers of Bermuda*, pp. 50–60; report of Cornelis Henricxs to the States General, Aug. 18, 1616, Edmund Bailey O'Callaghan and Berthold Fernow, eds., *Documents Relative to the Colonial History of the State of New York* I:12; Howard I. Chapelle, *The History of American Sailing Ships*, p. 6.
9. Philip Alexander Bruce, *Economic History of Virginia in the Seventeenth Century* 2:426–27; minutes of the Council and General Court, Dec. 11, 1623,

*Virginia Magazine of History and Biography* (hereafter *VMHB*) 19 (1911): 136n.

10. Pp. 47, 55, 127, 140, 146, 163.

11. Ibid., p. 178.

12. Ibid., p. 183.

13. Governor and Deputy of New England Company to Endecott, Apr. 17, May 28, 1629, in Nathaniel B. Shurtleff, ed., *Records of the Governor and Company of the Massachusetts Bay in New England* 1:394, 402–3.

14. John Winthrop, *The History of New England from 1630 to 1649*, ed. James Savage, 1:69; Chapelle, *Sailing Ships*, pp. 6–7.

15. 1:138, 230.

16. Edward Downinge to Sir John Coke, Jan. 3, 1633, *Calendar of State Papers, Colonial Series, America and the West Indies* 1:158; John J. Babson, *History of the Town of Gloucester, Cape Ann, Including the Town of Rockport*, p. 165; grant by town meeting to Stevens, Aug. 7, 1637, *Historical Collections of Essex Institute* (hereafter *HCEI*) 9 (1869):54; George F. Chever, "Some Remarks on the Commerce of Salem from 1626 to 1740," ibid., (1859): 73; Winthrop to Stevens, Feb. 20, 1638, Peter de Sallenova to Winthrop, Feb. 5, 1639, in Winthrop, *Papers*, ed. Allan B. Forbes, 4:15, 189–90.


CHAPTER II   Shipbuilding Patterns in Seventeenth-Century America

1. Darrett Bruce Rutman, *Winthrop's Boston: A Portrait of a Puritan Town, 1630–1649*, p. 183; Bernard Bailyn, *The New England Merchants in the Seventeenth Century*, p. 46.

2. Bailyn, p. 47; Rutman, *Boston*, p. 184.

3. Bailyn, pp. 48, 49, 62, 72; Winthrop, *History* 2:29.

4. Winthrop, *History* 2:29; ordinance passed by town meeting, Oct. 11, 1640, *HCEI* 9 (1869):107–8; Hugh Peter and Emmanuel Downing to Winthrop, Jan. 13, 1641, Winthrop, *Papers* 4:304–5; *Richard Hollingsworth v. Edward Payne and Joseph Yongs*, Jan. 1641, *Probate Records of Essex County, 1635–1681* 1:31; Chever, p. 75.

5. Winthrop, *History* 2:29, 91; grant by town meeting to Bourne, Jan. 25, 1641, *Reports of the Record Commissioners of the City of Boston* 2:58; order by town meeting to Wright, Jan. 25, 1641, ibid., p. 59.

6. Winthrop, *History* 2:181, 212, 292, 339; Samuel Wilson and Bourne contract, May 8, 1646, *Aspinwall Notarial Records from 1644 to 1651*, p. 46.

7. Chever, p. 139; Darrett Bruce Rutman, "Governor Winthrop's Garden Crop: The Significance of Agriculture in the Early Commerce of Massachusetts Bay," p. 413.

8. Grant by town meeting to Stevens, Aug. 7, 1637, *HCEI* 9 (1869):54; Chever, p. 73.

9. Minutes of General Court, May 22, 1639, in Shurtleff, 1:258.

10. Peters and Emmanuel Downing to Winthrop, Jan. 13, 1641, Endecott to Winthrop, Jan. 28, 1641, in Winthrop, *Papers* 4:304–5, 311–12; ordinance passed by town meeting, May 2, 1642, *HCEI* 9(1869):112.

11. Minutes of General Court, Oct. 7. 1641, in Shurtleff, 1:337–38; commissioners appointed to examine a bark, June 27, 1661, *Mordecha Craford* v. *Thomas Jeffords*, Mar. 27, 1663, *William Carr* v. *Robert Dutch*, Apr. 1679, *Records and Files of the Quarterly Courts of Essex County Massachusetts* 2:313; 3:43–44; 7:168; correspondence between Lt. Gov. William Stoughton, Thomas Johnson, and William Owen, shipwrights, in Jan. 1695, Miscellaneous, vol. 5, 1694–97, Massachusetts Historical Society.

12. An Act for Regulating and inspecting ye building of Ships, Dec. 5, 1698, vol. 62, Maritime, 1694–1706, pp. 294–96, Massachusetts Archives; repeal of certain laws passed in Massachusetts Bay between 1697 and 1700, at Hampton Court, Oct. 22, 1700, vol. 3, Colonial, Massachusetts Archives.

13. Order for formation of a shipwrights' company, May 29, 1644, in Shurtleff, 2:69; Davis, *English Shipping*, p. 54.

14. Committee of General Court appointed to present laws to prevent injury by unskilled shipwrights, Oct. 9, 1667, in Shurtleff, 4:345.

15. Declaration by General Court to encourage construction of a dry dock, Oct. 9, 1667, answer of General Court to petition of James Russell, John Heyman, John Phillips, and Samuel Ballatt, May 30, 1679, in Shurtleff, 4:346; 5:230.

16. Howard Irving Chapelle, *The National Watercraft Collection*, p. 14; *Wood* 1:13; Baker, p. 96; Holly, pp. 56–57, 62; William Falconer, *An Universal*

17. Robert Greenhalgh Albion, *Forests and Sea Power: The Timber Problem of the Royal Navy, 1652–1862*, pp. 101–2, 233.

18. William Sutherland, *Britain's Glory: Or, Shipbuilding Unvail'd*, p. 56; *Wood* 1:13; Baker, p. 96; Holly, pp. 56–57, 62; William Falconer, *An Universal Dictionary of the Marine*, s.v. "tree-nails."

19. Baker, p. 33; Sutherland, *Britain's Glory*, p. 110.

20. Bailyn, pp. 62–63; Paul Huffington and J. Nelson Clifford, "Evolution of Shipbuilding in Southeastern Massachusetts," p. 363; Arthur Cecil Bining, *British Regulations of the Colonial Iron Industry*, pp. 10, 12–13; Edward Neal Hartley, *Ironworks on the Saugus*, pp. 270, 279–80.

21. Bailyn, pp. 72–74; Baker, p. 98.

22. *History* 2:29.

23. Bailyn, pp. 78–79, 80–81.

24. David Kirke to John Bodington, Oct. 1, 1646, *Aspinwall Notarial Records*, p. 77.

25. Samuel Wilson and Nehemiah Bourne contract, May 8, 1646, *Aspinwall Notarial Records*, p. 46; John Brown and William Stevens contract, June 6, 1661, *HCEI* 13 (1877):135–36.

26. Randolph to Sir Henry Coventry, June 17, 1676, *Calendar of State Papers* 9:409.

27. The present state of New England, an answer to Lords of Trade and Plantations, Aug. 1, 1676, British Museum, Additional MSS 28089, pp. 39–40 (transcript in Library of Congress).

28. *Abraham Perkins* v. *John Cutt*, June 23, 1674, *Records and Files of the Quarterly Courts of Essex County* 5:339–40; Curwen Family MSS, vol. 2, Family Papers and Commercial 1664–1815, Essex Institute; Babson, p. 251.

29. Davis, *English Shipping*, pp. 51–52, 53, 61; Albion, pp. 217, 228; the present state of New England, 1676, pp. 39–40.

30. Samuel Ballat and Martin contract, 1676, Middlesex County Court Records, 1679, folio 86; Samuel Ballat and Zairiah Long account, 1679, ibid., 1679–86, folio 188; *Abraham Perkins* v. *John Cutt*, June 29, 1674, *William Carr* v. *Robert Dutch*, Apr. 1679, *Records and Files of the Quarterly Courts of Essex County* 5:339; 7:168.

31. Sidney Perley, *The History of Salem Massachusetts* 2:368; Robert Cheney, *Maritime History of the Merrimac and Shipbuilding*, p. 6; John James Currier, *Shipbuilding on the Merrimac River*, pp. 18–20; Thomas Franklin Waters, *Ipswich in the Massachusetts Bay Colony* 2:232; Albion, p. 238; Sampson Lane bill of sale, Mar. 22, 1649, in Nathaniel Bouton, *et al.*, eds., *Documents and Records Relating to the Province of New Hampshire* 40:65; John Mead Howells, *The Architectural Heritage of the Piscataqua*, p. 147.

32. William Stevens sentenced, June 26, 1667, *Records and Files of the Quarterly Courts of Essex County* 3:431; Babson, pp. 167, 186.

33. Chever, p. 80; William P. Upham, "Papers Relating to a Suit A.D. 1664 between John Pickering and the Owners of the New Mill in Salem," *HCEI* 8 (1866):22–23.

34. Perley, 2:350; 3:28; Upham, pp. 22–23.

35. Henry Fitzgilbert Waters, "The Gedney and Clarke Families of Salem, Mass.," *HCEI* 16 (1879):249; Perley, 2:252.

36. *Mordecha Craford* v. *Thomas Jeffords*, Mar. 27, 1663, *Records and Files of the Quarterly Courts of Essex County* 3:43; William Leavitt, "Retire Becket," *HCEI* 7 (1865):207; John Becket inventory, Nov. 26, 1683, Essex County Probate Records; Perley, 2:224–25.

37. *A New Discourse of Trade*, pp. 233–34.

38. "A Perfect Description of Virginia," in Peter Force, ed., *Tracts and Other Papers Relating Principally to the Colonies in North America* 2:65; Bining, pp. 6–7; Sir John Harvey to Sir Francis Windebank, July 14, 1634, *VMHB* 8 (1901):158; Bruce, 2:431–32; Susie M. Ames, *Studies of the Virginia Eastern Shore in the Seventeenth Century*, pp. 140–41; inventory of estate of Richard Wilson, May 1641, *Nathaniel Littleton* v. *William Stevens*, 1643, *Obedience Robins* v. *William Stevens*, 1644, *William Berry* v. *Philip Taylor*, Apr. 1644, Northampton County Court Records no. 2, 1640–45, pp. 65, 218, 278, 300, Virginia State Archives.

39. Berkeley, *A Discourse and View of Virginia*, pp. 8–9; an act for the encouragement of building vessels, Mar. 23, 1662, an act for the encouragement of builders to build vessels in Virginia, Dec. 14, 1662, in William Waller Hening, ed., *The Statutes at Large; being a Collection of all the Laws of Virginia from the First Session of the Legislature, in the Year 1619* 2:122–23, 204.

40. William Berkeley order, Sept. 16, 1663, in Hening, 2:204, 241–42; Fleming letter, Mar. 12, 1667, *VMHB* 20(1912):198.

41. Berkeley to Lords Commissioners of Foreign Plantations, 1671, in Hening, 2:515, 516; Berkeley, pp. 2–6; Bruce, 2:435.

42. Chapelle, *National Watercraft Collection*, p. 176.

43. Marion V. Brewington, "Shipbuilding in Maryland," in Morris L. Radoff, ed., *The Old Line State: A History of Maryland* 1:239.

44. Vice Director Alrichs to Commissioners of the Colony, Oct. 10, 1658, Tymen Jansen to Cornelis van Tienhoven, Mar. 22, 1639, Directors of Dutch West India Company to Stuyvesant, Apr. 4, 1652, in O'Callaghan and Fernow, 2:52; 14:17, 173; Isaac Newton Stokes, *The Iconography of Manhattan Island* 4:52.

45. Samuel Mavericke to Nicolls, Apr., July 5, Oct. 15, 1669, Andros to Committee of Privy Council on Trade and Plantations, Apr. 16, 1678, in O'Callaghan and Fernow, 3:183–85, 261.

46. Bining, pp. 12–13.

47. Edward E. Atwater, *History of the Colony of New Haven*, p. 219; Perley, 1:426.

48. Bailyn, p. 29; Henry T. Blake, *Chronicles of New Haven Green from 1638 to 1862*, pp. 53–54.

49. William Hubbard, "History of New England," *Collections of the Massachusetts Historical Society* 14:322; Charles McLean Andrews, *The Colonial Period of American History* 2:176n; Atwater, pp. 219–20; Blake, p. 228; Bailyn, p. 18.

50. Frances Manwaring Caulkins, *History of New London, Connecticut*, pp. 231, 232, 233–34; Pliny LeRoy Harwood, *History of Eastern Connecticut* 2:423.

51. Caulkins, p. 235; Leete and John Allyn to William Blathwayt, July 15, 1680, *Calendar of State Papers* 10:577.

52. Edward Field, ed., *State of Rhode Island and Providence Plantations at the End of the Century: A History* 3:327; John Harvey Chapman, *The Chapman Genealogy*, p. 4; Ralph Chapman and Joseph Mallison bill of sale for ship *Friends Adventure*, May 4, 1696, John Hicks and John Grove bill of sale for ship *Experiment*, May 10, 1696, Ralph Chapman and Francis Pope bill of sale for ship *Charles*, Dec. 31, 1696, Joseph Stafford and Sarah Fowler bill of sale for sloop *Scanderbage*, Sept. 8, 1697, vol. 2, Land Evidence, 1671–1708, Rhode Island Archives.

CHAPTER III   The Early Eighteenth-Century Expansion of Colonial
Shipbuilding

1. Data from these and other shipping records are presented in the shipping
tables in the Appendix.

2. See tables 1–4.

3. Davis, *English Shipping*, pp. 51, 67, 316, 317; Alfred Thayer Mahan, *The
Influence of Sea Power upon History, 1660–1783*, 12th ed. (Boston, 1918), p.
229; Ralph Davis, "Untapped Sources and Research Opportunities in the
Field of American Maritime History from the Beginning to about 1815,"
p. 7; Earl of Bellomont to Lords Commissioners for Trade and Plantations,
Nov. 28, 1700, in O'Callaghan and Fernow, 4:793.

4. See tables 1–4.

5. John Bonner, *The Town of Boston in New England, 1722* (plan); meet-
ings of selectmen, Mar. 2, 1721, Dec. 16, 1723, Apr. 30, 1724, *Reports of the
Record Commissioners of the City of Boston* 13:94, 121, 125, 143; William
Burgis, *A South East View of Ye Great Town of Boston in New England in
America* (engraving).

6. See tables 1–4; County Court order to attach the goods of Edward John-
son, Jr., Aug. 22, 1692, in Middlesex County Court Records, 1692, folio 172;
County Court order to attach the goods of Edward Johnson, 1699?, vol. 62,
Maritime, 1694–1706, pp. 328–29, Massachusetts Archives.

7. Moffat to Isaac Sperrin, June 9, July 9, 1715, Moffat to Stephen Perry
Nov. 22, 1715, Thomas Moffat Letter Book, New York Public Library.

8. L. Vernon Briggs, *History of Shipbuilding on North River, Plymouth
County, Massachusetts, 1640–1872*, pp. 366–68; Bernard and Lotte Bailyn,
*Massachusetts Shipping, 1697–1714, A Statistical Study*, p. 25.

9. See tables 1–4.

10. Registers of *America*, July 1, 1703, *Burnaby Gally*, Mar. 11, 1704, *Essex
Galley*, Aug. 21, 1704, *Prudent Hannah*, Mar. 5, 1705, *Dwall Frigat*, Oct. 6,
1705, *Friendship*, Nov. 28, 1705, *Stephen and Samuel*, Dec. 31, 1705, *Unity*,
Mar. 14, 1706, *Cumberland*, Nov. 2, 1706, *America*, Sept. 30, 1708, *Swan*, Oct.
1708, *Pelican*, July 1709, *Leopard*, Nov. 1709, *America*, Jan. 5, 1710, *Sarah*,
Dec. 8, 1712, Massachusetts register of shipping, 1697–1714, vol. 7, Commercial, 1685–1714, Massachusetts Archives.

11. Registers of *John and Mary*, July 11, 1701, *George*, Nov. 21, 1701, *Rebecca*, Dec. 19, 1701, *Samuel and David*, July 11, 1701, *Mary Fortune*, June 10,
1706, *Partridge*, Oct. 15, 1708, *John*, Nov. 1708, *Bond*, May 31, 1709, *Mary*,
May 20, 1705, *Eyton Frigat*, Oct. 31, 1705, *Olive Branch*, Aug. 5, 1706, *Blessing*,
Aug. 1706, *Rose*, Dec. 3, 1706, *Barbados Merchant*, Jan. 18, 1707, *Boston Merchant*, Feb. 10, 1707, *Margaret and Elinor*, Mar. 1707, *Mary*, Apr. 1713, *Union*,
Apr. 8, 1705, Massachusetts register of shipping.

12. Registers of *Leopard Galley*, July 27, 1709, *Prince Eugene*, Oct. 22,
1709, *Abigail and Rebecca*, Sept. 11, 1710, *Strawberry Galley*, Aug. 24, 1711,

*Nathaniel*, Aug. 4, 1712, *Rowlander*, Sept. 2, 1712, *Content*, Oct. 22, 1712, *Pannope*, July 7, 1713, *Samuel*, Aug. 28, 1713, *Sea Flower*, May 10, 1714, *Marlborough Galley*, Aug. 6, 1714, *Nicholson Frigat*, Sept. 11, 1710, *Barbados*, Aug. 24, 1711, *Lusitania Magna*, Mar. 6, 1712, *Daniel*, Aug. 4, 1712, *Guardian*, Dec. 2, 1712, Massachusetts register of shipping; see tables 1–4.

13. Moffat to Stephen Perry, Nov. 22, 1715, Thomas Moffat Letter Book.

14. *Dictionary of American Biography*, s.v. "Coram, Thomas"; Coram to Alured Popple, Mar. 12, 1731, *Calendar of State Papers* 38:58; see table 1.

15. See tables 2–3; Coram to Alured Popple, Mar. 12, 1731, *Calendar of State Papers* 38:58; registers of *Goodspeed*, June 9, 1698, *Two Brothers*, July 9, 1698, *Joseph's Adventure*, June 10, 1699, *Pelican*, June 18, 1700, *Goodwill*, Mar. 20, 1701, *Defiance*, Apr. 17, 1701, *Resignation*, Oct. 1, 1702, *Katherine*, Nov. 4, 1703, *Fountain*, Aug. 15, 1704, *Resolution Galley*, July 5, 1705, *Leeds Merchant*, Apr. 14, 1707, *Fame*, Oct. 9, 1708, Massachusetts register of shipping.

16. Hamilton Andrews Hill, "Thomas Coram in Boston and Taunton," *Proceedings of the American Antiquarian Society* 8 (1892):134–35, 144–45; Thomas Coram appeal to Superior Court, Sept. 2, 1701, *Proceedings of the Massachusetts Historical Society* 41:16–17; petition, Feb. 1701, and complaint, Mar. 5, 1701, of Thomas Coram, vol. 40, Judicial, 1683–1724, pp. 645–50, Massachusetts Archives; *Dictionary of American Biography*, s.v. "Coram, Thomas."

17. Registers of *Resolution Galley*, July 5, 1705, *Leeds Merchant*, Apr. 14, 1707, *Fame*, Oct. 9, 1708, *Louis*, June 1710, *Two Brothers*, Apr. 30, 1711, *Sarah*, Nov. 23, 1711, *Sea Nymph*, Feb. 7, 1712, *Thomas and Elizabeth*, Feb. 7, 1712, Massachusetts register of shipping; see tables 3–4.

18. Davis, *English Shipping*, p. 78; registers of *Sea Nymph*, Feb. 7, 1712, *Thomas and Elizabeth*, Feb. 7, 1712, Massachusetts register of shipping.

19. See tables 1–4.

20. See tables 1–4.

21. Bailyn and Bailyn, p. 109.

22. Davis, *English Shipping*, p. 34.

23. Bailyn and Bailyn, pp. 61–62, 90–91; registers of *Peregrine*, Mar. 10, 1698, *Swann*, Mar. 21, 1698, *Essex Galley*, Mar. 24, 1698, *Dolphin*, Mar. 25, 1698, *Prince Lewis of Baden*, Apr. 2, 1698, *Ann*, Apr. 14, 1698, *Endeavour*, May 2, 1698, *John and Ann*, May 11, 1698, *Industry*, June 1, 1698, *Essex*, June 2, 1698, *William and John Gally*, June 2, 1698, *Providence*, June 8, 1698, *Merry Frigate*, June 24, 1698, *May Flower*, June 27, 1698, *Hannah and Elizabeth*, June 30, 1698, *Lyon*, June 30, 1698, *Two Brothers*, July 9, 1698, *Jeremie*, Aug. 18, 1698, *Fame*, Aug. 20, 1698, *Swallow*, Sept. 22, 1698, *John and Abia*, Sept. 29, 1698, *Prudent Sarah*, Sept. 29, 1698, *Welcome*, Mar. 30, 1699, *Pelican*, Apr. 7, 1699, *Friendship*, May 18, 1699, *Society*, June 28, 1699, *Blossom*, June 30, 1699, *Ann*, July 15, 1699, *Dallmahoy*, Sept. 16, 1699, *Expedition*, Sept. 21, 1699, *Robert*, Oct. 16, 1699, *Amity*, Dec. 2, 1699, *John and Robert*, Apr. 29,

*1700, Joseph and Rebecca,* June 20, 1700, *Dolphin,* July 22, 1700, *Betty,* Aug. 15, 1700, *Samuel,* Sept. 5, 1700, *Elizabeth,* Sept. 26, 1700, *Katherine,* Jan. 23, 1701, *Lion,* May 26, 1701, *Port Royal Merchant,* June 30, 1701, *Samuel and Ann,* Sept. 6, 1701, *Three Friends,* Nov. 26, 1701, *Prince Eugene,* Apr. 9, 1702, *Speedwell,* July 2, 1702, *Content,* July 6, 1702, *Joseph and Rachel,* Feb. 4, 1703, *Reward,* Apr. 23, 1703, *Samuel and David,* May 20, 1703, *Adventure,* Nov. 3, 1703, *Swallow Galley,* Dec. 3, 1703, *John and Timothy,* Feb. 16, 1704, *William and Hannah,* Feb. 21, 1704, *Burnaby Gally,* Mar. 11, 1704, *America,* Aug. 15, 1704, *William and John,* Nov. 5, 1704, *Friendship,* Nov. 9, 1704, *Expedition,* Feb. 2, 1705, *Prudent Hannah,* Mar. 5, 1705, *Abigail,* Mar. 10, 1705, *Sarah Galley,* Mar. 21, 1705, *Union,* Apr. 8, 1705, *Colman Frigatt,* Apr. 19, 1705, *Resolution Galley,* July 5, 1705, *Dorothy,* July 9, 1705, *Swallow,* Aug. 8, 1705, *Globe Galley,* Aug. 20, 1705, *Golden Fleece,* Sept. 5, 1705, *Charles Galley,* Sept. 11, 1705, *Anne,* Sept. 12, 1705, *Dwaal Frigat,* Oct. 6, 1705, *Eyton Frigat,* Oct. 31, 1705, *Tryal,* Dec. 17, 1705, *Stephen and Samuel,* Dec. 31, 1705, *Adventure,* Jan. 21, 1706, *Unity,* Mar. 14, 1706, *Charles,* Mar. 22, 1706, *Boston Galley,* June 8, 1706, *Mary Fortune,* June 10, 1706, *Endfield Queen,* July 17, 1706, *Olive Branch,* Aug. 5, 1706, *Blessing,* Aug. 1706, *Adventure,* Sept. 17, 1706, *Cumberland,* Nov. 2, 1706, *Marlborough Galley,* Nov. 1706, *Belcher Frigat,* Nov. 1706, *Rose,* Dec. 3, 1706, *Barbados Merchant,* Jan. 18, 1707, *Jeremiah and Anna,* Jan. 31, 1707, *Boston Merchant,* Feb. 10, 1707, *Margaret and Elinor,* Mar. 1707, *Sarah and Francis,* Apr. 20, 1707, *Mary Galley,* June 13, 1707, *Susanna,* Aug. 14, 1707, *Churchill Frigat,* Sept. 6, 1707, *John,* Oct. 30, 1707, *Paul and Louis,* May 26, 1708, *Empresse Galley,* May 1708, *Joseph,* Aug. 13, 1708, *Florida,* Sept. 9, 1708, *Plymouth,* Sept. 13, 1708, *America,* Sept. 30, 1708, *Jeremiah,* Sept. 1708, *Fame,* Oct. 9, 1708, *Partridge,* Oct. 15, 1708, *Swan,* Oct. 1708, *Dolphin,* Nov. 10, 1708, *John,* Nov. 1708, *Success,* Dec. 1708, *Milford,* Jan. 1709, *Bond,* May 31, 1709, *Mulberry Tree Galley,* June 29, 1709, *Buckingham Frigat,* July 8, 1709, *Pelican,* July 1709, *Codegan Galley,* Aug. 8, 1709, *Prince Eugene,* Oct. 22, 1709, *Lake Frigat,* Oct. 22, 1709, *Eagle Galley,* Nov. 1709, *Queen of Spain,* Jan. 3, 1710, *America,* Jan. 5, 1710, *Resignation,* Jan. 1710, *Friends Adventure,* Mar. 20, 1710, *Friendly Galley,* Mar. 31, 1710, *King of Spain,* Apr. 5, 1710, *Edward,* Apr. 17, 1710, *Frederick of Hanover,* Apr. 28, 1710, *Dispatch Frigat,* June 22, 1710, *Louis,* June 1710, *Pembrook Galley,* July 1710, *Abigail and Rebecca,* Sept. 11, 1710, *Nicholson Frigat,* Sept. 11, 1710, *Triumph Galley,* Sept. 26, 1710, *John Galley,* Oct. 3, 1710, *Friendship,* Oct. 1710, *William,* Jan. 26, 1711, *Cambridge Frigat,* Jan. 27, 1711, *Silvester,* Feb 21, 1711, *Three Marys,* Mar. 10, 1711, *Hamilton Galley,* Mar. 23, 1711, *Rapahanac Frigat,* Apr. 6, 1711, *Charles and William,* May 1, 1711, *Right Dink,* June 14, 1711, *Ester,* Aug. 14, 1711, *Barbados,* Aug. 24, 1711, *Providence,* Sept. 3, 1711, *Sarah,* Nov. 23, 1711, *Caswell Frigat,* Nov. 25, 1711, *Lake Frigate,* Feb. 6, 1712, *Sea Nymph,* Feb. 7, 1712, *Thomas and Elizabeth,* Feb. 7, 1712, *Amity,* Feb. 27, 1712, *Lusitania Magna,* Mar. 6, 1712, *Choptank Frigate,* July 21, 1712, *Kingston Frigate,* July 26, 1712, *Daniel,* Aug.

4, 1712, *Bishop,* Aug. 25, 1712, *Rowlander,* Sept. 2, 1712, *Sarah,* Dec. 8, 1712, *Sea Horse,* Mar. 7, 1713, *Province Galley,* Mar. 11, 1713, *Mary,* Apr. 4, 1713, *Payne Frigatt,* May 19, 1713, *Eagle,* May 11, 1713, *Sagamour of Aggawan,* May 18, 1713, *Staple Grove Galley,* Aug. 13, 1713, *Vigilant,* Sept. 7, 1713, *Anna,* Sept. 1713, *George Augustus,* Nov. 19, 1713, *Abraham and Sarah,* Nov. 27, 1713, *Guardian,* Dec. 2, 1713, *Patience and Judith,* Jan. 7, 1714, *William and John,* Feb. 15, 1714, *Loyal Bartholomew,* Feb. 15, 1714, *Port Royall,* Feb. 18, 1714, *Endeavour,* Apr. 9, 1714, *Hayes Galley,* Apr. 27, 1714, *Marlborough Galley,* Aug. 6, 1714, *Prince Alexander,* Sept. 8, 1714, *Success,* Sept. 12, 1714, *Susannah,* Sept. 25, 1714, Massachusetts register of shipping.

24. Bailyn and Bailyn, pp. 20–21; Davis, *English Shipping,* p. 35.

25. Cumings to Council of Trade and Plantations, Sept. 17, 1717, *Calendar of State Papers* 30:30; report on colonies, Sept. 8, 1721, British Museum, King's MSS, 205 (transcript in Library of Congress); Davis, *English Shipping,* p. 67.

26. Report on colonies, Sept. 8, 1721, British Museum, King's MSS, 205 (transcript in Library of Congress); Saltonstall, p. 14; Howard Irving Chapelle, *The Search for Speed under Sail, 1700–1855,* p. 76.

27. Earl of Bellomont to Lords Commissioners for Trade and Plantations, Nov. 28, 1700, in O'Callaghan and Fernow, 4:790, 791; Dudley to Council of Trade and Plantations, Mar. 1, 1709, *Calendar of State Papers* 24:243; report on colonies, Sept. 8, 1721, British Museum, King's MSS, 205 (transcript in Library of Congress).

28. See tables 1–3; registers of *Eagle,* Nov. 1704, *Benjamin and Peter,* Oct. 8, 1705, *Sarah Galley,* Dec. 18, 1706, *Dudley Frigat,* Oct. 9, 1708, *Friends Adventure,* Oct. 22, 1709, *Neptune,* Oct. 22, 1709, *Edward,* Oct. 28, 1709, *William,* Feb. 1710, *William and John,* Apr. 1710, *Edward,* Aug. 24, 1711, Massachusetts register of shipping.

29. *News-Letter* (Boston), May 21, 1722, May 30, 1723; George Campbell to Hobhouse, Jan. 13, 1724, Hobhouse Letters, Central Reference Library, Bristol, England.

30. Peirce to Dolebra, Sept. 10, 1728, Peirce to Nathaniel Peirce, Apr. 24, 1729, Peirce to William Jacks, Dec. 22, 1730, Peirce to Capt. Thomas Simon, Dec. 18, 1732, Wendell Collection, Baker Library.

31. Field, 1:168.

32. Bills of sale by Ralph Chapman, May 4, 1696, Dec. 31, 1696, Nov. 17, 1702, bill of sale by John Hicks, May 10, 1696, vol. 2, Land Evidence, 1671–1708, Rhode Island Archives; see tables 2–3; Field, 1:168.

33. Richardson to Gilbert Higginson, Mar. 26, 1713, Richardson to Thomas Bond, Feb. 20, May 1, Nov. 21, 1713, Richardson to Joshua Byrch, Apr. or May 1714, Richardson to Stephen Webb and Nicholas Coleman, Oct. 21, 1714, Thomas Richardson Letter Book, 1712–15, Newport Historical Society.

34. Introduction to Robert Taylor will, Nov. 1762, *Newport Historical Magazine* 2 (1882):243; contract between John Barnes and Vrian Davis *et al.,*

Feb. 2, 1721, vol. 3, Rhode Island Historical Society MSS; Esek T. Delano, "The Early Development of Shipbuilding on Narragansett Bay," p. 2.

35. Gov. Joseph Jencks of Rhode Island to Lords of Trade, Nov. 9, 1731, British Museum, King's MSS, 205 (transcript in Library of Congress); J. P. Newell, *Newport, R. I., in 1730* (etching of a painting); William E. Minchinton, "Shipbuilding in Colonial Rhode Island," *Rhode Island History* 20 (1961):121–24; *News-Letter*, Apr. 23, 1716.

36. Carl Bridenbaugh, *Cities in the Wilderness: The First Century of Urban Life in America 1625–1742*, p. 177; report on colonies, Sept. 8, 1721, Gov. Joseph Jencks of Rhode Island to Lords of Trade, Nov. 9, 1731, British Museum, King's MSS, 205 (transcript in Library of Congress).

37. Gov. Joseph Talcot and Assembly of Connecticut to Council of Trade and Plantations, Sept. 9, 1730, *Calendar of State Papers* 37:271.

38. Ibid.; ship clearances from New London, July 18, 1726, Jan. 7, 1727, Shipping Papers, Connecticut Historical Society.

39. D. Hamilton Hurd, *History of New London County, Connecticut*, p. 207; *Diary of Joshua Hempstead of New London, Connecticut*, pp. 161, 266; Harwood, pp. 429–33.

40. Earl of Bellomont to Lords Commissioners for Trade and Plantations, Nov. 28, 1700, in O'Callaghan and Fernow, 4:790; Council of Trade and Plantations to the King, Sept. 8, 1721, Hunter to Council of Trade and Plantations, Nov. 12, 1715, *Calendar of State Papers* 28:337, 338, 340; 32:417.

41. Gov. Robert Hunter to Council of Trade and Plantations, Nov. 12, 1715, Caleb Heathcote to Lord Bolingbroke, Oct. 15, 1714, *Calendar of State Papers* 28:70, 388; see tables 2, 3, 35.

42. Charles Lyon Chandler, "Early Ship Building on the River Delaware," p. 516; William Penn to Committee of Free Society of Traders, Aug. 6, 1683, in Albert Cook Myers, "Narratives of Early Pennsylvania, West New Jersey, and Delaware, 1630–1707," p. 229; Frederick Barnes Tolles, *Meeting House and Counting House: The Quaker Merchants of Colonial Philadelphia, 1682–1763*, pp. 86–87; Struthers Burt, *Philadelphia, Holy Experiment*, p. 123.

43. William Penn to Committee of Free Society of Traders, Aug. 6, 1683, in Myers, p. 331; description of Philadelphia by Richard Castleman, 1710, in Albert Bushnell Hart, ed., *American History Told by Contemporaries* 2:75; Bridenbaugh, *Cities in the Wilderness*, p. 176.

44. Chandler, p. 522; Council of Trade and Plantations to the King, Sept. 8, 1721, *Calendar of State Papers* 32:419; Dickinson to Dickinson (a brother in Jamaica), Mar. 5, 1719, Jonathan Dickinson Letter Book, Historical Society of Pennsylvania.

45. See table 10; Samuel Reynell to Reynell, Nov. 9, 1730, Henry Bonnin to Reynell, May 16, 1733, Reynell to Michael Lee Dicker, Oct. 3, 1733, Coates, Reynell Papers, 1729–32, 1733–35, Historical Society of Pennsylvania; Patrick Gordon to Council of Trade and Plantations, Nov. 10, 1731, *Calendar of State Papers* 38:331.

46. See table 10.

47. Victor Selden Clark, *History of Manufactures in the United States* 1:95; sheriffs' returns, May 4, 1698, in William Hand Browne, ed., *Archives of Maryland* 25:595–601; John Seymour to Council of Trade and Plantations, June 23, 1708, Council of Trade and Plantations to the King, Sept. 8, 1721, *Calendar of State Papers* 23:760; 32:421.

48. Report on colonies, Sept. 8, 1721, British Museum, King's MSS, 205 (transcript in Library of Congress); see table 35; Bridenbaugh, *Cities in the Wilderness*, p. 178; Robert Johnson to Council of Trade and Plantations, Jan. 12, 1720, *Calendar of State Papers* 31:305–6.

49. Council of Trade and Plantations to Lord Townshend, Jan. 28, 1725, concerning shipwrights' petition of Oct. 19, 1724, Caleb Heathcote to Council of Trade and Plantations, Oct. 8, 1706, Joseph Dudley to Council of Trade and Plantations, Mar. 1, 1709, Thomas Bannister to Council of Trade and Plantations, July 7, 1715, *Calendar of State Papers* 34:316–17; 23:257; 24:236; 28:223; Andrews, 4:351; appearance of petitioning shipwrights before Commissioners for Trade and Plantations, Dec. 9, 1724, *Journal of the Commissioners for Trade and Plantations* 5:137; Davis, *English Shipping*, pp. 28, 67n, 68.

CHAPTER IV   Colonial Shipwrights

1. Albion, p. 56; Davis, *English Shipping*, p. 56.

2. Albion, pp. 68, 88; Davis, *English Shipping*, pp. 55, 62–66, 70.

3. Albion, pp. 72–73, 77–78; Chapelle, *Speed under Sail*, pp. 32–33.

4. Albion, p. 69.

5. Albion, p. 71; Davis, *English Shipping*, pp. 56, 121; Sutherland, *Britain's Glory*, pt. 2, p. 2.

6. Sutherland, *Britain's Glory*, pt. 2, p. 149.

7. Albion, p. 103.

8. Davis, *English Shipping*, pp. 54, 121; Sutherland, *Britain's Glory*, pt. 1, p. 73.

9. Davis, *English Shipping*, pp. 55, 56.

10. Ibid.

11. Clark, 1:67–68; Carl Bridenbaugh, *The Colonial Craftsman*, p. 130; Isaac Merrick indenture, Jan. 26, 1748, Gersham Burband indenture, May 14, 1751, Moses Dowing indenture, Aug. 28, 1752, John Swett indenture, 1752, Moses Weed indenture, June 15, 1754, Ebeneezer Chandler indenture, June 14, 1758, Joshua Coffin MSS, vol. 1, 1647–1777, Essex Institute.

12. Jonathan Hanson indenture, Dec. 12, 1745, Archibald Arksin indenture, May 8, 1746, "Accounts of Servants and Apprentices Bound and Assigned before James Hamilton, Mayor of Philadelphia, 1745 and 1746," Historical

Society of Pennsylvania; Gersham Burband indenture, May 14, 1751, Joshua Coffin MSS, vol. 1, 1647–1777; Thomas Beck writ, 10467, May 20, 1740, William Wills writ, 25872, Mar. 23, 1764, New Hampshire Archives; *John Dotrige* v. *Isaac Woodbery*, June 11, 1681, *Records and Files of the Quarterly Courts of Essex County* 8:109; Bridenbaugh, *Colonial Craftsman*, p. 133; Joseph Cottle account, Oct. 8, 1757, Capt. Gideon Woodwell Account Book, Essex Institute.

13. John Cruger to Charles Goulding, Oct. 6, 1766, Henry and John Cruger Letter Book, New York Historical Society; Robert Bulock indenture, Nov. 1, 1745, "Accounts of Servants and Apprentices Bound and Assigned before James Hamilton"; Thomas Clifford to Thomas Penrose, Oct. 8, 1760, Clifford Correspondence, vol. 3, 1760–62, Historical Society of Pennsylvania; Thomas Penrose and Thomas Clifford suit, Apr. 4, 1768, ibid., vol. 5, 1766–77.

14. William Piggott to Winthrop, May 4, 1647, Peter de Sallenova to Winthrop, Feb. 5, 1640, in Winthrop, *Papers* 5:154–55; 4:189–90; Thomas Beck writ, 10467, May 20, 1740, William Wills writ, 25872, Mar. 23, 1764, New Hampshire Archives; *John Dotrige* v. *Isaac Woodbery*, June 11, 1681, *Records and Files of the Quarterly Courts of Essex County* 8:109; Bridenbaugh, *Colonial Craftsman*, p. 133; *South Carolina Gazette* (Charleston), Sept. 6, 1742; *Virginia Gazette* (Williamsburg), Apr. 16, 1767; *Maryland Gazette* (Annapolis), July 19, 1753; *Pennsylvania Gazette* (Philadelphia), Apr. 24, 1760, Dec. 31, 1761, Apr. 7, 1768.

15. Simon Shirlock inventory, May 25, 1776, Probate Records, Philadelphia City Hall, Annex; Edward Snell inventory, Oct. 11, 1744, Inventories, 4 (1744–46):34–35, South Carolina Archives; *John Dotrige* v. *Isaac Woodbery*, June 11, 1681, *Records and Files of the Quarterly Courts of Essex County* 8:109.

16. Bridenbaugh, *Colonial Craftsman*, p. 134.

17. Abbot Emerson Smith, *Colonists in Bondage: White Servitude and Convict Labor in America, 1607–1776*, pp. 29, 33.

18. Smith, pp. 16–20, 117–119, 232.

19. Servants bound to Samuel Hastings, Michael Huling, John Lawton, Simon Shirlock, and Thomas Cuthbert, in "Accounts of Servants and Apprentices Bound and Assigned before James Hamilton"; Philadelphia Tax Record, 1767, Assessors' Returns, Rare Book Room, University of Pennsylvania Library; Provincial Tax Assessed the 13th day of March 1772, Historical Society of Pennsylvania; and Constables Returns, 1775, Philadelphia Archives, City Hall.

20. *Virginia Gazette*, Nov. 10, 1752, Sept. 28, 1769, July 9, 1772, Aug. 12, 1773, May 27, 1773; *Maryland Gazette*, Apr. 11, 1754, July 25, 1754, Aug. 28, 1755, Jan. 15, 1756, Apr. 29, 1756, Oct. 21, 1756; *Pennsylvania Gazette*, Aug. 1, 1751.

21. Carroll (Sr.) to Carrol (Jr.), May 8, 1754, Henry O. Thompson Papers, MS 821, Maryland Historical Society; *Maryland Gazette*, Aug. 28, 1755, Oct. 9, 1755, Jan. 15, 1756, Jan. 31, 1760.

22. Smith, p. 292.

23. Account of cost of brigantine *Fourtune*, Peter Papillon Account Book, Nov. 10, 1713, Essex Institute.

24. *South Carolina Gazette*, Dec. 9, 16, 1732, Apr. 14, 1733, Feb. 8, 1735, June 5, Dec. 24, 1736, Jan. 8, 1737.

25. Indenture of Ignatius Diggs' slave, Jack, to William Nicholls, July 31, 1771, Clement Hill Papers, MS 446, Maryland Historical Society; *Virginia Gazette*, May 2, Dec. 18, 1766, Dec. 19, 1771; *News-Letter*, Apr. 15, 1762; *South Carolina Gazette*, Dec. 16, 1732; Pollard to Samuel Inglis, Apr. 21, 1772, William Pollard Letter Book, Historical Society of Pennsylvania.

26. John Daniel inventory, Dec. 2, 1747, Alexander Russell inventory, Mar. 6, 1771, Inventories, 6:217–19; 16:12–13, South Carolina Archives; Mrs. Catherine Tweed schedule, Mar. 7, 1786, presented to the Commissioners on Loyalist Claims, transcribed in London, 1898–1903, 54:332–39 (microfilm copy in New York Public Library); *South Carolina Gazette*, Dec. 9, 1732, June 5, Nov. 20, 1736, Feb. 10, 1746, June 16, 1746; John Daniel, John Yarworth, George Heskett, John Scott, and David Brown remonstrance, Jan. 25, 1744, in James Harold Easterby, ed., *The Journals of the Commons House of Assembly* 4:547–48; Andrew Ruck petition in behalf of himself and several other shipwrights, Jan. 21, 1744, in Easterby, 4:541.

27. Committee report upon petition and remonstrance of Charleston shipwrights, Jan. 25, 1744, in Easterby, 4:549–50; recommendation of the Commons House, Jan. 25, 1744, ibid., p. 550; amendment defeated, Mar. 9, 1744, ibid., 5:56.

28. Norfolk Tithables, 1751, Virginia State Archives; William Ashley inventory, May 6, 1753, John Whiddon will, Nov. 7, 1748, Norfolk County Wills and Deeds, 1736–53, pp. 192–92a, 324–24a, Virginia State Archives; Thomas Herbert, Sr., will, Feb. 10, 1774, William Whitehurst will, Dec. 7, 1755, Norfolk County Will Book, no. 1, 1754–71, pp. 17, 32, Virginia State Archives; Philip Ludwell Lee inventory, Mar. 20, 1776, Virginia State Archives; *Maryland Gazette*, Apr. 25, 1765.

29. Philadelphia Tax Record, 1767, Assessors' Returns, Rare Book Room, University of Pennsylvania Library; Provincial Tax Assessed the 13th day of March, 1772, Historical Society of Pennsylvania.

30. Thomas Penrose will, Dec. 22, 1757, James West will and inventory, Mar. 8, 1762, Simon Shirlock will and inventory, May 25, 1776, Probate Records, Philadelphia City Hall, Annex.

31. *News-Letter*, Sept. 9, 1731, July 24, 1740; Valuation of Towns, Boston, vol. 132, Mass., 1768–71, Massachusetts Archives; Samuel Hood inventory, Apr. 1735 vol. 35, pp. 214–219, Suffolk County Probate Records; Ephram Jackson account, Aug. 15, 1740, John Moffat Accounts, vol. 3, 1725–50, New Hampshire Historical Society; ship *Sarah*, Jan. 19, 1742, snow *Lark*, Feb. 20, 1744, John Erving Journal, 1733–45, Baker Library; brig *Amilia*, Mar. 7, 1739, Commercial Papers, 1720–60, Hawthorne Family MSS, Essex Institute; ship *Berwick*, Dec. 5, 1740, ship *Newport*, Dec. 12, 1740, ship *Leathley*, Mar. 6,

1741, John Banister Daybook, Newport Historical Society; snow *Swan*, June 23, 1747, ship *Lee*, May 10, 1748, ship *Affrican*, Jan. 23, 1749, John Banister Letter Book, 1746–49, Newport Historical Society; sloop *Three Friends*, 1770, Ship Papers, Brown Papers, John Carter Brown Library; Jacob Shomaker account, 1762, Ledger, 1758–64, Brown Papers.

32. Ship *Sarah*, Jan. 19, 1742, John Erving Journal, 1733–45; John Peck account, 1770, Ship Papers, Brown Papers; Jacob Shomaker account, 1762, Ledger, 1758–44, Brown Papers; *David Brown* v. *Bryon Foskey*, 1756, 63A, *William Tweed* v. *William Maxwell*, 1774, 90A, Court Records of Common Pleas, South Carolina Archives; snow *Swan*, June 23, 1747, ship *Lee*, May 10, 1748, John Banister Letter Book, 1746–49; ship *Three Sisters*, Oct. 11, 1743, John Banister Daybook; George Dennistone account, Mar. 7, 1739, Commercial Papers, 1720–60, Hawthorne Family MSS.

33. John Daniel inventory, Dec. 2, 1747, Mary Yarworth inventory, Aug. 16, 1756, Thomas Middleton inventory, Feb. 3–5, 1767, David Brown inventory, June 10, 1765, Alexander Russell inventory, Mar. 6, 1771, Inventories, 6:217–27; 9:506–8; 13:399–403; 14:40–41; 16:12–13, South Carolina Archives; Pollard to Samuel Inglis, Apr. 21, 1772, William Pollard Letter Book; John Rose schedule, Mar. 21, 1784, Mrs. Catherine Tweed schedule, Mar. 7, 1786, John Immrie schedule, Mar. 27, 1786, presented to the Commissioners on Loyalist Claims, transcribed in London, 1898–1903, 53:272–77; 54:332–33; 55:35–36 (microfilm copy in New York Public Library); *South Carolina Gazette*, Dec. 9, 1732, June 5, 1736, July 2, 1741, June 25, 1750, June 28, 1760, Jan. 18, 1768; *Estate of John Daniel* v. *Thomas Headdy*, 1751, 17A, *Elias Vanderhorst* v. *George Monk*, 1769, 219A, Court Records of Common Pleas, South Carolina Archives.

34. Samuel Hood inventory, Apr. 1735, William Shute inventory, May 27, 1746, Caleb Eddy inventory, Feb. 16, 1747, Joseph Grant inventory, Sept. 3, 1756, Benjamin Hallowell inventory, May 3, 1773, Suffolk County Probate Records, 35:214–19; 39:38; 40: 433–34; 51:580–81; 72:579–82; Samuel Morgaridge inventory, Apr. 2, 1754, William Johnson inventory, July 20, 1741, Joseph Cottle inventory, July 6, 1765, Essex County Probate Records; Roger Kinnicut inventory, Aug. 10, 1751, Providence Probate Records; John Daniel inventory, Dec. 2, 1747, Thomas Middleton inventory, Feb. 3–5, 1767, Mary Yarworth inventory, Aug. 16, 1756, John Frink inventory, Aug. 18, 1761, Gideon Norton inventory, Apr. 14, 1762, Percival Pawley inventory, May 16, 1752, David Brown inventory, June 10, 1765, Alexander Russell inventory, Mar. 6, 1771, Edward Scull inventory, Dec. 18, 1744, Inventories, 6:217–27; 13:399–403; 9:506–8; 12:34–35, 209–11, 348–51; 14:40–41; 16:12–13; 4:34–35, South Carolina Archives.

35. *News-Letter*, Feb. 4, 1748, Apr. 15, 1762; *Maryland Gazette*, Apr. 25, 1765; *South Carolina Gazette*, Apr. 7, 14, 1733, Feb. 10, 1746, June 16, 1746; *Gazette* (Providence), July 25, 1767; *Virginia Gazette*, Sept. 10, 1733, Feb. 9, 1769; *Pennsylvania Gazette*, Feb. 2, 1769.

Papers; Ellis to Messrs. Leyborne, Rossey, and Rockless, Fe[b.] [Robe]rt Ellis Letter Book; W. Cathias Jones to Samuel and Willia[m] [...], 1748, Vernon Papers, box 49.

[...] Moffat to Isaac Sperrin, June 9, 1715, Thomas Moffat Lette[r] [...] to Elias Bland, Nov. 12, Dec. 3, 1746, Apr. 3, 1747, John Rey[nell] [...]ook, 1745–47, Coates, Reynell Papers; Powell to Robert Wheatle[y] [...], Samuel Powell, Jr., Letter Book, vol. 2, 1739–46; Richardson t[o] [...]lkinson, Nov. 1715, Thomas Richardson Letter Book, 1715–19[;] [...]inne and Walter Hawksworth to Coffin, Jan. 17, 1733, Joshua [...] vol. 1, 1647–1777; Lloyd to John Lloyd, May 9, 1765, Henry Lloyd [...]

[...]ell to Daniel Flexney, Jan. 4, 1741, Reynell to Elias Bland, Dec. [...] [Joh]n Reynell Letter Books, 1738–41, 1745–47, Coates, Reynell Papers; [...]burne to Joseph Harrison, Apr. 29, 1746, Foreign Letters, John [...] Letter Books; Timothy Orne, Benjamin Osgood, and Daniel Curtis [...] Sept. 5, 1751, Commercial Papers, box 2, 1751–56, Timothy Orne [...]than Miller and Aaron Lopez contract, Feb. 9, 1775, Aaron Lopez and [...] Child contract, Dec. 28, 1774, Aaron Lopez Papers, box 52, folio 4; [...]hillips and John Becket contract, June 23, 1721, Probate, Commissions, [...]gal, Curwen Family MSS, vol. 4, Essex Institute; Banister to James [...], Nov. 30, 1747, John Banister Letter Book, 1746–48.

[...]oshua Gee and Thomas Windsor contract, Oct. 30, 1701, vol. 62, Mari-[...] [16]94–1706, Massachusetts Archives; John Barnes, Vrian Davis, *et al.* con-[...] Feb. 2, 1721, Rhode Island Historical Society MSS, vol. 1; Jacob Phillips [...] [J]ohn Becket contract, June 23, 1721, Curwen Family MSS, vol. 4, Probate, [...]missions, and Legal; Andrew Webster, Jonathan Gardner, and Timothy [...] contract, Aug. 30, 1749, Commercial Papers, box 1, 1732–50, Timothy [...]e MSS; Benjamin Bowers and Aaron Lopez contract, May 30, 1764, Syl-[...]r Child, Aaron Lopez, and Benjamin Wright contract, Nov. 5, 1772, [...]ester Child and Aaron Lopez contract, Dec. 28, 1774, Aaron Lopez Papers, [...] 52, folio 4.

[2]0. Thomas Goldthwait petition, Samuel Vaughan and Moses Tyler reply, [De]c. 20, 1749, vol. 43, Judicial, 1749–54, pp. 30–32, 36–39, Massachusetts Ar-[ch]ives; John Banister to James Pardoe, July 23, 1748, John Banister Letter [Bo]ok, 1746–48.

21. Falconer, "Naval Architecture."

22. Chapelle, *Speed under Sail*, pp. 15, 150; Roger Charles Anderson, "Early Books on Shipbuilding and Rigging," *Mirror* 20(1924):53–64; Roger Charles Anderson, "Eighteenth-Century Books on Shipbuilding, Rigging and Seaman-ship"; Alexander Hunt inventory, Oct. 24, 1765, Suffolk County Probate Rec-ords, vol. 64; *News-Letter*, Feb. 3, 1726, Oct. 10, 1765; John Radburne to Joseph Harrison, Aug. 24, 1745, Foreign Letters, John Banister Letter Books; Nellson Rachlief account, Jan. 1747, Abner Dole Ledger, p. 5.

36. Sloop *Culloden* account, 1748, Vernon Papers, box 48, Newport Historical Society; sloop *Four Brothers*, Aug. 5, 1762, Ship Papers, Brown Papers; Prince Miller account, July 1768–Jan. 1771, Nicholas Brown Ledger, 1768–74, Brown Papers; unsigned letter to Aaron Lopez, Oct. 8, 1769, Wetmore Collection, 1768–69, Massachusetts Historical Society.

37. Burgis, *South East View of Boston*; Burgis, *A South Prospect of Ye Flourishing City of New York in America* (engraving); George Heap and Nicholas Scull, *An East Prospect of the City of Philadelphia* (engraving); Thomas Coram complaint, Mar. 5, 1701, vol. 40, Judicial, 1683–1724, pp. 649–50, Massachusetts Archives; *The shipyard at Spencer Hall, Kent Island, Maryland* (oil painting).

38. Philadelphia Historical Commission, "Southwark"; Philadelphia Tax Record, 1767, Assessors' Returns, Rare Book Room, University of Pennsylvania Lbrary.

39. Joseph F. W. Des Barres, "A Plan of the Town of Newport in the Province of Rhode Island."

40. John Decker account, May 5, 1735, Abner Dole Ledger, Essex Institute; Joseph Cottle account, Sept. 3, 1757, Oct. 10, 1759, Oct. 3, 1762, Capt. Gideon Woodwell Account Book; John Mitchell account, Nov. 24, 1755, Eliphalet Griffen Ledger, Baker Library; Dickinson to Dickinson (a brother in Jamaica), Mar. 5, 1719, Jonathan Dickinson Letter Book.

41. Thomas Lang writ, 24893, Feb. 18, 1744, New Hampshire Archives; Joshua Mitchel account, Nov. 1, 1756, Eliphalet Griffen Ledger; Stephen Cross account, Dec. 20, 1764, Capt. Gideon Woodwell Account Book.

42. Gershom Bradford, "The Ezra Westons, Shipbuilders of Duxbury," p. 35; Joseph Cottle accounts, Apr. 26, 1754, Mar. 15, 1759, two schooner accounts, June 19, Nov. 20, 1754, and Joshua Mitchel accounts, Nov. 24, 1754, Nov. 1, 1756, Eliphalet Griffen Ledger.

43. Ellis to ?, Apr. 17, 1741, Robert Ellis Letter Book, Historical Society of Pennsylvania; Boyd to Messrs. Lane, Son, and Fraser, July 5, 1773, George Boyd Letter Book, New Hampshire Historical Society; James Nelson writ, 22126, Nov. 17, 1743, New Hampshire Archives.

44. William Redwood to James Pemberton, Oct. 8, 1751, Pemberton Papers, vol. 7, 1750–52, Historical Society of Pennsylvania; Joseph Cottle account, Oct. 10, 1759, Capt. Gideon Woodwell Account Book; Boyd to Messrs. Lane, Son, and Fraser, July 5, 1773, George Boyd Letter Book; Benjamin Mifflin Journal, entry for Aug. 2, 1762, New York Public Library; Henry Springer inventory, Sept. 9, 1754, Essex County Probate Records.

45. Carroll (Sr.) to Carroll (Jr.), May 8, 1754, Henry O. Thompson Papers; Middleton, pp. 200, 261; Boyd to Samuel Grouble, Mar. 1, 1774, George Boyd Letter Book; Capt. Gideon Woodwell Account Book.

46. Moffat to Stephen Perry, July 1740, John Moffat Accounts, Waste Books, vol. A, July 1740–Jan. 1741; Dunlope and Glenholme to Andrew Orr, Nov. 9, 1767, Dunlope and Glenholme Letter Book, Historical Society of Pennsyl-

vania; Philadelphia Tax List, Mar. 31, 1775, Philadelphia Archives, City Hall; Allan Kuliloff, "The Progress of Inequality in Revolutionary Boston," pp. 385–86.

47. Bridenbaugh, *Colonial Craftsman*, pp. 134–35; Joseph Cottle inventory, July 8, 1765, Essex County Probate Records; Joshua Hemstead inventory, Jan. 5, 1759, Probate Records, Connecticut State Archives; Percival Pawley inventory, May 16, 1752, Inventories, 12:348–51, South Carolina Archives; Alexander Hunt inventory, Oct. 24, 1765, Benjamin Hallowell inventory, May 3, 1773, Suffolk County Probate Records, 64:595–98, 72:579–82; James West inventory, Mar. 8, 1762, Probate Records, Philadelphia City Hall, Annex; John Rose schedule, Mar. 21, 1784, presented to the Commissioners on Loyalist Claims, transcribed in London, 1898–1903, 53:272–77 (microfilm copy in New York Public Library); John Frink inventory, Aug. 18, 1761, Inventories 12:34–35, South Carolina Archives.

48. John James Currier, *History of Newburyport, Mass., 1764–1909* 2:207–9; *Dictionary of American Biography*, s.v. "Meserve, Nathaniel."

49. Cotton Mather, *The Life of Sir William Phips*, ed. Mark Van Doren, pp. 14–19; *Dictionary of American Biography*, s.v. "Phips, Sir William."

50. *Dictionary of American Biography*, s.v. "Partridge, Richard."

51. Cheney, pp. 14–25; Howells, pp. 141, 147; *Dictionary of American Biography*, s.v. "Meserve, Nathaniel"; Briggs, pp. 64, 65, 97, 287–324; administration of Samuel Hood estate, Apr. 1735, Benjamin Hallowell inventory, May 3, 1773, Suffolk County Probate Records, 35:214–19; 72:579–82; William Penrose Hallowell, *Record of the Hallowell Family including the Longstreet, Penrose and Norwood Branches*, pp. 147–51; Burt, p. 125.

## CHAPTER V    Ship Construction in Eighteenth-Century America

1. Chapelle, *Speed under Sail*, p. 33.
2. Ibid., pp. 70–73.
3. E. P. Morris, *The Fore-and-Aft Rig in America, A Sketch*, pp. 174–82.
4. See tables 6, 7, 12–19, 21, 22, 27, 29, 31, 39.
5. Chapelle, *Speed under Sail*, pp. 53, 56, 59, 62, 83, 85, 90; Chapelle, *Sailing Ships*, pp. 34, 37, 38; Jonathan Scott, Jr., to Christopher Champlin, Mar. 22, 1765, Wetmore Collection, 1755–65.
6. See tables 5–10, 12–18, 19, 21, 23, 25, 27, 29, 31, 33, 35, 39, 44–51; Voyages and Travels of Francis Goelet, 1746–58, entry for Oct. 21, 1750, New York Historical Society.
7. See tables 1–4, 5, 7, 9, 11, 13, 16, 18, 21, 23, 27, 33, 39, 52; Reynell to Daniel Flexney, Aug. 19, 1740, John Reynell Letter Book, 1737–38, Coates, Reynell Papers; Chapelle, *Sailing Ships*, p. 16.

8. Davis, *English Shipp.* 109–11, 118–21; Joseph Law vol. 8, 1765–67, Newport H.

9. See tables 18, 29, 51, 52

10. *News-Letter*, Apr. 28, 17 Smith, Jr., to John Smith, Jr., Southern Historical Collection, *ing Ships*, pp. 34, 38; Chapelle, 1768 Virginia sloop Mr. H. I. Cha Evers, Dec. 30, 1715, Thomas R. Winne and Walter Hawksworth to MSS, vol. 1, 1647–1777; Timothy 1751, Timothy Orne MSS, box 2, Aaron Lopez, and Archimedes Geor Papers, box 52, folio 4.

11. See table 55.

12. Jonathan Winne and Walter Haw Coffin MSS, vol. 1, 1647–1777; Daniel Fle Coates, Reynell Papers, Correspondence, to Joshua Way, Apr. 5, 1749, Hunt and Society of Pennsylvania.

13. Boyd to Thomas Fraser, Sept. 22, 1775 nell to Michael Lee Dicker, June 5, 1736, Jol Coates, Reynell Papers; John Baker Holroyd, *of the American States*, p. 98; W. Cathias Jones June 6, 1748, Vernon Papers, box 49; William Oct. 8, 1751, Pemberton Papers, vol. 7, 1750–5 Wyer, Apr. 29, 1754, Melatiah Bourn Papers, vo

14. John Hardman, Aaron, and Benjamin Heyw 9, 1746, Foreign Letters, John Banister Letter Boo Reynell, Dec. 20, 1739, Reynell Papers, 1738–39, Coa to David Barclay, Apr. 25, 1746, Samuel Powell, Jr., 46, Historical Society of Pennsylvania; Dunlope and Orr, Nov. 9, 1767, Dunlope and Glenholme Letter Bo

15. Richardson to Stephen Webb and Nicholas Co Thomas Richardson Letter Book, 1712–15; Thomas Fu 1738, John Moffat Accounts, journal for 1735–39; Pe Thomas Quayl, Oct. 29, 1737, Peter Faneuil Papers, L Hancock Collection, Baker Library.

16. Lloyd to John Lloyd, May 9, 1765, Henry Lloyd Library; John Barrell to Gerrish, Oct. 4, 1738, John Barrell York Historical Society; Daniel Flexney to John Reynell, M. Bland to John Reynell, Aug. 21, 1746, Reynell Papers, 1

Coates, Reynel 23, 1740, Robe Vernon, June 17. Thoma Book; Reynel nell Letter B Apr. 24, 174 William Wi Jonathan V Coffin MSS Letter Boo 18. Rey 3, 1746, Jo John Rad Banister contract, MSS; Na Sylveste Jacob P and Le Pardoe 19. time, tract, and J Com Orne Orn vest Syl bo

D cl B

36. Sloop *Culloden* account, 1748, Vernon Papers, box 48, Newport Historical Society; sloop *Four Brothers*, Aug. 5, 1762, Ship Papers, Brown Papers; Prince Miller account, July 1768–Jan. 1771, Nicholas Brown Ledger, 1768–74, Brown Papers; unsigned letter to Aaron Lopez, Oct. 8, 1769, Wetmore Collection, 1768–69, Massachusetts Historical Society.

37. Burgis, *South East View of Boston*; Burgis, *A South Prospect of Ye Flourishing City of New York in America* (engraving); George Heap and Nicholas Scull, *An East Prospect of the City of Philadelphia* (engraving); Thomas Coram complaint, Mar. 5, 1701, vol. 40, Judicial, 1683–1724, pp. 649–50, Massachusetts Archives; *The shipyard at Spencer Hall, Kent Island, Maryland* (oil painting).

38. Philadelphia Historical Commission, "Southwark"; Philadelphia Tax Record, 1767, Assessors' Returns, Rare Book Room, University of Pennsylvania Lbrary.

39. Joseph F. W. Des Barres, "A Plan of the Town of Newport in the Province of Rhode Island."

40. John Decker account, May 5, 1735, Abner Dole Ledger, Essex Institute; Joseph Cottle account, Sept. 3, 1757, Oct. 10, 1759, Oct. 3, 1762, Capt. Gideon Woodwell Account Book; John Mitchell account, Nov. 24, 1755, Eliphalet Griffen Ledger, Baker Library; Dickinson to Dickinson (a brother in Jamaica), Mar. 5, 1719, Jonathan Dickinson Letter Book.

41. Thomas Lang writ, 24893, Feb. 18, 1744, New Hampshire Archives; Joshua Mitchel account, Nov. 1, 1756, Eliphalet Griffen Ledger; Stephen Cross account, Dec. 20, 1764, Capt. Gideon Woodwell Account Book.

42. Gershom Bradford, "The Ezra Westons, Shipbuilders of Duxbury," p. 35; Joseph Cottle accounts, Apr. 26, 1754, Mar. 15, 1759, two schooner accounts, June 19, Nov. 20, 1754, and Joshua Mitchel accounts, Nov. 24, 1754, Nov. 1, 1756, Eliphalet Griffen Ledger.

43. Ellis to ?, Apr. 17, 1741, Robert Ellis Letter Book, Historical Society of Pennsylvania; Boyd to Messrs. Lane, Son, and Fraser, July 5, 1773, George Boyd Letter Book, New Hampshire Historical Society; James Nelson writ, 22126, Nov. 17, 1743, New Hampshire Archives.

44. William Redwood to James Pemberton, Oct. 8, 1751, Pemberton Papers, vol. 7, 1750–52, Historical Society of Pennsylvania; Joseph Cottle account, Oct. 10, 1759, Capt. Gideon Woodwell Account Book; Boyd to Messrs. Lane, Son, and Fraser, July 5, 1773, George Boyd Letter Book; Benjamin Mifflin Journal, entry for Aug. 2, 1762, New York Public Library; Henry Springer inventory, Sept. 9, 1754, Essex County Probate Records.

45. Carroll (Sr.) to Carroll (Jr.), May 8, 1754, Henry O. Thompson Papers; Middleton, pp. 200, 261; Boyd to Samuel Grouble, Mar. 1, 1774, George Boyd Letter Book; Capt. Gideon Woodwell Account Book.

46. Moffat to Stephen Perry, July 1740, John Moffat Accounts, Waste Books, vol. A, July 1740–Jan. 1741; Dunlope and Glenholme to Andrew Orr, Nov. 9, 1767, Dunlope and Glenholme Letter Book, Historical Society of Pennsyl-

vania; Philadelphia Tax List, Mar. 31, 1775, Philadelphia Archives, City Hall; Allan Kulifoff, "The Progress of Inequality in Revolutionary Boston," pp. 385–86.

47. Bridenbaugh, *Colonial Craftsman*, pp. 134–35; Joseph Cottle inventory, July 8, 1765, Essex County Probate Records; Joshua Hemstead inventory, Jan. 5, 1759, Probate Records, Connecticut State Archives; Percival Pawley inventory, May 16, 1752, Inventories, 12:348–51, South Carolina Archives; Alexander Hunt inventory, Oct. 24, 1765, Benjamin Hallowell inventory, May 3, 1773, Suffolk County Probate Records, 64:595–98, 72:579–82; James West inventory, Mar. 8, 1762, Probate Records, Philadelphia City Hall, Annex; John Rose schedule, Mar. 21, 1784, presented to the Commissioners on Loyalist Claims, transcribed in London, 1898–1903, 53:272–77 (microfilm copy in New York Public Library); John Frink inventory, Aug. 18, 1761, Inventories 12:34–35, South Carolina Archives.

48. John James Currier, *History of Newburyport, Mass., 1764–1909* 2:207–9; *Dictionary of American Biography*, s.v. "Meserve, Nathaniel."

49. Cotton Mather, *The Life of Sir William Phips*, ed. Mark Van Doren, pp. 14–19; *Dictionary of American Biography*, s.v. "Phips, Sir William."

50. *Dictionary of American Biography*, s.v. "Partridge, Richard."

51. Cheney, pp. 14–25; Howells, pp. 141, 147; *Dictionary of American Biography*, s.v. "Meserve, Nathaniel"; Briggs, pp. 64, 65, 97, 287–324; administration of Samuel Hood estate, Apr. 1735, Benjamin Hallowell inventory, May 3, 1773, Suffolk County Probate Records, 35:214–19; 72:579–82; William Penrose Hallowell, *Record of the Hallowell Family including the Longstreet, Penrose and Norwood Branches*, pp. 147–51; Burt, p. 125.

CHAPTER V    Ship Construction in Eighteenth-Century America

1. Chapelle, *Speed under Sail*, p. 33.
2. Ibid., pp. 70–73.
3. E. P. Morris, *The Fore-and-Aft Rig in America, A Sketch*, pp. 174–82.
4. See tables 6, 7, 12–19, 21, 22, 27, 29, 31, 39.
5. Chapelle, *Speed under Sail*, pp. 53, 56, 59, 62, 83, 85, 90; Chapelle, *Sailing Ships*, pp. 34, 37, 38; Jonathan Scott, Jr., to Christopher Champlin, Mar. 22, 1765, Wetmore Collection, 1755–65.
6. See tables 5–10, 12–18, 19, 21, 23, 25, 27, 29, 31, 33, 35, 39, 44–51; Voyages and Travels of Francis Goelet, 1746–58, entry for Oct. 21, 1750, New York Historical Society.
7. See tables 1–4, 5, 7, 9, 11, 13, 16, 18, 21, 23, 27, 33, 39, 52; Reynell to Daniel Flexney, Aug. 19, 1740, John Reynell Letter Book, 1737–38, Coates, Reynell Papers; Chapelle, *Sailing Ships*, p. 16.

8. Davis, *English Shipping*, pp. 65–66; Chapelle, *Speed under Sail*, pp. 79, 109–11, 118–21; Joseph Lawrence to Lopez, Nov. 18, 1767, Aaron Lopez Papers, vol. 8, 1765–67, Newport Historical Society.

9. See tables 18, 29, 51, 52.

10. *News-Letter*, Apr. 28, 1774; *South Carolina Gazette*, Apr. 23, 1754; Josiah Smith, Jr., to John Smith, Jr., Jan. 12, 1773, Josiah Smith, Jr., Letter Book, Southern Historical Collection, University of North Carolina; Chapelle, *Sailing Ships*, pp. 34, 38; Chapelle, *Speed under Sail*, pp. 71, 87, 110; plan of a 1768 Virginia sloop Mr. H. I. Chapelle lent the author; Richardson to William Evers, Dec. 30, 1715, Thomas Richardson Letter Book, 1715–19; Jonathan Winne and Walter Hawksworth to Joshua Coffin, Jan. 17, 1733, Joshua Coffin MSS, vol. 1, 1647–1777; Timothy Orne and Daniel Curtis contract, Sept. 5, 1751, Timothy Orne MSS, box 2, 1751–56, Essex Institute; Nathan Miller, Aaron Lopez, and Archimedes George contract, Feb. 9, 1775, Aaron Lopez Papers, box 52, folio 4.

11. See table 55.

12. Jonathan Winne and Walter Hawksworth to Coffin, Jan. 17, 1733, Joshua Coffin MSS, vol. 1, 1647–1777; Daniel Flexney to John Reynell, June 18, 1740, Coates, Reynell Papers, Correspondence, 1729–64; John Hunt and Greenleafe to Joshua Way, Apr. 5, 1749, Hunt and Greenleafe Letter Book, Historical Society of Pennsylvania.

13. Boyd to Thomas Fraser, Sept. 22, 1773, George Boyd Letter Book; Reynell to Michael Lee Dicker, June 5, 1736, John Reynell Letter Book, 1734–37, Coates, Reynell Papers; John Baker Holroyd, *Observations on the Commerce of the American States*, p. 98; W. Cathias Jones to Samuel and William Vernon, June 6, 1748, Vernon Papers, box 49; William Redwood to James Pemberton, Oct. 8, 1751, Pemberton Papers, vol. 7, 1750–52; Thomas Walker to Robert Wyer, Apr. 29, 1754, Melatiah Bourn Papers, vol. 1, 1751–87, Baker Library.

14. John Hardman, Aaron, and Benjamin Heywood to John Banister, Mar. 9, 1746, Foreign Letters, John Banister Letter Books; Daniel Flexney to John Reynell, Dec. 20, 1739, Reynell Papers, 1738–39, Coates, Reynell Papers; Powell to David Barclay, Apr. 25, 1746, Samuel Powell, Jr., Letter Book, vol. 2, 1739–46, Historical Society of Pennsylvania; Dunlope and Glenholme to Andrew Orr, Nov. 9, 1767, Dunlope and Glenholme Letter Book.

15. Richardson to Stephen Webb and Nicholas Coleman, May 24, 1715, Thomas Richardson Letter Book, 1712–15; Thomas Furnell account, Jan. 10, 1738, John Moffat Accounts, journal for 1735–39; Peter Faneuil to Capt. Thomas Quayl, Oct. 29, 1737, Peter Faneuil Papers, Letter Book, 1737–39, Hancock Collection, Baker Library.

16. Lloyd to John Lloyd, May 9, 1765, Henry Lloyd Letter Book, Baker Library; John Barrell to Gerrish, Oct. 4, 1738, John Barrell Letter Book, New York Historical Society; Daniel Flexney to John Reynell, Mar. 16, 1739, Elias Bland to John Reynell, Aug. 21, 1746, Reynell Papers, 1733–35, 1746–47,

Coates, Reynell Papers; Ellis to Messrs. Leyborne, Rossey, and Rockless, Feb. 23, 1740, Robert Ellis Letter Book; W. Cathias Jones to Samuel and William Vernon, June 6, 1748, Vernon Papers, box 49.

17. Thomas Moffat to Isaac Sperrin, June 9, 1715, Thomas Moffat Letter Book; Reynell to Elias Bland, Nov. 12, Dec. 3, 1746, Apr. 3, 1747, John Reynell Letter Book, 1745–47, Coates, Reynell Papers; Powell to Robert Wheatle, Apr. 24, 1746, Samuel Powell, Jr., Letter Book, vol. 2, 1739–46; Richardson to William Wilkinson, Nov. 1715, Thomas Richardson Letter Book, 1715–19; Jonathan Winne and Walter Hawksworth to Coffin, Jan. 17, 1733, Joshua Coffin MSS, vol. 1, 1647–1777; Lloyd to John Lloyd, May 9, 1765, Henry Lloyd Letter Book.

18. Reynell to Daniel Flexney, Jan. 4, 1741, Reynell to Elias Bland, Dec. 3, 1746, John Reynell Letter Books, 1738–41, 1745–47, Coates, Reynell Papers; John Radburne to Joseph Harrison, Apr. 29, 1746, Foreign Letters, John Banister Letter Books; Timothy Orne, Benjamin Osgood, and Daniel Curtis contract, Sept. 5, 1751, Commercial Papers, box 2, 1751–56, Timothy Orne MSS; Nathan Miller and Aaron Lopez contract, Feb. 9, 1775, Aaron Lopez and Sylvester Child contract, Dec. 28, 1774, Aaron Lopez Papers, box 52, folio 4; Jacob Phillips and John Becket contract, June 23, 1721, Probate, Commissions, and Legal, Curwen Family MSS, vol. 4, Essex Institute; Banister to James Pardoe, Nov. 30, 1747, John Banister Letter Book, 1746–48.

19. Joshua Gee and Thomas Windsor contract, Oct. 30, 1701, vol. 62, Maritime, 1694–1706, Massachusetts Archives; John Barnes, Vrian Davis, *et al.* contract, Feb. 2, 1721, Rhode Island Historical Society MSS, vol. 1; Jacob Phillips and John Becket contract, June 23, 1721, Curwen Family MSS, vol. 4, Probate, Commissions, and Legal; Andrew Webster, Jonathan Gardner, and Timothy Orne contract, Aug. 30, 1749, Commercial Papers, box 1, 1732–50, Timothy Orne MSS; Benjamin Bowers and Aaron Lopez contract, May 30, 1764, Sylvester Child, Aaron Lopez, and Benjamin Wright contract, Nov. 5, 1772, Sylvester Child and Aaron Lopez contract, Dec. 28, 1774, Aaron Lopez Papers, box 52, folio 4.

20. Thomas Goldthwait petition, Samuel Vaughan and Moses Tyler reply, Dec. 20, 1749, vol. 43, Judicial, 1749–54, pp. 30–32, 36–39, Massachusetts Archives; John Banister to James Pardoe, July 23, 1748, John Banister Letter Book, 1746–48.

21. Falconer, "Naval Architecture."

22. Chapelle, *Speed under Sail*, pp. 15, 150; Roger Charles Anderson, "Early Books on Shipbuilding and Rigging," *Mirror* 20(1924):53–64; Roger Charles Anderson, "Eighteenth-Century Books on Shipbuilding, Rigging and Seamanship"; Alexander Hunt inventory, Oct. 24, 1765, Suffolk County Probate Records, vol. 64; *News-Letter*, Feb. 3, 1726, Oct. 10, 1765; John Radburne to Joseph Harrison, Aug. 24, 1745, Foreign Letters, John Banister Letter Books; Nellson Rachlief account, Jan. 1747, Abner Dole Ledger, p. 5.

23. Falconer, "Naval Architecture."

24. Mungo Murray, *A Treatise on Shipbuilding and Navigation*, pp. 135, 145; Chapelle, *Speed under Sail*, p. 140.

25. Murray, pp. 142–44; Benjamin Burbank to John Wendell, Nov. 27, 1759, John Wendell Letters, 1745–1807, Wendell Collection.

26. Ephraim Robinson Ledger, vol. 2, 1759–72, New Hampshire Historical Society; Caleb Barker account, Apr. 9, 1765, Stephen Rusel account, June 1765, Capt. Gideon Woodwell Account Book, pp. 171, 215; Joshua Humphreys Ledger D, 1766–77, May 20, 1766, Joshua Humphreys Papers, Historical Society of Pennsylvania; *Diary of Joshua Hempstead*, p. 56; *News-Letter*, May 13, 1717; Samuel Vaughan and Moses Tyler to Thomas Goldthwait, Dec. 1749, vol. 43, Judicial, 1749–54, pp. 36–39, Massachusetts Archives; Boyd to Messrs. Lane, Son, and Fraser, July 5, Nov. 6, 1773, George Boyd Letter Book; Powell to Robert Wheatle, Aug. 5, 1746, Samuel Powell, Jr., Letter Book, vol. 2, 1739–46; Thomas Coram petition, Feb. 1701, vol. 40, Judicial, 1683–1724, pp. 645–47, Massachusetts Archives.

27. William Sutherland, *The Ship Builder's Assistant or Marine Architecture*, pp. 72–75; Falconer, "Shipbuilding."

28. John Yeates to Messrs. Chamber and Baker, Dec. 6, 1744, Correspondence, 1738–49, box 1, Yeates Papers, Historical Society of Pennsylvania; Moses Tyler account, 1770, vol. 24, Domestic Invoices and Receipts, John Hancock Papers, Hancock Collection; Bining, pp. 27–30; Chapelle, *Speed under Sail*, p. 14; ship *Triton* account, 1742, John Banister Daybook; account of tradesmens bills for a ship, undated list in Thomas Hancock Papers, Hancock Collection.

29. Richardson to William Evers, Dec. 30, 1715, Thomas Richardson Letter Book, 1715–19; Messrs. Barnard and Harrison to Hancock, Mar. 23, 1764, Thomas Hancock Papers, vol. 7, Foreign Letters, Hancock Collection; Bowles and Luckis account, Oct. 28, 1768, Thomas Edes account, Jan. 6, 1774, John Hancock Papers, vols. 20, 23, Bills, Hancock Collection; Samuel Appleton to Hugh Wentworth, Sept. 6, 1760, Larkin Papers, Portsmouth Atheneum.

30. Falconer, "Sheathing"; Martin Detchevery to Henry Guionneau and James Leblond, Nov. 4, 1729, Miscellaneous Papers, 1722–53, Chamberlain Collection of Autographs, Boston Public Library; Banister to James Pardoe, Nov. 30, 1747, John Banister Letter Book, 1746–48.

31. Falconer, "Black-Strakes," "Pay," "Stuff"; Henry Stanbridge account, June 5, 1766, John Hancock Papers, vol. 23, Bills, Hancock Collection.

32. Falconer, "Launch."

33. *Pennsylvania Gazette*, Mar. 4, 1731; *News-Letter*, Nov. 8, 1770; Daniel Wentworth to Messrs. Davenport and Wentworth, Feb. 17, 1759, Miscellaneous (Bound) MSS, vol. 12, 1749–60, Massachusetts Historical Society; ship *Delaware* accounts, May 1762, Wharton MSS, box 1762–66, Historical Society of Pennsylvania.

34. Banister to Thomas Hall, Oct. 8, 1739, Copy Book of Letters, 1739–42, John Banister Letter Books, Newport Historical Society; brigantine *Undutied Tea* bill of sale, Apr. 20, 1774, John Hancock Papers, vol. 25, Bills, Hancock Collection; Joseph A. Goldenberg, "Names and Numbers: Statistical Notes on Some Port Records of Colonial North Carolina," pp. 159–60.

35. *Maryland Gazette*, Jan. 6, 1747.

36. *News-Letter*, Jan. 30, 1735, Sept. 10, 1747, Mar. 17, Dec. 22, 1748, Apr. 5, 1753; *Gazette*, Dec. 21, 1771; *Maryland Gazette*, Apr. 7, 1747.

37. *Pennsylvania Gazette*, Oct. 21, Nov. 18, Dec. 21, 1731, Aug. 30, 1739; *News-Letter*, Apr. 3, 1735; Daniel Flexney to John Reynell, Feb. 8, 1744, Reynell Papers, 1742–43, Coates, Reynell Papers.

38. *News-Letter*, Aug. 19, 1773; *Pennsylvania Gazette*, Jan. 22, 1741; Richardson to Stephen Webb and Nicholas Coleman, Oct. 21, 1714, May 24, 1715, Thomas Richardson Letter Book, 1712–15; Banister to John and Abraham Blydesteen, Oct. 8, 1739, Copy Book of Letters, 1739–42, John Banister Letter Books; Powell to Robert Wheatle, Aug. 5, Dec. 5, 1746, Samuel Powell, Jr., Letter Book, vol. 2, 1739–46, vol. 3, 1746–47; Reynell to Elias Bland, Apr. 30, 1747, John Reynell Letter Book, 1744–45, Coates, Reynell Papers; Banister to John Radburn, Oct. 19, 1747, John Banister Letter Book, 1746–48.

39. Reynell to Elias Bland, Apr. 30, 1747, John Reynell Letter Book, 1745–47, Coates, Reynell Papers; Daniel Wentworth to Messrs. Davenport and Wentworth, Feb. 11, 1759, Miscellaneous (Bound) MSS, vol. 12, 1749–60, Massachusetts Historical Society.

40. Michael Lee Dicker to John Reynell, Sept. 13, 1739, Daniel Flexney to John Reynell, Sept. 24, 1739, Reynell Papers, 1738–39, Coates, Reynell Papers; Banister to Jonathan Rigg, June 10, 1739, Copy Book of Letters, 1739–42, John Banister Letter Books; *Proceedings of the Massachusetts Historical Society* 58 (1925):424–25; Davis, *English Shipping*, pp. 374–75.

41. Sloop *Swallow* account Jan.–Apr. 1700, Joseph Buckley Account Book, Massachusetts Historical Society; brigantine *Lark* account, May 11, 1732, brigantine *Amistad* account, Sept. 15, 1732, Peter Faneuil Account Book, 1731–32, Hancock Collection; brigantine *Ebenezer* account, Dec. 1738, sloop *Mermaid* account, Sept. 3, 1739, Thomas Hancock Day Book, 1737–39, Hancock Collection; ship *Cromwell* account, Nov. 8, 1743, sloop *St. Andrew* Account, Mar. 5, 1744, ship *Mary* account, Apr. 18, 1744, John Irving Journal, Accounts, 1733–67, Hancock Collection; brigantine account, Oct. 18, 1765, John Hancock Journal, 1764–82, Hancock Collection; brigantine *Lydia* account, May 25, 1765, John Hancock Waste Book, 1764–67, Hancock Collection; ship *Hermione* account, June 24, 1740, John Banister Daybook; ship *Mary* account, June 8, 1742, John Reynell Daybook, 1741–45, Coates, Reynell Papers; ship *Tetsworth* account, Apr. 27, 1748, snow *Mary* account, June 12, 1749, John Reynell Daybook, 1748–52, Coates, Reynell Papers.

42. Davis, *English Shipping*, p. 375; Banister to James Pardoe, July 23, 1748, John Banister Letter Book, 1746–48.

CHAPTER VI   The Markets for Colonial-built Vessels

1. *News-Letter*, Oct. 22, 1716, Mar. 10, 1743, Sept. 11, 1760, July 2, 1761, Sept. 17, 1767; *Pennsylvania Gazette*, Oct. 4, 1753, May 19, 1762, Jan. 24, 1765; *Maryland Gazette*, July 27, 1748, May 17, 1749, Aug. 15, 1750, July 25, 1754; *Virginia Gazette*, Feb. 21, 1751, Oct. 13, 1769, Sept. 13, 1770, Mar. 5, 1772; *South Carolina Gazette*, Dec. 8, 1746, Apr. 16, 1750; advertisements in the *News-Letter, Pennsylvania Gazette, Maryland Gazette, Virginia Gazette,* and *South Carolina Gazette* average slightly less than one each year, with concentrations in certain periods, for the entire series of each newspaper.

2. Carl Bridenbaugh, *Cities in Revolt: Urban Life in America, 1743–1776,* pp. 44, 47, 257; Robert Willing to Thomas Greenough, June 10, 1743, Greenough Papers, box 1, Massachusetts Historical Society; Lloyd to David Beveridge, Apr. 27, 1765, Henry Lloyd Letter Book; William Redwood to James Pemberton, Oct. 31, 1751, Pemberton Papers, vol. 7, 1750–52; Henry Lloyd to Thomas Clifford, May 26, June 2, 1760, Clifford Correspondence, vol. 3, 1760–62; see tables 17, 18.

3. See tables 21–35, 38, 39, 42, 46–51; Clark, 1:113; Bridenbaugh, *Cities in Revolt,* p. 257; Middleton, pp. 237, 252.

4. See table 52; Lawrence Henry Gipson, *The British Empire before the American Revolution* 3:6–7; John Greenwood Brown Hutchins, *The American Maritime Industries and Public Policy, 1789–1914,* p. 192.

5. Robert Willing to Thomas Greenough, June 10, 1743, Greenough Papers, box 1; William Redwood to James Pemberton, Oct. 31, 1751, Pemberton Papers, vol. 7, 1750–52; Christopher Starbuck to Thomas Wharton, Dec. 3, 1761, Wharton MSS, box 1760–61; Scott to Christopher Champlin, Mar. 22, 1765, Wetmore Collection, 1755–65; Richardson to William Evers, Dec. 30, 1715, Thomas Richardson Letter Book, 1715–19; Bridenbaugh, *Cities in Revolt,* pp. 46–47; Lopez to Henry Cruger, Sr., Oct. 13, 1767, Aaron Lopez Letter Book, 1767, Aaron Lopez Papers.

6. Cravath and Dugan to Caleb Davis, Feb. 16, Oct. 11, 1771, Davis Papers, vols. 7b, 7c, 1770–72, Massachusetts Historical Society; Abraham Van Bibber and Crockett to Lopez, July 14, 1773, Aaron Lopez Papers, vol. 15, 1773–74; Starbuck to Wharton, Mar. 2, Dec. 3, 1761, Wharton MSS, box 1760–61; Osborn to Hancock, Feb. 18, 1755, Hancock to Osborn, Feb. 24, 1755, Thomas Hancock Papers, vol. 1, Domestic Letters, Hancock Collection.

7. Bridenbaugh, *Cities in Revolt,* pp. 330–31; Middleton, p. 199; Richard Pares, *Yankees and Creoles: The Trade between North America and the West Indies before the American Revolution,* p. 26; Richardson to Stephen Webb and Nicholas Coleman, Oct. 21, 1714, Thomas Richardson Letter Book, 1712–15; W. Cathias Jones to Messrs. Samuel and William Vernon, June 6, 1748, Vernon Papers, box 49; Lopez to Abraham Mendes, Dec. 10, 1767, Aaron Lopez Letter Book, 1767, Aaron Lopez Papers; Peter Faneuil to Thomas

Quayl, Oct. 29, 1737, Peter Faneuil Papers, Letter Book, 1737–39, Hancock Collection; Daniel Rindge to Langdon, June 30, Dec. 9, 1763, Henry Sherburne and Woodbury Langdon to Langdon, Dec. 7, 1764, John Langdon Papers, box 3, Correspondence, 1760–1832, New Hampshire Historical Society; Boyd to John Cruger, July 23, 1773, George Boyd Letter Book; Orne, Jonathan Gardner, and George Dodge to John Gardner, Jan. 30, 1763, Timothy Orne MSS, Ledger 6, 1762–68; William Threipland Baxter, *The House of Hancock: Business in Boston, 1724–1775*, p. 85.

8. Faneuil to Thomas Quayl, Dec. 12, 1737, Peter Faneuil Papers, Letter Book, 1737–39, Hancock Collection; Richardson to Joshua Byrk, Mar. 1714, Richardson to Stephen Webb and Nicholas Coleman, Oct. 21, 1714, Thomas Richardson Letter Book, 1712–15; W. Cathias Jones to Messrs. Vernon, June 6, 1748, Vernon Papers, box 49; Rindge to Langdon, June 30, Dec. 9, 1763, Henry Sherburne and Woodbury Langdon to Langdon, Dec. 7, 1764, John Langdon Papers, box 3, Correspondence, 1760–1832.

9. Clark, 1:95; Gipson, 3:6–7; Davis, *English Shipping*, pp. 291–92; see table 52.

10. Hutchins, p. 154; Benjamin Landon to John Cranch, Mar. 31, 1743, Hawthorne Family MSS, vol. 2; Boyd to Messrs. Lane, Son and Fraser, Nov. 6, 1773, Boyd to Cruger, Sept. 23, Nov. 1, 1773, Mar. 4, 1774, George Boyd Letter Book; Woodbury Langdon to John Langdon, Apr. 28, 1766, Langdon, Peabody, and Kittery Papers, New Hampshire Historical Society; Lopez to Cruger, May 24, July 16, 1765, Aaron Lopez Papers, box 52; Byron Fairchild, *Messrs. William Pepperrell: Merchants at Piscataqua*, p. 101; William Palfrey to George Hayley and Hopkins, Jan. 10, 1774, John Hancock Papers, Letter Book, 1763–83, Hancock Collection.

11. Lopez to Cruger, Mar. 20, May 24, Aug. 12, 22, 1765, Lopez to William Stead, Apr. 23, July 22, 1765, Cruger to Lopez, Sept. 4, 1766, Aaron Lopez Papers, box 52; Cruger to Lopez, Apr. 9, May 20, 1766, Feb. 20, Nov. 1, 1769, Feb. 1, Dec. 1, 1772, *Collections of the Massachusetts Historical Society* 69:151–57, 160, 266–67, 295, 388, 421–22; Baxter, pp. 246–50.

12. Barrell to John Gerrish, Oct. 4, 1738, John Barrell Letter Book; Joseph Harrison to Banister, July 29, Sept. 27, 1743, John Kempland to Banister, Sept. 25, 1745, William Eaton to Banister, Aug. 8, 1745, John Hardman, Abraham and Benjamin Heywood to Banister, Mar. 9, 1746, Foreign Letters, John Banister Letter Books.

13. Boyd to Samuel Grouble, Mar. 1, 1774, Boyd to Henry Cruger, Jr., Mar. 25, 1774, George Boyd Letter Book; Boyd to John Wendell, June 27, Aug. 26, 1774, *Proceedings of the Massachusetts Historical Society* 48:335–36, 337–38, 340.

14. Clark, 1:95; Radburn to Banister, Aug. 24, 1745, Manesty to Banister, Aug. 2, 1745, Aug. 15, 1746, Foreign Letters, John Banister Letter Books; David Flexney to John Reynell, Aug. 2, 1740, Correspondence, 1729–64, Coates,

Reynell Papers; John Hunt and Greenleafe to James Pemberton, June 6, 1749, Hunt and Greenleafe Letter Book.

15. Samuel Clarke account, Aug. 18, 1742, John Erving Journal, Baker Library; Faneuil to Messrs. Lane and Smethurst, Jan. 10, 1739, Apr. 4, 1739, Peter Faneuil Papers, Letter Book, 1737–39, Hancock Collection; Christopher Kilby and John Barnard to Hancock, Feb. 11, 1750, Thomas Hancock Papers, vol. 7, Foreign Letters, Hancock Collection; Reynell to Daniel Flexney, Dec. 5, 1739, John Reynell Letter Book, 1738–41, Coates, Reynell Papers; Henry Cruger, Jr., to John Hancock, Jan. 13, 1772, John Hancock Papers, vol. 27, Foreign Letters, Hancock Collection.

16. Bland to Reynell, Aug. 21, 1746, Edward Wilson to Reynell, Apr. 30, 1747, John Reynell Papers, 1746–47, Coates, Reynell Papers; John Reynell to Bland, Apr. 25, Nov. 12, Dec. 3, 1746, Apr. 30, 1747, John Reynell Letter Book, 1745–47, Coates, Reynell Papers; Tolles, pp. 88, 93.

17. Reynell to Daniel Flexney, Oct. 19, 1741, John Reynell Letter Book, 1741–44, Coates, Reynell Papers; Powell to Thomas Plumstead, July 16, 1740, Powell to Robert Wheatle, Dec. 30, 1745, Aug. 11, 1746; Samuel Powell, Jr., Letter Book, vol. 2, 1739–46; Dunlope and Glenholme to William Beath and George Anderson, Oct. 5, 1767, Dunlope and Glenholme Letter Book; Gov. James Glen of South Carolina to Lords of Trade, 1749, British Museum, King's MSS, 205, p. 560 (transcript in Library of Congress); Davis, *English Shipping*, p. 281; Hutchins, p. 154; Boyd to Daniel Delany, Oct. 10, 1773, George Boyd Letter Book; Radburne to John Banister, Aug. 24, 1745, Foreign Letters, John Banister Letter Book; Richardson to Thomas Bond, May 1, 1713, Thomas Richardson Letter Book, 1712–15; Ellis to Lawrence Williams, Aug. 7, 1741, Ellis to John Savage, Apr. 9, 1743, Robert Ellis Letter Book; Reynell to Richard Deeble, Sept. 10, 1735, John Reynell Letter Book, 1734–37, Coates, Reynell Papers.

18. Banister to John Radburn, Oct. 27, 1747, John Banister Letter Book, 1746–48; Moffat to Joseph Robinson, May 22, 1716, Moffat to Stephen Perry, Mar. 8, 1716, Thomas Moffat Letter Book, 1714–16; John Hunt and Greenleafe to Joshua Way, May 31, 1749, John Hunt and Greenleafe to Capt. Nicholas Stephenson, June 6, 1749, Hunt and Greenleafe Letter Book; Holroyd p. 309; Daniel Flexney to Reynell, June 18, 1740, Commercial 1729–64, Coates, Reynell Papers; Banister to John Radburn, Oct. 19, 27, 1747, Banister to James Pardoe, July 23, 1748, John Banister Letter Book, 1746–48; Powell to Robert Wheatle, Apr. 24, 1746, Samuel Powell, Jr., Letter Book, Vol. 2, 1739–46; Reynell to Daniel Flexney, Oct. 19, 1741, May 10, 1742, John Reynell Letter Book, 1741–44, Coates, Reynell Papers.

19. Accounts of nameless ship, 1736, and ship *Two Friends*, July 1737, Journal, 1735–39, John Moffat Accounts; accounts of brig *Lark*, May 11, 1732, brig *Amistad*, Sept. 1, 1732, Peter Faneuil Account Book, 1731–32, Hancock Collection; account of ship *Friendship*, May 27, 1738, Thomas Hancock Day-

book, 1737–39, Hancock Collection; account of brig *Lydia*, May 25, 1765, John Hancock Waste Book 1764–67, Hancock Collection; accounts of ship *Hermione*, June 24, 1740, ship *Berwick Galley*, Dec. 5, 1740, John Banister Daybook; accounts of ship *Mary*, June 8, 1742, ship *Tetsworth*, Apr. 27, 1748, John Reynell Daybooks, 1741–45, 1748–52, Coates, Reynell Papers; Reynell to Richard Deeble, Sept. 10, 1735, John Reynell Letter Book, 1734–37, Coates. Reynell Papers; Richard Deeble to Reynell, May 15, 1736, John Reynell Papers, 1736–37, Coates, Reynell Papers; Reynell to Richard Deeble, Aug. 11, 1736, Reynell to Michael Lee Dicker, June 28, 1738, John Reynell Letter Books, 1736–37, 1737–38, Coates, Reynell Papers.

20. Michael Lee Dicker to Reynell, Sept. 13, 1739, Daniel Flexney to Reynell, Sept. 24, 1739, John Reynell Papers, 1738–39, Coates, Reynell Papers; Reynell to Josiah Knight, Aug. 7, 1741, John Reynell Letter Book, 1738–41, Coates, Reynell Papers; Powell to Robert Wheatle, Dec. 10, 1745, Samuel Powell, Jr., Letter Book, vol. 2, 1739–46; Gov. Francis Bernard of Massachusetts to Lords Commissioners for Trade and Plantations, Sept. 5, 1763, King's MSS, 205 (transcript in Library of Congress); Holroyd, p. 98; Clark, 1:95; Reynell to Richard Deeble, Sept. 10, 1735, John Reynell Letter Book, 1734–37, Coates, Reynell Papers; Dunlope and Glenholme to Andrew Orr, Nov. 9, 1767, Dunlope and Glenholme Letter Book; Powell to David Barclay, Apr. 25, 1746, Powell to Wheatle, Aug. 5, Sept. 5, Nov. 8, Dec. 5, 1746, Samuel Powell, Jr., Letter Book, vol. 2, 1739–46.

21. Carroll (Sr.) to Carroll (Jr.), May 5, 1754, Carroll to John Hanbury, Nov. 15, 1755, Cough-Carroll Correspondence, MS 821, Henry O. Thompson Papers; Silvester Grove to Samuel Galloway, Dec. 3, 1759, William Tippell to Samuel Galloway, Oct. 8, 1760, Apr. 18, 1763, Galloway-Maxcy-Markoe Papers, vols. 3, 6, 1759–61, 1764, Library of Congress; Davis, *English Shipping*, pp. 68, 197–98; Hutchins, pp. 154–55.

22. Col. David Dunbar to Alured Popple, Aug. 19, 1730, *Calendar of State Papers* 37:241; Committee . . . to inquire into a Declaration or Evidence of Mr. Jeremiah Dunbar, Jan. 2, 1733, *Journals of the House of Representatives of Massachusetts* 11:163–66; Martin Detchevery to Henry Guionneau and James Leblond, Nov. 4, 1729, Miscellaneous Papers, vol. 3, Chamberlain Collection of Autographs.

23. David Macpherson, *Annals of Commerce, Manufacturers, Fisheries, and Navigation* 3:397.

24. Joshua Gee to Council of Trade and Plantations, Oct. 27, 1721, *Calendar of State Papers* 32:474; Macpherson, 30:164, 165–66; Fairchild, p. 76; Ellis to Mannock and Ryan, Nov. 24, 1737, Ellis to Capt. Edward Dover, May 27, 1740, Ellis to Lawrence Williams, June 20, 1744, Ellis to Leybourne and Stubbs, July 4, Dec. 18, 1744, Robert Ellis Letter Book; Stamper to Capt. Thomas Stamper, Apr. 27, 1752, John Stamper Letter Book; John Srizoll and John Legg to Capt. John Tussell, May 31, 1718, Hawthorne Family MSS, vol. 1, 1664–1730.

CHAPTER VII   Colonial Warships

1. Albion, pp. 42–43; Michael Lewis, *The Navy of Britain: A Historical Portrait,* pp. 364–65.

2. Howard Irving Chapelle, *The History of the American Sailing Navy: The Ships and Their Development,* pp. 11–16; Albion, pp. 43, 88; Davis, *English Shipping,* p. 67n; Lewis p. 374.

3. Albion, pp. 74–75, 244–46.

4. Ibid., p. 76; Lords of Admiralty to Navy Board, Nov. 9, 1691, Adm 2/171, British Public Record Office (hereafter BPRO); Chapelle, *American Sailing Navy,* pp. 5, 47; Chapelle, *Speed under Sail,* p. 76; Mr. Chapelle generously lent the author transcripts of the documents from the British Public Record Office used in this chapter.

5. Lords of Admiralty to Navy Board, Apr. 16, 1694, June 7, 1695, Adm 2/174–75, Navy Board to Lords of Admiralty, June 10, 1695, Adm 1/3576, BPRO; Offices of the Deptford Yard to Navy Board, Mar. 5, 1697, Adm 106/3292, BPRO; Albion, p. 56; Chapelle, *Speed under Sail,* pp. 76–77.

6. Albion, p. 244; Chapelle, *Speed under Sail,* pp. 70, 78.

7 Albion, p. 245; Adm. Peter Warren to Lords of Admiralty, June 26, 1746, Lords of Admiralty to Navy Board, Sept. 1, 1746, Navy Board to Lords of Admiralty, Sept. 19, Oct. 10, 17, 1746, Aug. 28, 1747, Adm 1/480, 2/210, 106/2182–83, BPRO.

8. Navy Board to Lords of Admiralty, Sept. 19, Dec. 31, 1746, June 19, 1747, Adm 106/2183, BPRO.

9. Chapelle, *Speed under Sail,* pp. 64, 77; Navy Board to Lords of Admiralty, Oct. 16, Nov. 12, 1747, Mar. 28, 1748, Adm 106/2183, BPRO; Chapelle, *American Sailing Navy,* pp. 45, 47.

10. Pepperrell to Thomas Corbett, Sept. 12, 17??, Sir William Pepperrell Papers, box 2, folio 6, Maine Historical Society; Chapelle, *Speed under Sail,* p. 77.

11. Chapelle, *Speed under Sail,* pp. 82–84; Lords of Admiralty to Navy Board, Jan. 7, 1764, May 25, 1769, Adm. William Parry to Lords of Admiralty, Nov. 20, 1767, Adm 2/233, 2/238, 1/238, BPRO; *Virginia Gazette,* July 20, 1767.

12. Offices of Deptford Yard to Navy Board, May 7, 16, 1764, Adm 106/3314, BPRO; Chapelle, *Speed under Sail,* pp. 84, 90.

13. Offices of Deptford Yard to Navy Board, Sept. 2, 7, 12, 1774, Nov. 16, 1769, Adm 106/3402, 106/3316, BPRO; *South Carolina Gazette,* June 9, 1766; Chapelle, *Speed under Sail,* pp. 118–21; Piers Mackesy, *The War for America, 1775–1783,* pp. 62–68.

14. Geoffrey J. Marcus, *A Naval History of England* 1:274; *Pennsylvania Gazette,* Apr. 10, May 22, Aug. 7, Sept. 11, 1740, Aug. 6, 1741; *South Carolina Gazette,* Mar. 13, 1742.

15. Lt. Gov. William Shirley to Sheriff of Suffolk County and constables of Boston, July 31, 1740, vol. 63, Maritime, 1706–40, Massachusetts Archives.

16. Account of ship *King George*, Jan. 2, 1758, vol. 65, Maritime, 1753–59, Massachusetts Archives; *Pennsylvania Gazette*, May 5, 1757; Chapelle, *Sailing Ships*, pp. 62–63, 138–42; Lt. Gov. John Wentworth to Council of Trade and Plantations, Apr. 6, 1724, *Calendar of State Papers* 34:78; *Pennsylvania Gazette*, May 24, Dec. 6, 1744, Feb. 19, Mar. 26, 1745, Nov. 25, 1756, May 5, 1757, June 24, 1762, Aug. 11, 1763.

17. Chapelle, *Sailing Ships*, pp. 131–33; Bridenbaugh, *Cities in Revolt*, pp. 61–63.

18. William S. Sachs and Ari Hoogenboom, *The Enterprising Colonials: Society on the Eve of the Revolution*, p. 114; Baxter, pp. 80–81, 94–95; Powell to Thomas Hyman, Dec. 21, 1744, Powell to Robert Wheatle, Dec. 10, 1745, Samuel Powell, Jr., Letter Book, vol. 2, 1739–46; Bridenbaugh, *Cities in Revolt*, p. 65.

19. Benjamin Glasier Diary, Mar. 14, 15, June 22, July 2, 20, Aug. 23, Sept. 6, 1758, Essex Institute.

20. Chapelle, *Speed under Sail*, p. 79; Herbert Levi Osgood, *The American Colonies in the Eighteenth Century* 4:380.

21. William Alexander to Gov. William Shirley, May 10, 17, 1755, Alexander Papers, MSS vol. 1, 1717–56, New York Historical Society; Osgood, 4:380; Chapelle, *Speed under Sail*, p. 79.

22. Osgood, 4:380; Diary of Stephen Cross, Mar. 1, Apr. 29, Aug. 14, Sept. 4, Oct. 22, 1756, Newburyport Historical Society; John Andrews petition, Feb. 1764, Petitions to the Rhode Island General Assembly, vol. 2, 1762–65, Rhode Island Archives; Francis Parkman, *Montcalm and Wolfe* 2:132–33.

CHAPTER VIII   The Development of Shipbuilding in the South

1. Davis, *English Shipping*, pp. 286–87; Middleton, pp. 246–48, 254; Stuart to Andrew Armour, Feb. 14, 1752, Charles Stuart Letter Book, 1751–53, Historical Society of Pennsylvania; Moses Lopez to Lopez, May 3, 1764, Aaron Lopez Papers, vol. 2, 1762–65.

2. Bordley to Slowerdewe and Norton, Oct. 31, 1750, Stephen Bordley Letter Book, Maryland Historical Society; Laurens to Dennistoun Monroe, Feb. 29, 1764, Laurens to Reynolds Getly, Jan. 23, 1771, Laurens to James Laurens, Dec. 18, 1771, Henry Laurens Letter Books, 1762–64, 1767–71, 1771–72, Henry Laurens Papers, South Carolina Historical Society; Middleton, pp. 259–63.

3. Carroll (Sr.) to Carroll (Jr.), May 8, 1754, Carroll (Sr.) to John Hanbury, Aug. 29, 1754, Nov. 15, 1755, Henry O. Thompson Papers; William Teppell to Samuel Galloway, Oct. 8, 1760, James Russell to Samuel Galloway and Stephen Stewart, May 7, 1770, Galloway-Maxcy-Markoe Papers, vol. 2, 1759–61, vol. 10, 1769–70; *Pennsylvania Gazette*, Aug. 1, 1751; *Maryland*

*Gazette*, Apr. 11, July 25, 1754, Aug. 28, 1755, Jan. 15, Apr. 29, Oct. 21, 1756; *Virginia Gazette*, Sept. 28, 1769, May 27, Aug. 12, 1773.

4. See tables 19, 21–34.

5. See tables 20–34.

6. *Virginia Gazette*, Feb. 21, June 6, Sept. 12, 1751, Sept. 22, 1752, Apr. 4, 1756, Nov. 4, 1763, Apr. 11, June 27, Aug. 1, Sept. 19, Dec. 4, 1766, Jan. 29, Mar. 5, 26, June 4, 1767, June 9, 16, Aug. 4, 18, Sept. 29, 1768, May 11, Oct. 19, 1769; Middleton, pp. 234, 237–38, 260, 263; Lt. Gov. Francis Fauquier of Virginia to Lords Commissioners for Trade and Plantations, 1763, British Museum, King's MSS, 205 (transcript in Library of Congress); see table 52; Holroyd, p. 96.

7. See tables 11–19, 21, 23, 25, 27, 29, 31, 33, 49–52; Davis, *English Shipping*, pp. 286, 361; Middleton, pp. 218–19; Chapelle, *Speed under Sail*, pp. 65, 70–71, 78, 83, 84, 93–94.

8. Middleton, p. 243; see table 52; Holroyd, p. 96.

9. See tables 39, 43, 52; Charles Christopher Crittenden, *The Commerce of Colonial North Carolina, 1763–1789*, pp. 72, 78.

10. See tables 44–51; Governor Glen of South Carolina to Lords Commissioners for Trade and Plantations, 1749, British Museum, King's MSS, 205 (transcript in Library of Congress); Laurens to Lachin McIntosh, Oct. 11, 1764, Laurens to James Baillie, Mar. 28, 1763, Henry Laurens Letter Book, 1762–64, Henry Laurens Papers; the remonstrance of John Daniell, John Yerworth, George Heskett, John Scott, and David Brown, Jan. 25, 1744, in Easterby, 4:547–48.

11. See tables 49–52; *South Carolina Gazette*, Oct. 25, 1773.

12. Moses Lopez to Lopez, May 3, 1764, Aaron Lopez Papers, vol. 2, 1762–65; Laurens to Reynolds Getly, Jan. 23, 1771, Laurens to James Laurens, Dec. 18, 1771, Laurens to Thomas Courtin, Mar. 10, July 28, Aug. 29, 1763, Henry Laurens Letter Books, 1767–71, 1771–72, 1762–64, Henry Laurens Papers.

13. Jonathan Pierpoint to Caleb Davis, Dec. 18, 1771, Davis Papers, vol. 7c, 1771–72; *South Carolina Gazette*, Dec. 5, 1771, Oct. 25, 1773; Laurens to William Cowles, May 31, June 4, 1771, Laurens to Reynolds Getly, Dec. 23, 1773, Laurens to James Laurens, Jan. 3, 1774, Laurens to John Rose, Jan. 3, 1774, Henry Laurens Letter Books, 1771–72, 1772–74, Henry Laurens Papers; see tables 49–51.

14. Lloyd to Thomas Lynch, June 20, Nov. 8, 13, 1766, Henry Lloyd Letter Book; Laurens to William Cowles, May 31, 1771, Henry Laurens Letter Book, 1771–72, Henry Laurens Papers; John Immrie schedule, Mar. 27, 1786, Daniel Manson and William Begbie schedule, Mar. 1786, Mrs. Catherine Tweed schedule, Mar. 7, 1786, presented to the Commissioners on Loyalist Claims, transcribed in London, 1898–1903, 55:32–45, 293–319; 54:327–33 (microfilm copy in New York Public Library); *South Carolina Gazette*, May 21, 1763, Feb. 1, 1770, Jan. 17, Nov. 14, 1771, Oct. 18, 1773.

15. See table 52; Holroyd, p. 96; Bridenbaugh, *Cities in Revolt*, p. 262; Sachs and Hoogenboom, p. 116.

## CHAPTER IX   Conclusion

1. Governor Bernard of Massachusetts to Lords Commissioners for Trade and Plantations, Sept. 5, 1763, British Museum, King's MSS, 205 (transcript in Library of Congress).

# Bibliography

PRIMARY SOURCES

Manuscripts

*Baker Library, Harvard Business School, Cambridge*

Melatiah Bourn Papers, 1727–1803. 10 vols. The accounts and bills of a colonial merchant.

John Erving Journal, 1733–45. Detailed shipping accounts of a Boston merchant.

Eliphalet Griffen Ledger, 1751–75. The daily work record of a Newbury shipwright.

Hancock Collection, 1712–83. 29 vols. and 53 boxes. Includes the business papers of Peter Faneuil, John Hancock, Thomas Hancock, and Daniel Henchman.

Henry Lloyd Letter Book, 1765–67. The letters of a Boston merchant to colonial and English correspondents.

Wendell Collection, 1722–1808. 10 vols. The letters and account books of two Portsmouth, New Hampshire, merchants, Joshua Pierce and John Wendell.

*British Public Record Office, London*

Admiralty Letters, Adm 1/, Adm 2/, Adm 106/. Correspondence between the Admiralty and Navy boards. Mr. Howard I. Chapelle lent the author transcripts of these documents.

Shipping Returns, Port of Boston Records, 1753; Port of Piscataqua Records, 1744–45, 1756–57, 1768. Prof. Lawrence A. Harper lent the author transcripts of these documents, listing 840 colonial-built vessels.

*Essex Institute, Salem*

Joshua Coffin MSS, 1647–1862. 3 vols. Includes the colonial business correspondence of Joseph and David Coffin of Newbury.

Curwen Family MSS, 1653–1815. 38 vols. Includes the letters and accounts of three merchants of colonial Salem: George, Jonathan, and Samuel Curwen.

Abner Dole Ledger, 1730–60. The daily work record of a Newbury shipwright.

Benjamin Glasier Diary, 1758–60. This diary of a Salem shipwright includes his daily work accounts to 1771.

Hawthorne Family MSS, 1664–1760. 2 vols. Includes the correspondence of Jonathan Cranston and Benjamin Landon, two Boston merchants.

Timothy Orne MSS, 1738–68. 16 vols. and 2 boxes. Excellent records of a Salem merchant.

Peter Papillon Account Book, 1713–25. The shipping accounts of a Boston merchant.

Capt. Gideon Woodwell Account Book, 1757–66. The records of a Newbury shipwright and shipyard owner.

*Historical Society of Pennsylvania, Philadelphia*

"Accounts of Servants and Apprentices Bound and Assigned before James Hamilton, Mayor of Philadelphia, 1745 and 1746." 2 vols.

Clifford Correspondence, 1722–77. 5 vols. The correspondence and accounts of Thomas Clifford, a Philadelphia merchant.

Coates, Reynell Papers, 1729–84. 12,000 items. Includes 21 vols. of the John Reynell letter books and papers, and the business records of Samuel Coates.

Jonathan Dickinson Letter Book, 1718–19. Correspondence of an early Philadelphia merchant.

Dunlope and Glenholme Letter Book, 1767–69. Describes the shipping activities of two Philadelphia merchants.

Robert Ellis Letter Book, 1736–48. Contains good information about Philadelphia trade with other colonies and with England.

Joshua Humphreys Papers, 1682–1835. 20 vols. Contains 3 ledgers of a colonial shipyard.

Hunt and Greenleafe Letter Book, 1747–49. Letters of two London tobacco merchants to correspondents in Philadelphia and Annapolis.

Pemberton Papers, 1641–1880. 70 vols. Includes 24 vols. of colonial correspondence, with excellent material on Quaker family life and the iron industry.

William Pollard Letter Book, 1772–74. Correspondence of a Philadelphia merchant.

Samuel Powell, Jr., Letter Books, 1724–47. 3 vols. The letters of a Philadelphia merchant to correspondents in Barbados, Ireland, and London.

Ship Register Books of the Province of Pennsylvania, 1722–76. 21 vols. Includes the registers of 2,251 colonial-built vessels.

John Stamper Letter Book, 1751–70. Letters of a Philadelphia merchant to West Indian correspondents.

Charles Stuart Letter Books, 1751–63. 2 vols. The correspondence of a Portsmouth, Virginia, merchant engaged in the grain, rum, tobacco, and wine trades.

Wharton MSS, 1679–1834. 2,000 items. The letters and accounts of Thomas Wharton, a late colonial merchant, form the bulk of this collection.

Yeates Papers, 1718–1876. 7,500 items. Includes the correspondence of John Yeates of Philadelphia with West Indian merchants.

*Library of Congress, Washington, D.C.*

British Museum, Additional MSS, transcripts. Includes the present state of New England, an answer to the Lords of Trade and Plantations, Aug. 1, 1676, and the general reports of the state of the American colonies, 1721–66.

Galloway-Maxcy-Markoe Papers, 1738–1858. 79 vols. Includes 12 vols. of the letters of Samuel Galloway, an Annapolis merchant, received 1754–75.

*Maryland Historical Society, Baltimore*

Stephen Bordley Letter Book, 1727–59. A typescript of 5 MS vols. bound in 1 book. The letters of a Maryland merchant.

Clement Hill Papers, 1670–1805. 9 vols. Letter books, business papers, and legal documents of a Maryland family.

Henry O. Thompson Papers. Transcripts made by Henry O. Thompson in 1879 of the Dr. Charles Carroll [Sr.] and Charles Carroll [Jr.] Letters, 1752–69.

*Massachusetts Historical Society, Boston*

Joseph Buckley Account Book, 1693–1701. Detailed accounts of a Boston merchant.

Davis Papers, 1684–1828. 38 vols. Includes 7 vols. of the Caleb Davis accounts and letters, 1761–74.

Greenough Papers, 1653–1782. 3 boxes. Includes the accounts and correspondence of Thomas Greenough, a Boston merchant.

Miscellaneous (Bound) MSS, 1629–1908. 21 vols. Includes contracts; the correspondence of Davenport and Wentworth, Portsmouth (New Hampshire) merchants; and legal disputes.

Wetmore Collection, 1706–1835. 21 vols. Papers on Rhode Island commerce, including some correspondence of Christopher Champlin and Aaron Lopez, Newport merchants.

*New Hampshire Historical Society, Concord*

George Boyd Letter Book, 1773–75. Business correspondence of a Portsmouth merchant.

John Langdon Papers, 1760–1832. 4 boxes. The correspondence of John Langdon, a New Hampshire sea captain, merchant, governor, and United States senator.

Langdon, Peabody, and Kittery Papers, 1765–75. Includes some business records of the Langdon family.

John Moffat Accounts, 1725–75. 10 vols. The ledgers of a leading Portsmouth merchant.

Ephraim Robinson Ledger, 1748–72. 2 vols. The ledger of a New Hampshire timber merchant.

*Newport Historical Society*

John Banister Letter Books, 1739–48, and Daybook, 1739–43. 3 vols. and 1 vol. Excellent letters between a Newport merchant and his correspondents in England, and unusually detailed accounts of shipbuilding costs.

Aaron Lopez Papers, 1744–1812. 17 vols. and 33 boxes. An extensive collection of the business papers of a Newport merchant.

Thomas Richardson Letter Books, 1712–19. 2 vols. The letters of a Newport merchant to West Indian and English correspondents.

Vernon Papers, 1747–76. 3 vols. and 4 boxes. The business papers of Samuel and William Vernon.

*New-York Historical Society*

Alexander Papers, 1717–73. 69 boxes. Includes 3 letter books of William Alexander (Lord Stirling).

John Barrell Letter Book, 1738–60. Correspondence of a Boston merchant.

Henry and John Cruger Letter Book, 1766–67. Contains good detail on trade between New York and the West Indies.

Voyages and Travels of Francis Goelet, 1746–58. Journal of a New York City merchant.

*New York Public Library, Manuscript Room*

Books and Papers of the Commission of Enquiry into the Losses and Services of the American Loyalists, 1783–90. 60 vols. Transcribed in London, 1898–1903.

Benjamin Mifflin Journal, 1762. Account of the tour of a Philadelphia merchant through Delaware and Maryland.

Thomas Moffat Letter Book, 1714/15–1716. The letters of a Boston merchant to his British correspondents.


*Rhode Island Archives, Providence*

Land Evidence, 1646–1741. 4 vols. Includes, among other legal documents, shipbuilding contracts and bills of sale.

Petitions to the Rhode Island General Assembly, 1728–65. 11 vols.

Rhode Island Law Cases, File Papers, 1725–50. 10 vols. Includes shipbuilding contracts and accounts.

Rhode Island Register of Shipping, 1776–78. Contains the registers of 64 colonial vessels built before 1776.


*South Carolina Archives, Columbia*

Court Records of Common Pleas, 1703–90. Loose documents in process of being bound. Includes valuable material on the cost of free and slave labor in South Carolina shipyards.

Inventories, 1736–84. 20 vols.

South Carolina Ship Register, 1734–83, 2 vols. Includes the registers of 468 colonial-built vessels.


*Southern Historical Collection, University of North Carolina, Chapel Hill*

Brunswick Port Records, 1767–75. Transcript; original is in the North Carolina State Archives. Includes valuable information about Massachusetts shipbuilding.

James Iredell, Sr., Notebooks, 1759–87. 23 vols. Includes 5 vols. of the records of Port Roanoke, Edenton, 1771–75.

Josiah Smith, Jr., Letter Book, 1771–84. The correspondence of a Charleston merchant.


*Miscellaneous*

Boston Public Library, Rare Book Room. Chamberlain Collection of Autographs, Miscellaneous Papers, 1722–53.

Central Reference Library, Bristol, England. Hobhouse Letters, 1722–25. The correspondence of two Bristol merchants.

Connecticut Historical Society, Hartford. Shipping Papers, 1726–1810. 1 box. Miscellaneous items, including the clearance papers for several ships departing New London.

Connecticut State Archives, Hartford. Probate records.

Essex County Courthouse, Salem. Probate records.

John Carter Brown Library, Providence. Brown Papers, 1730–1910 (app.) 100 vols. Includes 8 account books, 1767–74, and 1 box of ship papers, all of which provide excellent material on the shipping activities of Nicholas Brown and Company.

Maine Historical Society, Portland. Sir William Pepperrell Papers, 1707–ca. 1750. 2 boxes. Includes some business papers of the Pepperrell family.

Massachusetts Archives, Boston. Files of the General Court of Massachusetts, 1628–present. Includes the colonial, commercial, judicial, and maritime records of Massachusetts.

Middlesex County Courthouse, Cambridge, Mass. Probate Records.

Newburyport Historical Society. Stephen Cross Diary, 1756. The diary of a Newbury shipwright captured by the French at Oswego.

New Hampshire Archives, Concord. Court Records, writs.

North Carolina State Archives, Raleigh. Port of Roanoke, Book of Registers, 1725–51. A combination of ship register and port record. Includes 250 registers of vessels trading with North Carolina and built 1710–51. Especially useful for its detailed information about Massachusetts shipbuilding.

Philadelphia Archives, City Hall. Philadelphia Tax List, Mar. 31, 1775.

Philadelphia City Hall, Annex. Probate Records.

Portsmouth [New Hampshire] Atheneum. Larkin Papers, 1770. Includes a few letters belonging to Hugh Hall Wentworth, a Portsmouth merchant.

Rhode Island Historical Society, Providence. Rhode Island Historical Society MSS, 1630–1865. 19 vols.

South Carolina Historical Society, Charleston. Henry Laurens Papers, 1747–1801. 6,500 items. Includes 12 letter books, 1747–76, which contain excellent business and political material on the leading merchant in Charleston.

Suffolk County Courthouse, Boston. Probate Records.

University of Pennsylvania Library, Rare Book Room. Philadelphia Tax Record, 1767, Assessors Returns.

Virginia State Archives, Richmond. Northampton County Court Records, 1640–45.


Published Primary Sources

*Aspinwall Notarial Records from 1644 to 1651.* Boston: Municipal Printing Office, 1903.

Birket, James. *Some Cursory Remarks Made by James Birket in His Voyage to North America, 1750–1751.* New Haven: Yale University Press, 1916.

Bouton, Nathaniel, *et al.*, eds. *Documents and Records Relating to the Province of New Hampshire.* 40 vols. Concord, N.H.: State Printer, 1867–1943.

Bradford, William. *Of Plymouth Plantation, 1620–1647.* Ed. Samuel Eliot Morison. New York: Alfred A. Knopf, 1952.

Browne, William Hand, ed. *Archives of Maryland.* 65 vols. Baltimore: Maryland Historical Society, 1883–1952.

*Calendar of State Papers, Colonial Series, America and the West Indies.* 43 vols. London: Her Majesty's Stationery Office, 1860–1963.

*Collections of the Massachusetts Historical Society.* 79 vols. Boston: Massachusetts Historical Society, 1792–1941.

*Diary of Joshua Hempstead of New London, Connecticut.* New London: New London Historical Society, 1901.

Eagle, William Henry, and Reed, George Edward, eds. *Pennsylvania Archives, Third Series.* 30 vols. Harrisburg: Clarence M. Busch and William Stanley Rays, 1894–99.

Easterby, James Harold, ed. *The Journals of the Commons.* 9 vols. Columbia: Historical Commission of South Carolina and South Carolina Archives Department, 1951–62.

Force, Peter, ed. *Tracts and Other Papers Relating Principally to the Colonies in North America.* 4 vols. Washington, D.C.: Peter Force, 1836–46.

Hart, Albert Bushnell, ed. *American History Told by Contemporaries.* 4 vols. New York: Macmillan, 1897–1901.

Hening, William Waller, ed. *The Statutes at Large: Being a Collection of All the Laws of Virginia from the First Session of the Legislature, in the Year 1619.* 13 vols., 1809–23. Reprint. Charlottesville: University Press of Virginia, 1969.

*Historical Collections of Essex Institute.* 104 vols. Salem: Essex Institute, 1859–1968.

*Journal of the Commissioners for Trade and Plantations.* 12 vols. London: Her Majesty's Stationery Office, 1920–36.

*Lloyd's Register of Shipping,* 1776. Reprint. Ridgewood, N.J.: Gregg Press, 1964.

Myers, Albert Cook. "Narratives of Early Pennsylvania, West New Jersey, and Delaware." In *Original Narratives of Early American History.* Ed. John Franklin Jameson. Vol. 11. New York: Charles Scribner's Sons, 1912.

*Newport Historical Magazine.* 7 vols. Newport: Newport Historical Society, 1880–87.

O'Callaghan, Edmund Bailey, and Fernow, Berthold, eds. *Documents Relative to the Colonial History of the State of New York.* 15 vols. Albany: Weed, Parsons, 1856–87.

*Probate Records of Essex County, 1635–1681.* 3 vols. Salem: Essex Institute, 1916–20.

*Proceedings of the Massachusetts Historical Society.* 72 vols. Boston: Massachusetts Historical Society, 1859–1963.

*Records and Files of the Quarterly Courts of Essex County Massachusetts.*
8 vols. Salem: Essex Institute, 1911–21.

*Reports of the Record Commissioners of the City of Boston.* 39 vols. Boston:
Rockwell and Churchill, 1876–1909.

Shurtleff, Nathaniel Bradstreet, ed. *Records of the Governor and Company
of the Massachusetts Bay in New England.* 12 vols. Boston: William White,
1853–61.

*Virginia Magazine of History and Biography.* 76 vols. Richmond: Virginia
Historical Society, 1893–1968.

Winthrop, John. *The History of New England from 1630 to 1649.* Ed. James
Savage. 2 vols. Boston: Little, Brown, 1853.

———. *Papers.* Ed. Allan B. Forbes. 5 vols. Boston: Massachusetts Historical
Society, 1929–47.

Newspapers

*Gazette* (Providence), 1762–75.
*Maryland Gazette* (Annapolis), 1745–75.
*News-Letter* (Boston), 1704–75.
*Pennsylvania Gazette* (Philadelphia), 1728–75.
*South Carolina Gazette* (Charleston), 1731–75.
*Virginia Gazette* (Williamsburg), 1736–75.

SECONDARY SOURCES

General Works and Special Studies

Albion, Robert Greenhalgh. *Forests and Sea Power: The Timber Problem
of the Royal Navy, 1652–1862.* Cambridge: Harvard University Press, 1926.

Ames, Susie M. *Studies of the Virginia Eastern Shore in the Seventeenth
Century.* Richmond: Dietz Press, 1940.

Andrews, Charles McLean. *The Colonial Period of American History.* 4
vols. New Haven: Yale University Press, 1934–38.

Atwater, Edward E. *History of the Colony of New Haven.* Meriden, Conn.:
Journal Publishing Co., 1902.

Babson, John J. *History of the Town of Gloucester, Cape Ann, Including
the Town of Rockport.* Gloucester, Mass.: Procter Brothers, 1860.

Bailyn, Bernard. *The New England Merchants in the Seventeenth Century.* Cambridge: Harvard University Press, 1955.

and Bailyn, Lotte. *Massachusetts Shipping, 1697–1714: A Statistical Study.* Cambridge: Harvard University Press, 1959.

Baker, William A. *Colonial Vessels: Some Seventeenth-Century Sailing Craft.* Barre, Mass.: Barre Publishing Co., 1962.

*A Maritime History of Bath, Maine, and the Kennebec River Region.* Bath, Maine: Marine Research Society of Bath, 1973.

Baxter, William Threipland. *The House of Hancock: Business in Boston, 1724–1775.* Cambridge: Harvard University Press, 1945.

Berkeley, Sir William. *A Discourse and View of Virginia.* Reprint. Norwalk, Conn.: William H. Smith, Jr., 1914.

Bining, Arthur Cecil. *British Regulation of the Colonial Iron Industry.* Philadelphia: University of Pennsylvania Press, 1933.

Blake, Henry T. *Chronicles of New Haven Green from 1638 to 1862.* New Haven: Tuttle, Morehouse and Taylor, 1898.

Brewington, Marion V. "Shipbuilding in Maryland." In *The Old Line State: A History of Maryland.* Ed. Morris L. Radoff. Vol. 1. Baltimore: Historical Record Association, 1956.

Bridenbaugh, Carl. *Cities in Revolt: Urban Life in America, 1743–1776.* New York: Alfred A. Knopf, 1955.

*Cities in the Wilderness: The First Century of Urban Life in America, 1625–1742.* 2d ed. New York: Alfred A. Knopf, 1955.

*The Colonial Craftsman.* New York: New York University Press, 1950.

Briggs, L. Vernon. *History of Shipbuilding on North River, Plymouth County, Massachusetts, 1640–1872.* Boston: Coburn Brothers, 1889.

Brown, Vaughan W. *Shipping in the Port of Annapolis, 1748–1775.* Annapolis: United States Naval Institute, 1965. The volume is based on Annapolis port records in the Maryland Historical Society and the Maryland Archives.

Bruce, Philip Alexander. *Economic History of Virginia in the Seventeenth Century.* 2 vols. New York: Macmillan, 1896.

Burt, Struthers. *Philadelphia, Holy Experiment.* Garden City, N.Y.: Doubleday, 1945.

Caulkins, Frances Manwaring. *History of New London, Connecticut.* New London: H. D. Utley, 1895.

Chapelle, Howard Irving. *The History of American Sailing Ships.* New York: W. W. Norton, 1935.

*The History of the American Sailing Navy: The Ships and Their Development.* New York: W. W. Norton, 1949.

*The National Watercraft Collection.* Washington, D.C.: United States National Museum, 1960.

*The Search for Speed under Sail, 1700–1855.* New York: W. W. Norton, 1967.

Chapman, John Harvey. *The Chapman Genealogy.* Newburgh, N.Y.: Commercial Offset Printers, 1963.

Cheney, Robert. *Maritime History of the Merrimac and Shipbuilding.* Newburyport, Mass.: Newburyport Press, Inc., 1964.

Child, Sir Josiah, Baronet. *A New Discourse of Trade.* 4th ed. London: J. Hodges, 1740.

Clark, Victor Selden. *History of Manufactures in the United States.* 3 vols. Washington, D.C.: Carnegie Institution of Washington, 1929.

Crittenden, Charles Christopher. *The Commerce of Colonial North Carolina, 1763–1789.* New Haven: Yale University Press, 1936.

Currier, John James. *History of Newburyport, Mass., 1764–1909.* 3 vols. Newburyport, Mass.: Printed for the author, 1909.

*Shipbuilding on the Merrimac River.* Newburyport, Mass.: n.p., 1877.

Davis, Ralph. *The Rise of the English Shipping Industry in the Seventeenth and Eighteenth Centuries.* London: Macmillan, 1962.

*Dictionary of American Biography.* Ed. Allen Johnson and Dumas Malone. 21 vols. New York: Charles Scribner's Sons, 1928–37.

Fairchild, Byron. *Messrs. William Pepperrell: Merchants at Piscataqua.* Ithaca, N.Y.: Cornell University Press, 1954.

Falconer, William. *An Universal Dictionary of the Marine.* 2d ed. London: T. Cadell, 1789.

Field, Edward, ed. *State of Rhode Island and Providence Plantations at the End of the Century: A History.* 3 vols. Boston: Mason Publishing Co., 1902.

Gipson, Lawrence Henry. *The British Empire before the American Revolution.* 13 vols. New York: Alfred A. Knopf, 1936–67.

Hallowell, William Penrose. *Record of the Hallowell Family Including the Longstreet, Penrose and Norwood Branches.* Philadelphia: Hallowell, 1893.

Harper, Lawrence Averell. *The English Navigation Laws.* New York: Columbia University Press, 1939.

Hartley, Edward Neal. *Ironworks on the Saugus.* Norman: University of Oklahoma Press, 1957.

Harwood, Pliny LeRoy. *History of Eastern Connecticut.* 3 vols. New Haven: Pioneer Historical Publishing Co., 1932.

Holroyd, John Baker, first earl of Sheffield. *Observations on the Commerce of the American States.* 6th ed. London: J. Debrett, 1784.

Howells, John Mead. *The Architectual Heritage of the Piscataqua.* New York: Architectural Book Publishing Co., 1937.

Hurd, D. Hamilton. *History of New London County, Connecticut.* Philadelphia: J. W. Lewis, 1882.

Hutchins, John Greenwood Brown. *The American Maritime Industries and Public Policy, 1789–1914.* Cambridge: Harvard University Press, 1941.

Lefler, Hugh Talmage, and Newsome, Albert Ray. *The History of a Southern State: North Carolina.* Chapel Hill: University of North Carolina Press, 1954.

Lewis, Michael. *The Navy of Britain: A Historical Portrait.* London: George Allen and Unwin, 1948.

Mackesy, Piers. *The War for America, 1775–1783.* Cambridge: Harvard University Press, 1964.

Macpherson, David. *Annals of Commerce, Manufacturers, Fisheries, and Navigation.* 4 vols. London: Nichols and Son, 1805.

Mahan, Alfred Thayer. *The Influence of Sea Power upon History, 1660–1783.* 12th ed. Boston: Little, Brown, 1918.

Major, R. H., ed. *The Historie of Travaile into Virginia Britania.* London: Hakluyt Society, 1849.

Marcus, Geoffrey J. *A Naval History of England.* 3 vols. Boston: Little, Brown, 1961–.

Mather, Cotton. *The Life of Sir William Phips.* Ed. Mark Van Doren. New York: Stratford Press, 1929.

Middleton, Arthur Pierce. *Tobacco Coast: A Maritime History of Chesapeake Bay in the Colonial Era.* Newport New, Va.: The Mariners Museum, 1953.

Morris, E. P. *The Fore-and-Aft Rig in America, A Sketch.* New Haven: Yale University Press, 1927.

Murray, Mungo. *A Treatise on Shipbuilding and Navigation.* London: D. Henry and R. Cave, 1754.

Osgood, Herbert Levi. *The American Colonies in the Eighteenth Century.* 4 vols. New York: Columbia University Press, 1924–25.

Owen, Henry Wilson. *The Edward Clarence Plummer History of Bath, Maine.* Bath: Times Co., 1936.

Pares, Richard. *Yankees and Creoles: The Trade between North America and the West Indies before the American Revolution.* Cambridge: Harvard University Press, 1956.

Parkman, Francis. *Montcalm and Wolfe.* 2 vols. Boston: Little, Brown, 1884.

Perley, Sidney. *The History of Salem Massachusetts.* 3 vols. Salem: Sidney Perley, 1924–26.

Phillips-Birt, Douglas. *Fore and Aft Sailing Craft and the Development of the Modern Yacht.* London: Seeley, Service, 1962.

Rowe, William Hutchinson. *The Maritime History of Maine, Three Centuries of Shipbuilding and Seafaring.* New York: W. W. Norton, 1948.

Rutman, Darrett Bruce. *Winthrop's Boston: Portrait of a Puritan Town, 1630–1649.* Chapel Hill: University of North Carolina Press, 1965.

Sachs, William S., and Hoogenboom, Ari. *The Enterprising Colonials: Society on the Eve of the Revolution.* Chicago: Argonaut, 1965.

Saltonstall, William G. *Ports of Piscataqua.* Cambridge: Harvard University Press, 1941.

Smith, Abbot Emerson. *Colonists in Bondage: White Servitude and Convict Labor in America, 1607–1776.* Chapel Hill: University of North Carolina Press, 1947.

Stokes, Isaac Newton. *The Iconography of Manhattan Island.* 6 vols. New York: Robert H. Dodd, 1895–1928.

Sutherland, William. *Britian's Glory: Or, Ship-Building Unvail'd.* 2d ed. London: A. Bettesworth, 1729.

The Ship Builder's Assistant or Marine Architecture. 6th ed. London: Mount and Davidson, 1794.

Tolles, Frederick Barnes. *Meeting House and Counting House: The Quaker Merchants of Colonial Philadelphia, 1682–1763.* Chapel Hill: University of North Carolina Press, 1948.

Waters, Thomas Franklin. *Ipswich in the Massachusetts Bay Colony.* 2 vols. Ipswich, Mass., Ipswich Historical Society, 1905–17.

Wilkinson, Henry. *The Adventurers of Bermuda.* London: Oxford University Press, 1953.

*Wood: A Manual for Its Use as Shipbuilding Material.* 4 vols. Washington, D.C.: Department of the Navy, 1957.


Articles


Anderson, Roger Charles, "Early Books on Shipbuilding and Rigging." *Mariner's Mirror 20* (1924):53–64.

"Eighteenth-Century Books on Shipbuilding, Rigging and Seamanship." *Mariner's Mirror 33* (1947):218–25.

Bradford, Gershom. "The Ezra Westons, Shipbuilders of Duxbury." *American Neptune 14* (1954):29–41.

Chandler, Charles Lyon. "Early Ship Building on the River Delaware." *Journal of the Franklin Institute 213* (1932):515–45.

Chever, George F. "Some Remarks on the Commerce of Salem from 1626 to 1740." *Historical Collections of Essex Institute* 1 (Apr.–Nov. 1859):67–181.

Goldenberg, Joseph A. "Names and Numbers: Statistical Notes on Some Port Records of Colonial North Carolina." *American Neptune 29* (1969):155–66.

"A Forgotten Dry Dock in Colonial Charlestown." *American Neptune 30* (1970):56–61.

Hill, Hamilton Andrews. "Thomas Coram in Boston and Taunton." *Proceedings of the American Antiquarian Society* 8 (Apr. 1892):133–48.

Holly, Hobart H. "Sparrow-Hawk: A Seventeenth-Century Vessel in Twentieth-Century America." *American Neptune 13* (1953):51–64.

Huffington, Paul, and Clifford, J. Nelson. "Evolution of Shipbuilding in Southeastern Massachusetts." *Economic Geography* 15 (Oct. 1939):362–78.

Kelso, William M. "Shipbuilding in Virginia, 1763–1774." *Records of the Columbia Historical Society of Washington, D.C., 1971–1972.* Baltimore: for the Society by the Waverly Press, 1973.

Kulifoff, Allan. "The Progress of Inequality in Revolutionary Boston." *William and Mary Quarterly* 28(1971):375–412.

Leavitt, William. "Retire Becket." *Historical Collections of Essex Institute* 7 (Oct. 1865):207–8.

Minchinton, William E. "Shipbuilding in Colonial Rhode Island." *Rhode Island History* 20 (1961):119–24.

Rutman, Darrett Bruce. "Governor Winthrop's Garden Crop: The Significance of Agriculture in the Early Commerce of Massachusetts Bay." *William and Mary Quarterly* 20 (July 1963):396–415.

Salisbury, William. "Early Tonnage Measurement in England." *Mariner's Mirror* 52 (1966):41–51.

Upham, William P. "Papers Relating to a Suit A.D. 1664 between John Pickering and the Owners of the New Mill in Salem." *Historical Collections of Essex Institute* 8 (Mar. 1866):21–28.

Waters, Henry Fitzgilbert. "The Gedney and Clarke Families of Salem, Mass." *Historical Collections of Essex Institute* 16 (Oct. 1879):241–78.


Miscellaneous


Bonner, John. *The Town of Boston in New England, 1722.* Boston: Francis Dewing, 1722. This plan of Boston is in the Massachusetts Historical Society.

Burgis, William. *A South East View of Ye Great Town of Boston in New England in America.* Boston: William Price, ca. 1722. This engraving is in the New-York Historical Society.

*A South Prospect of Ye Fourishing City of New York in America.* Ca. 1717. London: Thomas Bakewell, 1746. This engraving is in the New-York Historical Society.

Davis, Ralph. "Untapped Sources and Research Opportunities in the Field of American Maritime History from the Beginning to about 1815." Paper presented at Mystic Seaport Seminar, Mystic, Conn., 1966.

Delano, Esek T. "The Early Development of Shipbuilding on Narragansett Bay." Paper presented to the Rhode Island Historical Society, May 14, 1920.

Des Barres, Joseph F. W. "A Plan of the Town of Newport in the Province of Rhode Island." *Atlantic Neptune.* London: Joseph F. W. Des Barres, 1774–84. Reprint. Barre Publishers, Barre, Mass., 1966.

Heap, George, and Scull, Nicholas. *An East Prospect of the City of Philadelphia.* London: Gerard Vandergucht, 1754. This engraving is in the Historical Society of Pennsylvania.

J. P. Newell, *Newport, R.I., in 1730.* 1884. Reprint. Greenwich, Conn.. New York Graphic Society, 1961. Etching of a painting in the possession of James Phillips.

Philadelphia Historical Commission. "Southwark." 1966. Survey of colonial buildings in the Southwark district of Philadelphia.

*The Shipyard at Spencer Hall, Kent Island, Maryland.* Ca. 1770. This oil painting on a mantel panel is in the Maryland Historical Society.

# Index

# Index

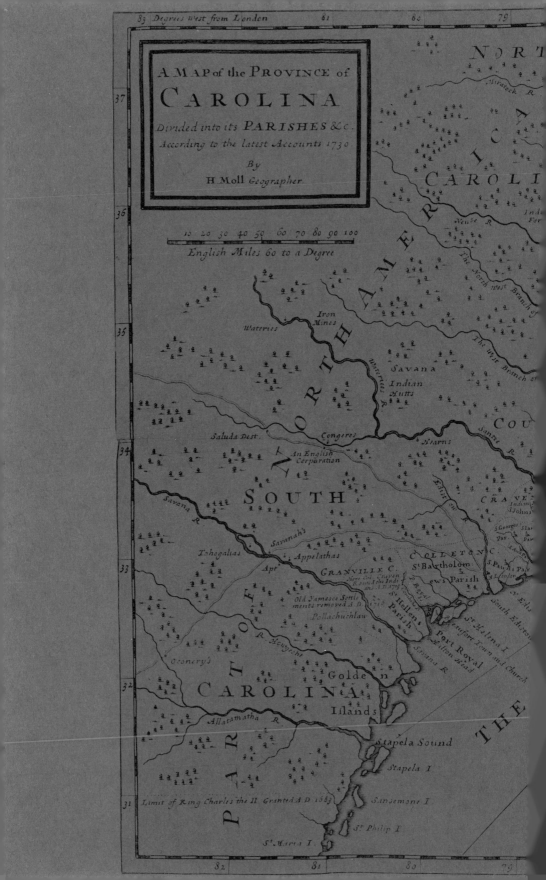

A MAP of the PROVINCE of

# CAROLINA

Divided into its PARISHES &c.

According to the latest Accounts 1730.

By

H. Moll Geographer.

10 20 30 40 50 60 70 80 90 100

English Miles 60 to a Degree

NORT

CAROLI

AMERICA

Miratock R.

Inde
For

Neuse R.

The North West Branch of

The West Branch of

Iron
Mines

Wateries

Savana
Indian
Hutts

COU

Wateries R.

Saluda Dest.

Congeres

Stearns

Santee R.

An English
Corporation

SOUTH

CRAVE

Indian
S.John's

S.Georges Star
Par

Savana R.

Tshogalias

Savanah's

Appelathas

COLLETON C.

St Bartholom
ews Parish

S.Pauls Par

S.Sander

Apt

GRANVILLE C.

Here Col. Craven
Routed the Indi
and A.D. 1715

St Ellena

S.Georges

S.Ellis

R. Hougche

Old Yamesee Settle
ments removed A.D. 1718

Pollachuchlau

St Hellen
Parish

Royal

South Edistow

St Helena I.

Beaufort Town and Church

Oconery's

Golden

Port Royal

Hilton Head

Savana R.

CAROLINA

Islands

Allatamatha R.

PART OF

Stapela Sound

THE

Stapela I.

Sansemone I.

St Philip I.

St Marra I.